Dissertations
in
American Economic History

This is a volume in the Arno Press collection

Dissertations in American Economic History

Advisory Editor
Stuart Bruchey

Research Associate
Eleanor Bruchey

See last pages of this volume for a complete list of titles.

LABOR ON THE ILLINOIS CENTRAL RAILROAD 1852-1900

The Evolution of an Industrial Environment

David L. Lightner

With a New Index

ARNO PRESS

A New York Times Company

New York / 1977

Editorial Supervision: LUCILLE MAIORCA

First publication in book form, Arno Press, 1977

DISSERTATIONS IN AMERICAN ECONOMIC HISTORY
ISBN for complete set: 0-405-09900-2
See last pages of this volume for titles.

Manufactured in the United States of America

Library of Congress Cataloging in Publication Data

Lightner, David L
Labor on the Illinois Central Railroad, 1852-1900.

(Dissertations in American economic history)
Originally presented as the author's thesis, Cornell, 1969.
Bibliography: p.
Includes index.
1. Illinois Central Railroad--Personnel management--History. 2. Railroads--United States--Employees--History. I. Title. II. Series.
HE2791.I3L54 1977 658.3'7'38509773 76-39834
ISBN 0-405-09914-2

LABOR ON THE ILLINOIS CENTRAL RAILROAD, 1852-1900: THE EVOLUTION OF AN INDUSTRIAL ENVIRONMENT

David L. Lightner

In memory of E.

PREFACE

In this study of labor on the Illinois Central, I have sought to depart from traditional labor history, with its heavy emphasis upon trade unions, their institutional development and conflicts with capital. Labor historians have written adequate histories of most railroad unions and some interesting accounts of major railroad strikes, but there has been little investigation of the wages, hours, and working conditions of railroaders; of the attitude of railroad managers toward their work force; and of the methods by which employers endeavored to recruit, train, discipline, and provide for the safety and welfare of their employees. Surely these subjects deserve attention, and much can be learned about them from the correspondence and corporate records of the Illinois Central company.

The following pages do not contain the full story of labor on the Illinois Central. Rather, they present that story insofar as I have been able to reconstruct it from scraps of information widely scattered among the writings of company officials to whom labor problems were, except on rare occasions, matters of only incidental concern. Some subjects are overemphasized and others neglected because company officers recorded that which was of immediate concern to themselves, not to the long-range interest of the social historian. To some extent the prejudices and rationalizations of the railroad managers may have influenced my conclusions, although I have tried to allow for the bias of my sources, a task made easier by the fact that railroad officers of the nineteenth century were quite open about many actions that a modern manager might wish to conceal. Moreover, the Illinois Central archives include a great many private and confidential documents that provide information even on those aspects of labor policy that were not publicly divulged. I have tried to portray accurately the attitudes and actions of the men whose correspondence is the basis of this study. There is, after all, much value in seeing how labor problems appeared from the management point of view.

***

Working on the railroad has been a pleasant experience, thanks to many kind persons.

Hours were long but working conditions superb at the Newberry Library, where Director Lawrence W. Towner and his fine staff gave me every aid and encouragement. The officers of the Illinois Central Railroad graciously allowed me free access to their records both in the Newberry Library and at Central Station.

To receive wages while pursuing one's own ends is rare indeed, yet such was my good fortune thanks to a New York State Herbert H. Lehman Fellowship and an Associated Colleges of the Midwest Junior Fellowship. Through the latter grant I was privileged to participate in the 1968-69 Newberry Library Seminar in the Humanities. My associates in the seminar, both teachers and students, were generous with advice, sympathy, and good fellowship.

The management policies of my graduate committee, to whom an earlier version of this study was presented as a Cornell University doctoral dissertation, were both fair and humane. I have benefitted from the thoughtful comments of Professor Gerd Korman, who originally suggested this project. To my mentor, Professor Paul W. Gates, I am indebted not only for helpful criticism but also for his fine example as teacher and scholar.

All accidents which may mar the following pages are the result of my own negligence and are not to be blamed upon my managers, fellow servants, or financiers.

TABLE OF CONTENTS

LIST OF TABLES

LIST OF ILLUSTRATIONS

INTRODUCTION

In 1850 the United States was, as it had always been, a nation of farmers. The American economy was based upon agriculture, and most of the nation's exports consisted of the raw products of farm and plantation. America's imports, on the other hand, included numerous manufactured articles which domestic workshops could not supply.[1] The growth of the American economy depended upon the importation of these manufactured goods, and also upon a steady inflow of immigrants, investments, and ideas from overseas.

Yet amid these signs of immaturity there were indications that this young land was moving toward a new economic way of life. In the North-east, the factory system already was eclipsing household production of textiles, and technological innovations were permitting increased use of steam-powered machinery in the making of cloth, iron, and other commodities. The emergence of mechanized production had been accompanied by remarkable improvements in transportation facilities, so that by mid-century manufacturers were afforded comparatively cheap, rapid, and regular freightage of raw materials and finished goods. In earth and forest abundant resources awaited exploitation, while the burgeoning population of farm and village promised an expanding market for the fruits of capitalist enterprise. All of these developments were much in evidence by 1850, and their combination was to bring about the industrialization of the United States at a pace so pronounced as to alter the American way of life in the next fifty years.

To study this nation's history from 1850 to 1900 is to study the impact of industrialization on American society. In the space of a few decades large corporations arose, grew, and were consolidated into still larger ones. The industrial labor force expanded rapidly, and workers increasingly banded together in national unions to protect their interests in the new industrial environment. While leaders in government, religion, and social thought tried to adjust to these startling developments, the nation's farmers rebelled against the new order of economic life, which tore away their status as America's social paragon. Thus, in their various ways, businessmen and politicians, laborers and farmers, clergymen and intellectuals all responded to the onrushing tide of industrialization.[2]

An important factor in the rise of the new industrial economy was the spread of the national railway network, for railroads carried the goods which industry consumed and produced. Also, the railroads comprised an important market for new industry by absorbing large quantities of iron, coal, wood, machinery, glass, felt, rubber, and brass. Perhaps most significant of all, railroading was the nation's first really big business, and so it was compelled to deal with problems that had not existed in the pre-industrial era. New methods had to be found to meet huge capital requirements, to manage enterprises of vast territorial extent and organizational complexity, and to deal with the needs of customers, the pressure of competitors, and the demands of governmental authority. Finally, the railroads had to learn how to handle the problem of labor management, for the successful operation of a railroad demanded the services of a veritable army of employees.[3]

The railroads had to recruit large numbers of unskilled laborers to build their lines and to repair and improve them when built. Skilled men were needed as brakemen, firemen, conductors, and engineers; and swarms of machinists, boilermakers, blacksmiths, masons, painters, and carpenters were required to maintain locomotives, rolling stock, bridges, and buildings. These men had to be trained and their efforts coordinated, and rigid discipline was necessary in order to meet timed schedules and avoid accidents. Wages, hours, and working conditions needed continual review and adjustment, especially when the intervention of labor unions made workers less subservient to the will of their employers. Experience taught railroad managers that they also had to concern themselves with the health and welfare of their employees. Because railroading pioneered in meeting all of these problems and served as a model for other industries, the origins of many aspects of modern industrial relations may be found in the nineteenth century railroad industry.

A detailed examination of the evolution of labor policy on one railroad may afford insight into the effect of the industrial environment upon the work force of other railroads and other industries. The Illinois Central Railroad is particularly suitable for such a case study. Unlike many other railroads, the Illinois Central was not created through the consolidation of several local projects; instead, it was from its beginning a big business, a railway planned to extend over 700 miles and to employ a labor force numbering in the thousands. Because the Illinois Central was built through sparsely settled territory, unlike the earlier lines which linked the population centers of the East, the problems encountered in its construction were accentuated and thereby rendered more amenable to study. Finally, it may be noted that the story of the Illinois Central spans the entire second half of the nineteenth century, coincides with the industrialization of the United States, and therefore provides a continuous setting in which to examine the impact of industrialization upon one set of managers and employees.[4]

[1]In 1850 total U.S. exports were valued at $135,000,000, of which $92,000,000 was in the form of raw materials. In the same year U.S. imports totalled $174,000,000, of which $142,000,000 consisted of manufactured goods. U.S. Bureau of the Census, _Historical Statistics of the United States, Colonial Times to 1957_ (Washington: Government Printing Office, 1960), p. 545.

[2]Samuel P. Hays, _The Response to Industrialism 1885-1914_ (Chicago: University of Chicago Press, 1957) is an interpretive survey based on this theme. Robert H. Wiebe, _The Search for Order 1877-1920_ (New York: Hill and Wang, 1967) stresses the emergence of bureaucratic structure in response to the needs of urban-industrial life, while Kenneth E. Boulding, _The Organizational Revolution: A Study in the Ethics of Economic Organization_ (New York: Harper and Brothers, 1953) thoughtfully examines the growth of organizations as a result, in part, of improvements in transportation and communications.

[3]Alfred D. Chandler Jr., _The Railroads: The Nation's First Big Business_ (New York: Harcourt, Brace, and World, 1965), p. 9. W. Fred Cottrell, _The Railroader_ (Stanford: Stanford University Press, 1940), p. 2.

[4]The archives of the Illinois Central Railroad are located in the Newberry Library, Chicago, Illinois. Because the materials used in the present study are scattered among the 400,000 letters, 126 bundles, and 2,000 bound volumes which constitute this collection, I have in my notes followed each citation of an item in the archives with the initials "IC," together with the catalog number under which the item is classified in Carolyn C. Mohr, _Guide to the Illinois Central Archives in the Newberry Library 1851-1906_ (Chicago: Newberry Library, 1951). In a few instances I have cited materials which are located in the Chicago offices of the Illinois Central Railroad Company. Although these items remain in the possession of the company, they have been cataloged by the Newberry Library. When reference is made to these materials, the initials IC and the catalog number are given as usual, but they are preceded by an asterisk.

CHAPTER I

BUILDING THE CHARTER LINES

The building of the Illinois Central Railroad was an ambitious, some said foolish, project. The Central line was to be longer than any railroad then in existence, and it was to pass through lands but thinly settled and far removed from the main paths of American commerce. "Here is a vast work," said the nation's leading authority on railroads, ". . . which when completed will be without use or function. . . . The road by universal consent, is a superfluous addition to the railroad system of the country."[1] Only men possessed of much imagination could discern potential profit in the scheme by forseeing the economic development of Illinois that would result from railroad construction. Such men were the promoters of the Illinois Central: George Griswold, David Neal, Robert Rantoul, Robert Schuyler, Jonathan Sturges, and a handful of other merchants and financiers who were practical enough to recognize the obstacles in their way but visionary enough to see that the Illinois Central's ribbons of iron could bind Illinois into an economic unit, open her interior lands to agriculture, and, in time, give rise to a growing volume of railroad traffic. This vision had sustained them as they struggled to obtain from the State of Illinois a corporate charter establishing the Illinois Central Railroad Company, granting its promoters the power to build and operate the road, and donating to them a huge quantity of public land which the federal government had conveyed to Illinois for the encouragement of railroad construction. They had succeeded in this effort. The charter had been won.[2] Now, in 1851, they were ready to build.

The promoters intended to construct a road that would endure until the economic development of interior Illinois had generated sufficient traffic to make it pay. "If the Road is to do a <u>small</u> business <u>badly</u>," wrote Robert Rantoul, "it is not worth building; if it is to do a <u>large</u> business <u>well</u>, it must be well built and well equipped."[3] Realizing the importance of proper construction but lacking familiarity with such matters, the promoters sought to place the task of construction into more experienced hands. They soon discovered that the building of 700 miles of railroad was too big a project for any single construction firm to carry out alone. And so they decided to parcel the work among a number of firms, each responsible for a portion of the total project.[4]

The proposed route of the Illinois Central, a giant Y-shaped plan linking the southern tip of Illinois with the extreme northeast and northwest corners of the state, was cut into a dozen numbered divisions, ranging in length from less than fifty to nearly eighty miles. The divisions numbered one and two carried the road from Cairo, a Mississippi riverport in the extreme south of the state, northward to the town of Centralia. From Centralia, divisions three and four continued on through the center of the state to the village of Decatur. The fifth division proceeded from there to Bloomington, and division six went on to La Salle. At La Salle junction was made with the Illinois and Michigan Canal, and the main line of the Illinois Central came to an end. This termination was a legal technicality, however, for from La Salle the so-called Galena branch continued on in an irregular northwesterly course through Freeport (northern limit of division seven) to Dunleith (end of division eight), just across the Mississippi from Dubuque, Iowa. The remaining four divisions of the charter route consisted in the Chicago branch, a line which ran southwest from Chicago until it struck the Illinois Central main line at Centralia. The divisions of this branch were numbered nine through twelve, beginning at Chicago.[5]

To coordinate work on the various divisions, the promoters hired an unusually able and vigorous agent in the person of Roswell B. Mason, an engineer with nearly thirty years' experience in the building and management of canals and railways. His most recent position had been with the New York and New Haven Railroad, of which he was chief engineer and superintendent from 1848 until he left for service with the Illinois Central. Mason arrived in Illinois in May, 1851, bringing with him a corps of engineers, and immediately organized surveying parties to lay out the precise route of the charter lines. The

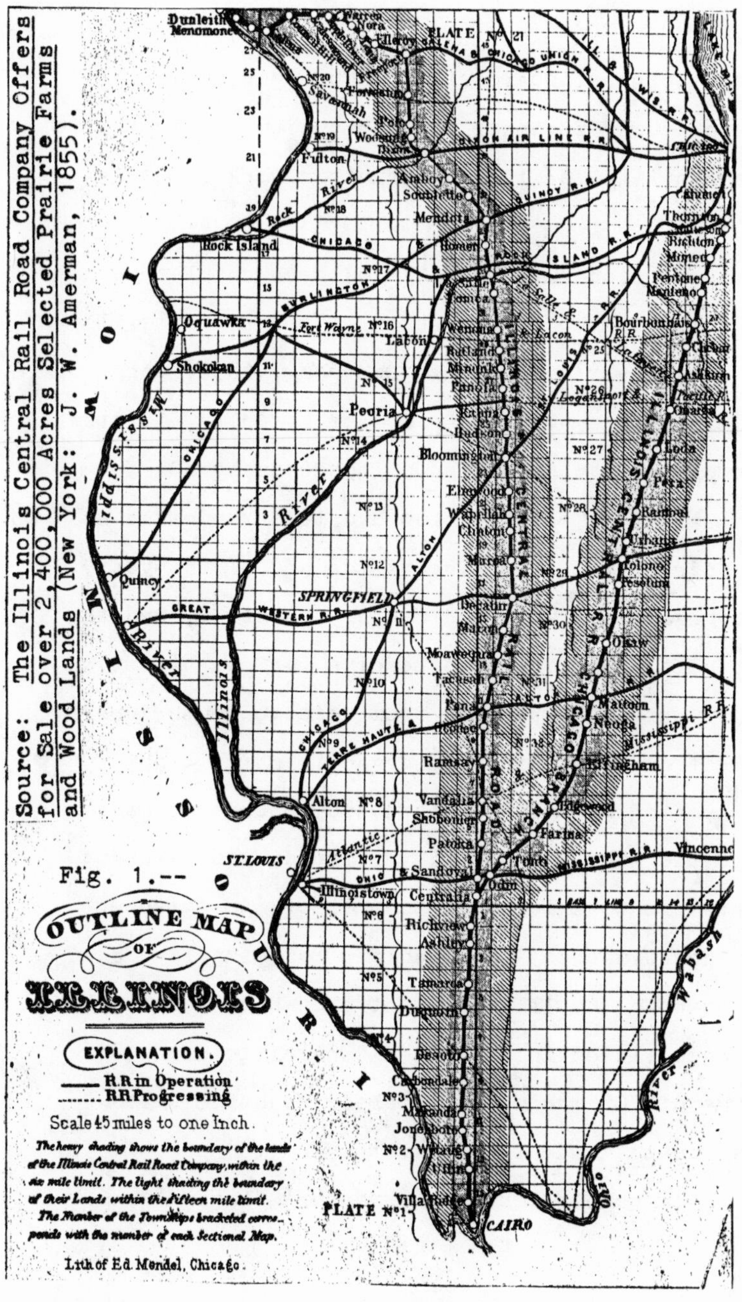

Fig. 1.--

Source: The Illinois Central Rail Road Company Offers for Sale over 2,400,000 Acres Selected Prairie Farms and Wood Lands (New York: J. W. Amerman, 1855).

Illinois Central board of directors gave him the title of chief engineer and bestowed upon him entire responsibility for the construction work in Illinois.[6]

As soon as surveying had been completed, Mason ordered the first use of laborers on the Illinois Central line. Late in December, 1851, gangs of men were set to work at Cairo and La Salle, in order to comply with a provision of the company charter which said that construction had to be underway at both ends of the main line by the end of the year.[7] These beginnings were rudimentary, however, and the first part of the line to receive serious attention was a twenty mile stretch from Chicago south, where preparation of the roadbed began in March, 1852.[8] This section was given precedence in order to accommodate the Michigan Central Railroad, which sought an entrance to Chicago at that time. An agreement was reached whereby the Michigan road supplied a cash loan to the Illinois Central, which built the line and allowed the Michigan Central to use it. A force of 700 men was assembled, shanties were thrown up to house the laborers, and the project was pressed to completion in two months' time.[9]

Meanwhile, Mason was interviewing prospective contractors in order that work might begin elsewhere on the charter lines.[10] He felt sure that favorable word-of-mouth advertising of the opportunity for employment would induce a strong influx of men to the various construction sites, but he was anxious that construction get underway as soon as possible, for any delay might cloud the general expectation among laborers that plenty of jobs would be available along the Illinois Central route.[11] By mid-June Mason's efforts were rewarded with the signing of contracts for divisions one and two, and within a month four other divisions had been let to builders.[12] Half of the charter lines now were taken up, and company officials were confident that the six sections under contract possessed a potential for immediate profit. The first two divisions, extending well over a hundred miles north of Cairo, were expected to carry considerable shipments of farm products, timber, and coal. Divison six, from Bloomington to La Salle, passed through a rich farming area already fairly well settled, while division eight would carry east-west traffic from Dunleith to Freeport, where junction would be made with the Galena and Chicago Union Railroad. The remaining two segments under contract, divisions nine and ten, extended south from Chicago to Urbana and would open up a fertile country at relatively small expense because of the regularity of the terrain in that region.[13]

Recruiting the Construction Labor Force

With surveys completed and contracts signed, Mason turned his attention to the most difficult problem of the construction period: the recruitment of a labor force. Thousands of men were needed to dig cuts, raise embankments, lay rails, and pound spikes in order to push the railroad line across the marshy lowlands, rolling prairies, and gentle hills of interior Illinois. Not only was a large force needed at the outset, but also there was a high turnover among the construction laborers. The work force suffered constant attrition as a result of illness and accident, temporary cessations of work caused by material shortages, and defections to other employers.

The Illinois Central was only one of many railroads under construction between 1852 and 1856. In those same years other companies built some 1,600 miles of line within Illinois and more than 3,800 miles in other states of the Old Northwest.[14] Three lines were pushed westward from Chicago in the early years of the decade: the Galena and Chicago Union Railroad, begun in 1850 and completed as far as Freeport by 1853; the Rock Island Railroad, built at about the same time; and the Dixon Air Line, which reached the Mississippi River at Fulton in 1855. Meanwhile, the Alton Railroad was completed from Bloomington to Alton, and work was begun on the Aurora branch of the Michigan Central Railroad and on what were to become known as the Joy lines, in the western part of the state. The success of these early ventures prompted still more construction, as four roads were built across the state south of Chicago: the Peoria and Oquawka, the Great Western, the Terre Haute and Alton, and the Ohio and Mississippi. By 1860 Illinois had more than 2,800 miles of railroad, more than any other state except Ohio; and Chicago, the terminus of eleven major lines, had become the railroad center of the United States.[15] The surge in railroad construction generated severe competition for a limited labor supply and compelled the Illinois Central company to mount a vigorous recruitment campaign. In June 1852, the company advertised that it had work for a thousand men. Two months later a single contractor--the firm in charge of division one, the southernmost section--was employing between 800 and 1,000 hands and offering jobs for up to 3,000 more. By September the company was promising two to three years' work for 10,000 men.[16]

All efforts to recruit men for work on the first division were embarrassed by the widespread belief that the southern part of Illinois was an unhealthy region.[17] For many workingmen, even the lure of relatively high wages and year-round employment could not overcome the fear of sickness--not when other railroad projects, busy farms, and thriving cities offered a host of employment opportunities in localities of better reputation. On other divisions of the line the recruitment problem was not quite so acute, but everywhere there was a need for far more men than the local populace could supply. At Roswell Mason's suggestion, contractors used horse-drawn scrapers in order to reduce the number of men needed to level the roadbed, and wherever possible local farmers were persuaded to devote whatever time they could spare to assisting in the work.[18] But such expedients could not overcome the shortage of laborers within the state. Clearly, it was necessary to look for available manpower beyond the borders of Illinois.

One place to look was obvious at this time. In the port cities of the United States, the newest sons of the Republic, their ranks swelled each year by hundreds of thousands of still newer arrivals, formed a vast pool of prospective laborers. In 1852 alone, more than 150,000 Irishmen and nearly as many Germans debarked on American soil.[19] These immigrants were mostly poor and unskilled, but they were eager for jobs, accustomed to hard work, and willing to accept conditions unappealing to the spoiled natives of the land of plenty. In Illinois there was work in abundance for all who would have it. "So come along, strangers," called the publicists of the Illinois Central.[20] "Come forward and assist in laying this mighty track," receive the "bountiful monthly dispensations" of the contractors, "and when the road is finished, purchase a farm, marry a wife, and dwell contented" under your "own vine and fig tree."[21]

Newspaper notices and word of mouth advertising had been sufficient to make Illinois workingmen aware of the employment opportunities available on the Central road. But to appeal to the immigrant laborers of the eastern cities and induce them to travel far into the interior of the country, more formal arrangements were necessary. In the spring of 1853, Roswell Mason believed that there were not a fourth as many men in Illinois as would be needed for work in the coming season. "My only hope," he wrote, "is in a large emigration from the East--I have an arrangement with one concern in N[ew] York to send 1500 Germans and with an Irish Emigrant Society to send a large number."[22] A month later he lamented that no workmen had arrived as yet but said he had sent a labor recruiter to New York, and that this agent had informed him that large numbers of Germans and Irish were arriving there and that arrangements had been made to transport them to Chicago at a fare of $4.50[23] By late summer the agent also was sending men from New York to Kankakee at a fare of $4.75 for employment on the lower end of the Chicago branch, where a contractor had promised to pay any foreman bringing a labor gang to his work a bonus of $1.00 for each man so delivered. Mason had a few qualms about his agent's advertising claims and he objected to shipping men to Kankakee, which was 100 miles away from the place they were to work, but he needed the men desperately.[24]

Eight thousand laborers were then at work on the Illinois Central, and by autumn the work force totalled approximately 10,000 men.[25] The latter figure was probably the greatest number employed at any one time in the building of the charter lines, although large forces continued to be employed in 1854. From 1854 to the completion of construction in 1856, contractors sent agents to Missouri and even as far as Ohio to round up men, but the company itself did not find it necessary to recruit immigrants from the East.[27] The struggle to maintain an adequate construction labor force did not fully cease until the last rail of the charter lines was put in place on

September 27, 1856.[28]

The Laborer Is Worthy of His Hire

The dearth of laborers which plagued railroad builders in the 1850's was a blessing to the workingmen whose services were solicited so assiduously. The great demand for labor meant that discipline could not be too severe nor working conditions too harsh at any job, lest the men go elsewhere. Above all, it meant that employers had to compete with one another for the limited labor supply, and the only really effective means of attracting men was to spread the word that high wages would be paid to those who would come where they were needed. Thus, when the Illinois Central first advertised for men, it announced that $1.00 a day would be paid to construction laborers.[29] Since a range of $0.75 to $1.00 was then considered normal pay for day laborers in Illinois, the Central's offer seemed generous enough.[30] But experience showed that the offer of a dollar a day was insufficient to attract men to the work on the first division, and a company official on the scene concluded that to retain men at that point steps would have to be taken that would, he feared, consume money.[31] Wages on the first division were raised to as much as $1.25, but even this did not attract so many men as could have been put to use.[32]

Soon the trend toward higher wages spread to other parts of the state, as the competition of contractors, farmers, and other employers for man-power became more and more severe. "Men are scarce," wrote an exasperated Roswell Mason in April, 1853. "Contractors are bidding against each other and . . . south of the 6th Division contractors are paying all prices from $1 to $1.25 per day. . . . It is a constant struggle to get men--and they are constantly changing from one place to another."[33] The contractors on the fifth division--Decatur to Bloomington--were still holding the line at $1.00, but Mason did not think they could do so much longer; their reputation for promptness in paying wages was the only thing that had delayed the departure of their workmen for greener pastures. It was rumored that at St. Louis railroad contractors were offering wages as high as $1.37-1/2 to men who would agree to come to their works in Illinois. "I do not believe this but still it may come to that," exclaimed Mason. "There's so many roads and such a strife for men and so little honor and fair dealing among contractors particularly on different roads that they send agents out to each others work and entice men away."[34]

The problem of high wages and labor scarcity was so severe that Mason confessed that he hardly knew what to do. After considering the situation, however, he arrived at an idea: why could not the various railroad companies get together and agree upon a common wage for laborers? This would end the cutthroat competition for men that was causing so much trouble to all the companies and would permit wages to be reduced to more acceptable levels. At first Mason thought that $1.00 a day might be made the standard wage, but he quickly conceded that a higher price would have to be paid in the southern part of the state. "As some contractors are working 11 hours some 11-1/2 some 12 and 12-1/2 hours I have thought that 10 cts. per hour would be a fair thing for the men," he wrote. "Then if they worked 12-1/2 hours they would get $1.25"[35] Most of the contractors on the Central road approved of Mason's idea, although a few feared it would lead to disputes with their men over time worked. As it turned out, nobody got the chance to see how the laborers would have reacted to the scheme, for Mason did not succeed in putting it into effect. He was able to persuade only one other railroad official to go along with his plan, and even that small try at cooperation proved unsuccessful. In Mason's words, "Mr. Lee of the Chicago and Mississippi road after agreeing with Mr. Plant one of my assistants not to go above 1.12-1/2 unless our contractors paid more, raised the next day to $1.20." Lee claimed that he had taken this step because an Illinois Central contractor had offered $1.25. The I.C. man "positively declared he did not offer it," but his denial did not convince Lee. The experiment ended with heightened wage costs and bruised feelings on both sides.[36] Mason's proposal that the various railroads unite in a common effort to reduce wages is a good illustration of his pragmatic approach to problems. If the law of supply and demand said that laborers should cost twenty-five per cent more than he was willing to pay, then he was perfectly willing to try to obviate the effects of that law.

Once high wages had become general throughout the state, they could not be reduced without creating great dissatisfaction among the workers. An Illinois Central contractor at La Salle learned that fact at high cost in December of 1853, when he and other employers in the vicinity tried to reduce wages from $1.25 to $1.00 a day. Announcement of the pay cut touched off a riot in which the contractor was beaten to death by a mob of Irish laborers.[37] The continued scarcity of men on some parts of the line led to wages as high as $1.50 in 1854, and even that was not always enough to satisfy the men. One contractor complained bitterly:

> When we took the contract Labor and Provisions were at reasonable rates . . . since which time labor has risen at least 33 per cent and provisions more than that. When I commenced the work, I paid one dollar per day for laborers and one dollar fifty for experienced track layers and now I am paying one dollar and a half for laborers and from one seventy-five to two fifty for track layers. . . . I have been obliged to increase the price of my men as the warm weather made its appearance and now my foreman informs me that my men will leave there the 20th of June and . . . larger prices must be paid for men or it will be impossible to get men enough to finish the work.[38]

"I find in looking over the reports of my assistants that our work is going slowly everywhere . . . in many cases at this time on acc[oun]t of the harvest," wrote Mason in August 1854. "Farmers come onto the work and offer the Irishmen $2 per day and board to work at harvest."[39]

Clearly the men who built the Illinois Central were well paid according to the standards of the time. Because they toiled out of doors, they lost many a day's wages when bad weather prevented work. But on the days when they did work, their wages of $1.00 to as much as $1.50 a day for unskilled labor compared rather favorably with those of many inside workers with skill and training (see Table 1). Illinois was in a period of great growth and demand for all classes of workmen was high. According to one newspaper editor, in 1853 and 1854 "those who worked by the day or week were the real masters, for good mechanics could command almost any price they chose to ask."[40] There probably was little basis for another editor's contention that increased wages merely gave the workingmen money to squander on liquor, cigars, chewing tobacco, and other extrava-

TABLE 1

WAGES OF JOURNEYMEN EMPLOYED IN VARIOUS TRADES AT CHICAGO IN MAY, 1854

Occupation	Wages per Day	Earnings per Week for Piece Work
Blacksmiths	$1.25-$2.00	. .
Butchers	1.00- 3.00	. .
Carpenters	1.50- 2.00	. .
Cabinet Makers	1.00- 2.00	$ 9-$18
Coopers	. .	9- 12
Curriers	. .	9- 12
Day Laborers	1.00- 1.50	. .
Harness Makers	. .	6- 15
Hatters	. .	12- 20
House Painters	1.25- 1.75	. .
Machinists	1.00- 2.00	12- 18
Marble Cutters	1.75- 2.00	. .
Masons and Plasterers . .	1.50- 2.00	. .
Printers	1.67	12- 18
Rope Makers	1.50	. .
Ship Caulkers	2.25- 2.50	. .
Shoemakers	. .	6- 12
Stone Cutters	1.75- 2.00	. .
Tailors	. .	7- 11
Tanners	1.00- 1.25	. .
Trunk Makers	. .	8- 15
Wire Workers	1.00- 1.50	14- 15
Wagon Makers	1.25- 2.00	. .

Source: [William Bross], The Rail-Roads, History, and Commerce of Chicago (Chicago: Democratic Press, 1854), p. 48. "The range is large, but it is not wider than the difference in the skill and capacity of different men in every occupation."

gances; but there certainly was truth in his statement that wage earners had seldom had it so good: "These are decidedly good times--every one is doing well in this glorious country, who <u>tries</u>. 'The laborer is worthy of his hire'--and we will add to that, that we believe he <u>gets</u> his hire, in these days."[41]

Working Conditions in the Construction Period

If the wages of construction laborers were high, they also were amply earned. In the 1850's railroad building was heavy, arduous work, and most of it was accomplished by sheer physical exertion with little assistance from mechanical devices. Iron and timber might be hauled about in carts pulled by teams of oxen, and horse-drawn scrapers could be used to advantage in the grading of fairly level areas. But where earthen embankments, cuts, or drainage ditches were needed, the necessary work was done by men with shovels; and everywhere the iron rails were fastened down by spikes driven home in a cacaphony of hammer blows.[42] The men who wielded shovel and sledge toiled eleven or twelve hours a day, six days a week, often under conditions of great hardship.[43]

In the summer months the sun beat down endlessly upon backs already sweltering in the heat of labor. Of the construction camps in southern Illinois, an observer said:

> When summer comes drouth prevails and the weather is intensely hot. The thermometer ranged from 101 to 105 in the shade every day we were there and had done so for two weeks previous. In addition to this the drouth is so severe that the men have no water to drink except what is hauled by teams from 3 to 10 miles.[44]

When the sun did not shine, the men sometimes were no less miserable, for, said the same witness, "When it rains long, the bottoms are covered by water, and it becomes unhealthy."[45] Moreover, heavy rain brought the threat of flood in low-lying areas. Wrote a company officer from Vandalia, a town on the third division:

> The Okaw or Kaskaskia bottom 4 miles in width immediately south of this place is a most abominable place to work. A large force has been started there three or four times, and as many times driven off by high water. During the winter some 400 or 500 men were there and after working a little more than a month, they were so completely flooded that every shanty had 3 or 4 feet of water on its floor, and it became necessary to build flat boats to bring the men off which occupied 2 days, and two were drowned.

> They all refused to go back, and now they are preparing to pile and trestle for part of the distance. . . . It is impossible to conceive the difficulties attending the execution of the work in the southern part of the state without coming here and going over the ground.[46]

Excessive heat and rainfall helped bring on the danger most feared by the construction laborers: the threat of sickness in the labor camps. Hot weather brought the possibility of illness resulting from tainted food or from sanitation problems, which increased as water supplies dwindled. Wet weather, on the other hand, contributed to outbreaks of chills and fevers among men who ceased their daily labors in rain and mud only to sleep in drafty shanties, sometimes not much drier than the open air. Malaria was spread among the laborers by clouds of mosquitoes, and dysentery and other diseases flourished because of crowded, unsanitary conditions, as at Cairo, where the railroad men were said to "sleep five in a bed, and drink very harmoniously out of the same jug."[47] Small wonder that waves of sickness frequently engulfed the labor camps. "So much sickness I never saw before among so small a population," was a typical comment from one of Mason's assistants. Mason himself said that "sickness of the most violent character on many parts of the line" was the most serious of all the difficulties that hampered construction.[48] There was one disease that was feared above all others: the dreadful scourge of cholera.

Asiatic cholera had not been unknown in Illinois in earlier decades, but it raged with particular fury in the 1850's, the years of the great boom in railway construction. Cholera struck swiftly and without warning and often claimed the life of its victim in a matter of days, sometimes only hours.[49] In 1852 there were two outbreaks of the disease at La Salle, the terminus of the Illinois Central main line. In the second outbreak, which occurred in August, the victims were all Irish laborers who had come to the vicinity in order to secure employment on the railroad. About thirty workers were seized with premonitory symptoms, and of these sixteen or more died after only a few hours of illness.[50] The disease also occurred at other locations. A company official recalled many years later that on the Chicago branch cholera had broken out in the summers of both 1852 and 1853 and that in an effort to combat it he had ordered the removal of the labor camp to a new location on several occasions.[51]

By far the worst ravages of cholera occurred in the year 1854, when an epidemic broke out in the northwestern part of the state and spread southward during the early summer. The first cases appeared in the town of Galena in late May. This was a minor outbreak and did not affect the railroad laborers of the area; in fact, it had a tendency to induce laborers to leave the city and go out on the work.[52] In mid-June, however, the disease struck with a vengeance on the fifth and sixth divisions. It appeared suddenly among a gang of men manning a gravel train near Clinton, killing a foreman and one laborer.[53] At the same time, there was a terrible outbreak at a construction camp near La Salle. Between seventy and eighty laborers died there, half of them while at work and the other half after they fled in terror from the work camp into the town. Three laborers at the La Salle station also fell victims to the disease. One of the three, after seeing his brother die, was so frightened that he drew his pay and started for Iowa, but before leaving La Salle, he himself fell ill and died. The president of the Illinois Central wrote that all of the deaths at La Salle had resulted from "real malignant cholera, killing in 3 to 8 hours." He added that he considered it neither politic nor humane to attempt to increase the work force until the epidemic had run its course.[54]

Before conditions at La Salle had returned to normal, cholera occurred again at Galena, and this time it broke out within the construction camp outside the city, causing the laborers to abandon the work and flee for their lives. The disease also appeared in a nearby camp at Scales Mound, where the men became so excited that their employer hired a physician in an attempt to forestall panic.[55] In July, cholera came to Chicago, and nearly all of the Illinois Central employees--laborers, mechanics, stonecutters, and even draftsmen and office workers--joined other citizens in a pell-mell exodus to the countryside.[56] In August there was still considerable cholera in the vicinity of Centralia, causing great fright on the lower end of the third division.[57]

Cholera or other illness was the greatest threat to the health of the construction laborer, but it was not the only one. There was also the danger of physical injury while on the job. It is not possible to give precise information on the nature and frequency of such mishaps, but obviously accidents did occur, and a few of them were reported in the newspapers of Chicago and other cities. For example, in the Chicago Tribune appeared the following news item, a model of concise reporting:

> A laborer by the name of John Morgan was injured last week on the Illinois Central R. R. Both of his legs were crushed by coming against a tree as they were hanging on the side of a gravel car in which he was riding. How careless every body is getting to be.[58]

The Tribune also carried accounts of an accident in which a Michigan Central passenger train ran into an Illinois Central construction train--"but to the surprise of all it was found that only one man was killed and comparatively few were injured"[59]--and of an explosion which crippled two workmen in the employ of an Illinois Central contractor:

> Two employees of Bailey, Broad, & Co., R.R. contractors, were blown up at Stony Island by the premature discharge of a keg of gunpowder. Richard Andrews, it is thought, will not live. John McCay is severely injured but probably will recover.[60]

Among other accidents reported in Illinois newspapers were the plunge of a gravel train from a trestle, crushing one laborer and drowning another; the cave-in of an excavation, burying alive three workmen; and the collision of a train and a handcar carrying nine tracklayers, of whom three were killed.[61]

Accident or illness endangered not only the life and limb of the construction laborer, but also his livelihood. A man who was sick or injured could not work, and when a man did not work he received no wages. There was no sick pay or other compensation for men incapacitated by accident or disease; once dropped from the payroll they might as well have ceased to exist so far as the railroad company and its contractors were concerned. The employers' indifference towards these unfortunates was but one facet of their general policy of unconcern for the welfare of the construction laborers. Other manifestations of this attitude were plentiful.

When construction first began on the Illinois Central, a company agent in New York recruited 600 immigrants, promised them jobs in Illinois, and shipped them to Chicago. There many of them found themselves distitute and unable to secure work because no provision had been made for their transportation from Chicago to the construction sites. The company did nothing for them until the mayor of the city insisted that they be put to work, lest they become public charges.[62] When a laborer obtained a job with the railroad company or with one of its contractors, he acquired no guarantee of steady employment. Any cessation of construction work because of material shortages, weather conditions, or other cause could bring the prompt dismissal of those men whose services were not of immediate use. However, the manpower shortage in Illinois made contractors reluctant to discharge men as long as they could find something for them to do. The lament of a contractor responsible for laying track on the Chicago branch illustrates this point:

> There have been frequent delays[,] sometimes for want of the grading being done[;] at other times we have been out of iron and the first six months out of chairs a great portion of the time[;] to say the least I laid over fifty miles without them. . . . When delayed for want of grading or iron I have several times been obliged to break up my gang, keep my teams at expense and pay my foreman or should lose him. . . . Besides after a gang is broken up and scattered it is no small matter and attended with no small expense to get up another gang and break them in.[63]

The contractor's remarks indicate that he kept his men at work despite a shortage of "chairs," the iron clamps used to fasten rails to ties. He did not break up his gang until an ungraded roadbed or shortage of rails made tracklaying impossible. It is interesting, though perhaps unfair, to notice that while the contractor took care of his work animals during the stoppages, he expected his men to shift for themselves.

The Illinois Central and its contractors displayed only a minimal interest in the personal comfort of their laborers. In unsettled areas they found it necessary to erect shanties and cart in provisions, but where possible they left these matters to profit-seeking individuals who came to the construction sites, threw up a few rough buildings, and began selling food, lodging, and ample quantities of whisky to a more or less captive clientele.[64] Even the foreman of an individual labor gang was expected to devote his full energies to the interests of his employer and not involve himself with the personal welfare of the workmen under his charge. On one occasion Roswell Mason ordered a contractor to discharge a foreman whom Mason believed to be in collusion with his men.[65] Throughout the construction period the only responsibility toward its laborers which was consistently recognized by the Illinois Central company was the obligation to pay them promptly, and in cash, the wages which they had earned. In this matter the company went so far as to guarantee to redeem at par value all banknotes paid to the men as wages.[66] Once a man had performed his work and pocketed his pay, his relations with the Illinois Central were at an end, and his health, livelihood, and mode of life were his own concern.

A Reputation for Violence

If the worker's welfare was of little moment to his employer, it was of still less concern to the society into whose midst he had come. The native population of Illinois welcomed the building of railroads and accepted the influx of foreign-born laborers as a necessary accompaniment, but the newcomers were viewed as a group apart, and they seemed strange and sometimes even frightening to the farmers and townsfolk who lived in the vicinity of the construction camps. The community response to the coming of the railroad laborers did not consist in any demonstrations of concern for the welfare of the newcomers, but rather in defensive measures against what was commonly viewed as a threat to the social order. Townspeople frequently became alarmed at brawls, riots, and other manifestations of violence among the railroad laborers. Such disturbances did not occur with unwonted frequency, considering the thousands of men involved in railroad building and the harsh conditions under which they lived and worked, but there was sufficient violence to cause near panic in some communities and to arouse hostile sentiments in a good many others.[67] In 1853, there were apprehensions of difficulties between the laborers and the citizens on the first division and fears of real terrorism on the fourth, where a citizen of Decatur reported that that village frequently was thrown into confusion by reports that the Irish were determined to burn it down, and that a volunteer company had been formed "of a number of our best citizens, to prevent disturbances."[68] The Decatur volunteers were not a very effective outfit, if we are to judge from an event that occurred soon after the formation of that company of the elite:

> On last Saturday night, about twelve o'clock, the citizens of Decatur were awakened from their peaceful slumbers by the violent ringing of the town bells, and the report immediately spread that the Irish railroad laborers were rising _en masse_ to burn down the town. The terrified citizens rushed to the Irish shanties to beg for quarters, but soon learned that they had been most unmercifully hoaxed by some wag of a fellow. Every Irishman was sound asleep.[69]

Decatur's citizens acquitted themselves more creditably on a later occasion, when a series of clashes between Irish and German laborers threatened to erupt into a battle royal. A Decatur store clerk described this affair, which involved laborers on both the Illinois Central and Great Western railroads. On the Great Western line there were two contractors, one on each side of Stevens Creek. One contractor employed all Irish laborers, and the other all Germans. On the Illinois Central there was a large gang of Irishmen in the employ of John Post, who had the grading contract for one mile of road at Decatur. There had been constant friction and several fights between the two gangs at work on the Great Western, and one day a rumor reached Decatur that the German gang was exterminating the Irish. The Irishmen at work on the Illinois Central immediately determined to rescue their countrymen. They armed themselves with pickaxes, shovels, and shillalahs, and marched up Decatur's Main Street, enroute to the "Battle of Stevens Creek." But the people of the town saw to it that they never got there. When they reached the courthouse square, the Irishmen encountered a solid phalanx of citizens armed to the teeth with muskets and bayonets. The workmen were cowed by this display of superior weaponry and soon decided to return peacably to their own camp. Had they but known that the formidable looking weapons of the Decatur volunteers were mostly rusted flintlocks left over from the Indian and Mexican wars, the affair might well have ended differently.[70]

Affrays between laborers of differing backgrounds were common. Usually such imbroglios pitted Irish against German immigrants, as in the affair just described, but there also is record of a fight which involved one Irish laborer versus half a dozen assailants, also Irish but "from a different county of Ireland from where this unfortunate man was born."[71] One characteristic common to nearly all these conflicts was that in virtually every case, no matter what its origin, the inebriation of the participants was cited by witnesses as a major factor in converting bad feelings into bloodshed.

"These scenes of violence," said Roswell Mason, "are the result in most cases of the free use of whiskey by the men. This cursed stuff has been the cause of more delay, more violence, and bloodshed, than any one thing."[72] In an attempt to deal with the problem of drunkenness and rioting, Mason, with characteristic decisiveness, forbade the transportation of intoxicants on Illinois Central construction trains, but he found it impossible to cut off the supply in that way.[73] At least one Illinois Central contractor forbade the use of spirits at his camp and begged the citizens of nearby towns not to sell alcoholic beverages to his men.[74] But such efforts were usually in vain. Nearly every village along the Central route was, like Vandalia, "blessed with the presence of several doggeries, where rot gut is dealt out with impunity to those whose appetites are stronger by fearful odds than their judgments."[75] Occasionally local citizens took direct action to deal with the liquor problem. A few weeks after authorities at La Salle visited a grogshop and discovered ten men lying on the floor dead drunk--one of them with his stomach stretched across a barrel of whisky--there was a flurry of vigilante activity which resulted in the destruction of $2,000 worth of alcoholic beverages. "Openings were made in the casks to permit the liquor to run off," said a newspaper account of the incident. "The ladies are strongly suspected of having had something to do with it."[76] A few communities along the railroad line escaped the consequences of drinking by prohibiting the sale of alcohol within their town limits. The founder of Carbondale, a village laid out along the first division while the Illinois Central was being built, recalled in his memoirs that many laborers were employed in the vicinity of the town, but "Carbondale, having no tippling shops, was free from drunken brawls and riots at all times, and the Sabbaths were as quiet as in any other part of the country. Those who desired to put in time spreeing away their health and hard-earned wages were compelled to go elsewhere to do so."[77]

The most serious outbreak of violence at an Illinois Central construction camp occurred near the town of La Salle in December, 1853.[78] Nearly 2,000 hands were employed in railroad construction in that locality, and of these about 400 were working on an embankment contracted to the firm of Story, Talmadge, and Conklin by the Illinois Central company. A series of disturbances had occurred among these laborers in 1852 and 1853, including a riot in which one German worker was killed and several others seriously injured.[79] A company officer wrote that there had always been "a bad Set of men about the heavy work at Lasalle" and that the ease with which whisky had been obtainable had paved the way for "the brutal and murderous character" of their actions of December 16, 1853.[80] On that day, Albert Story, of the firm working under contract with the Illinois Central, announced a reduction in wages from $1.25 to $1.00 per day. Other contractors in the area had agreed to make the same pay cut, so Story did not expect his employees to put up any serious resistance to the move. But he was mistaken.

A number of Story's hands refused to work at the new price and demanded that they be paid off immediately so that they might leave the camp. Story, no doubt sensing that the situation was becoming dangerous, agreed to this demand, but not quickly enough to satisfy one John Ryan, who demanded his wages in a violent manner.

> Story told him he should have them, when his turn came round, whereupon the man seized Story by the throat, a struggle ensued, Story snatched his revolver and levelled him with the ground. A number of Irishmen then rushed on Story, drove him from his store to his house, thence to his barn, where they most brutally knocked him down, beat his brains out, dragged him to the door, and then with large stones crushed his skull to a mummy. Consternation spread like a prairie on fire. The Irish assembled in great numbers, many of them in a fury of drunkenness.[81]

The people of La Salle were terrified by this event and immediately called for the intervention of Shield's Guards, an eighty-man military company from the nearby village of Ottawa. Meanwhile, the citizens of La Salle armed themselves and hastened to the scene of the crime. When the citizens and soldiers arrived, the Irishmen hid among their shanties. But they soon were rounded up and forced to pass in a file, while Story's foreman identified those who had participated in the outrage. The men so identified were arrested by the sheriff and examined on the spot by a local magistrate.[82]

Many of the people from La Salle--the large majority, according to one report--favored "instant jury" for the rioters "and if found guilty, instant suspension on the first tree."[83] However, cooler heads prevailed and the prisoners were not molested. If a lynching had occurred, it would have aroused little indignation elsewhere in Illinois. At Chicago, for example:

> The riot at La Salle, and the murder of a contractor by a set of brutish Irishmen, caused considerable excitement. . . . There was more indignation manifest than we have seen lately, and had the whole thirty-two prisoners that were taken, been marched out and shot on the spot, . . . the public judgment would have sanctioned it at once. There appears to be a growing feeling against Irish riots, and a determination to use strong measures to put them down hereafter.[84]

The excitement at La Salle subsided within a few weeks, but repercussions of the affair were felt for months afterwards. Eleven men were tried for the murder of Albert Story, and six of them were convicted and sentenced to hang.[85] A campaign to secure clemency for the doomed men was instigated on the grounds that they were merely a few individuals among a mob of hundreds of rioters and that they had taken no direct part in the murder of Story. But many Illinoisans shared the view of the Chicago Tribune that the accomplices to the murder were as guilty as the persons who had struck the fatal blow, and that the effort to secure commutation from the governor was a dangerous machination of the Roman Catholic Church.

The _Tribune_ alleged that its files were crimson with the bloody record of awful crimes, "nine cases out of ten committed by 'noble Celts,' and almost invariably accompanied with circumstances of diabolical atrocity and cruelty," and claimed that the pardon campaign was being promoted secretly by the _Tablet_, Chicago's Roman Catholic newspaper.[86] These charges provoked a vigorous reply from J. F. Farnsworth, attorney for the accused, who argued that the condemned men were "poor Railroad Irishmen" who had been convicted because railroad companies and contractors had spent money lavishly in behalf of the prosecution. "If these men must be hanged," said Farnsworth, "then the State should immediately set to work and hunt down and hang the whole three hundred men who were there."[87]

The clemency campaign was successful, perhaps partly because Mason Brayman, solicitor for the Illinois Central, supported the petition for executive intervention.[88] In July, 1854,

Governor Joel A. Matteson commuted the sentences of the rioters from death to life imprisonment. For this act of mercy the governor was burned in effigy at La Salle, Joliet, and Chicago.[89]

Most of the hostile sentiment which the citizenry of Illinois displayed toward the railroad laborers derived from a natural distrust of these rough-mannered "foreigners" whose overwhelming numbers and boisterous behavior had disrupted the tranquil life of the prairie communities. When the construction work was finished and the labor camps broken up, this distrust subsided and resentment of the newcomers declined rapidly.

Many of the immigrant laborers had come to Illinois in hopes of amassing savings sufficient to acquire farms of their own, a goal beyond the dreams of poor men in Ireland or Germany. Some of them fulfilled this ambition, buying land from the railroad or the government and settling down to a fuller life than they had previously known. Other laborers remained in the service of the Illinois Central Railroad, signing on as section hands and perhaps hoping for better positions later on.[90] There were still others, those to whom illness, intemperance, or family responsibilities had denied the opportunity to accumulate savings. For those unfortunate souls there were other labor camps on other railroads.

***

The construction years were a unique period in the history of the Illinois Central company. The building of the world's longest railway, through a region largely unpopulated and undeveloped, required the employment of laborers in numbers far exceeding those obtainable in local markets. The company and its contractors were compelled to mount a vigorous recruitment campaign in order to draw Irish and German immigrants from the port cities of New York and New Orleans. They also had to pay their workmen relatively high wages in order to avoid losing them to competing employers.

Conditions of life and toil were hard for the construction laborers. The work day was long and arduous, and most tasks were accomplished by unaided muscle power. Makeshift housing provided only rudimentary protection against the vagaries of nature, so that both spring rain and summer heat caused hardship and contributed to outbreaks of sickness in the labor camps. Epidemics of cholera took the lives of scores of men in 1853 and 1854. Those unfortunate enough to be incapacitated by illness or accident received no assistance from the railroad company, which displayed minimal interest in the welfare of the construction labor force. The harsh quality of their environment caused many workers to seek escape in drunkenness and rowdyism, and this in turn contributed to fights and riots among rival gangs of Irish and German workers. These disturbances frightened the townsfolk and farmers of Illinois and reinforced the negative attitude of the native population toward the immigrant laborers.

The experience of the construction laborers is interesting in its own right, and it is a significant facet of the saga of the immigrant worker in antebellum America. But it has little direct connection with the later, larger story of labor on the Illinois Central. Most of the construction hands were hired by local contractors and thus had no direct affiliation with the Illinois Central company. Even those who were in the immediate employ of the corporation were regarded as temporary workers, in whose welfare the company had no permanent interest. The building of the charter lines required a large labor force, but that was virtually the only characteristic of modern industrialism that was present in the job environment of the construction era. Not until the railroad began its traffic operations would it have need for a regular labor force. It would be for these men, the first permanent Illinois Central employees, to face the demands of a nascent industrial environment.

[1]Henry V. Poor in American Railroad Journal, XXVII (March 18, 1854), 162. The north-south route of the Illinois Central made it an anomaly among railroad projects of the 1850's, when the development of the great east-west trunk lines occupied the attention of most railroad men.

[2]The origin of the federal land grant and the struggle for the charter are described in Paul W. Gates, The Illinois Central Railroad and Its Colonization Work (Cambridge: Harvard University Press, 1934), pp. 21-65.

[3]Robert Rantoul Jr. to Hon. U. F. Linder of the House, Springfield, February 1, 1851, Mason Brayman papers, Chicago Historical Society. This letter was printed in Illinois State Journal (Springfield), February 5, 1851.

[4]A New York syndicate expressed interest in building the line, and efforts were made to secure bids from English contractors, but both of these possibilities came to naught. Minutes of the Board of Directors, December 12, 1851; January 29, 1852, *IC-+3.1.

[5]Roswell B. Mason, Chief Engineer, to Pres. and Directors, Chicago, January 1, 1854, IC-2.12, gives the locations of the twelve divisions.

[6]William K. Ackerman, Historical Sketch of the Illinois Central Railroad (Chicago: Fergus Printing Co., 1890), p. 82. During the next few years, Mason proved such an asset to the I.C. that its president said the loss of his services would cost the company $100,000. William H. Osborn, Pres., to Jonathan Perkins, Treas., La Salle, June 11, 1856, IC-106.2. See also Ebenezer Lane, Counsel for I.C., to Edward Cron, n.p., September 11, 1856, Lane papers, University of Chicago Library.

[7]Mason to Mason Brayman, Solicitor, Chicago, December 8, 1851; December 31, 1851, Brayman papers, Chicago Historical Society. Cairo Sun, December 25, 1851.

[8]Robert Schuyler, Pres., to Brayman, New York, March 6, 1852, Brayman papers, Chicago Historical Society.

[9]Mason to Schuyler, Chicago, March 27, 1852, IC-1M3.1. Brayman to Mason, Chicago, May 10, 1852, Brayman papers, Chicago Historical Society. Carleton J. Corliss, Main Line of Mid-America: The Story of the Illinois Central (New York: Creative Age Press, 1950), p. 56.

[10]Mason to Schuyler, Chicago, March 30, 1852, IC-1M3.1.

[11]Mason to Schuyler, Chicago, April 6, 1852, IC-1M3.1.

[12]James F. Joy, Counsel, to W. Sloan et al., members of Illinois legislature, Springfield, June 17, 1852, printed in Salem Advocate, July 1, 1852, clipping in IC-3.6. Unsigned letter to C. Devaux and Co. of London, New York, July 9, 1852, IC-11N1.5.

[13]Letter to Devaux and Co., July 9, 1852, IC-11N1.5. The firms receiving the contracts are listed in Minutes of the Board of Directors, September 2, 1852, *IC-+3.1.

[14]Frederick L. Paxson, "The Rail-roads of the 'Old Northwest' Before the Civil War," Wisconsin Academy of Sciences, Arts, and Letters, Transactions, Vol. XVII (1911), Part II, statistical tables, pp. 269-273.

[15]Gates, Illinois Central, pp. 85-90.

[16]Alton Daily Morning Courier, June 21, 1852. Ibid., August 27, 1852, copying Jonesboro Gazette. Bloomington Intelligencer, September 8, 1852.

[17]The Alton paper denied reports of high mortality in the South but admitted that they were responsible for labor shortages at Jonesboro and Cairo. Alton Daily Morning Courier, November 13, 1852; December 2, 1852.

[18]Mason to Schuyler, Chicago, April 22, 1853, IC-1M3.1. On the use of scrapers, see also Chicago Daily Tribune, April 13, 1853, and Mason to Schuyler, Chicago, May 22, 1853, IC-1M3.1.

[19]U.S. Bureau of the Census, Historical Statistics of the U.S, p. 57.

[20]Alton Daily Morning Courier, December 2, 1852. See also Chicago Daily Tribune, March 30, 1853.

[21]Chicago Daily Tribune, January 18, 1853, copying Railroad Times.

[22]Mason to Schuyler, Chicago, April 18, 1853, IC-1M3.1.

[23]Mason to Schuyler, Chicago, May 22, 1853, IC-1M3.1. An agent also was sent to New Orleans to recruit immigrants arriving there, according to Mason Brayman, quoted in Alton Daily Morning Courier, April 25, 1853. Charlotte Erickson, American Industry and the European Immigrant 1860-1885 (Cambridge: Harvard University Press, 1957), pp. 71-72, says that Mason appointed Henry Phelps as agent in New York in 1852 with instructions to recruit immigrants.

[24]Mason to William P. Burrall, Treas., Chicago, August 10, 1853, IC-1M3.3. Contract between Henry Phelps, agent for I.C., and Richard Mead, August 4, 1853, IC-3.92. Gates, Illinois Central, p. 96, reproduces a broadside issued by Phelps in July 1853, calling for 3,000 laborers to work on the twelfth division.

[25]Alton Daily Morning Courier, August 16, 1853, quoting Mason Brayman. Chicago Daily Tribune, May 4, 1853; October 28, 1853.

[26]According to the editor of the Chicago Daily Democratic Press, 7,000 were at work in May 1854. [William Bross], The Rail-Roads, History and Commerce of Chicago (Chicago: Democratic Press, 1854), p. 14.

[27]George Watson, Supt. of southern division, to Mason, Ewington, March 28, 1854, IC-1B7.1. Osborn to Perkins, Centralia, June 7, 1856; June 9, 1856, IC-106.2. Benjamin F. Johnson, Assistant to Pres., to Osborn, Chicago, June 30, 1856, IC-1J6.2.

[28]Johnson to Osborn, Chicago, September 27, 1856, IC-1J6.2. By November 1853, about 125 miles of track were built. Another 125 were finished the following year. The main line was completed in the last few days of 1854 and the Galena branch was opened six months later. On September 27, 1856, the last rail was placed on the Chicago branch, thus ending the construction of the charter lines. _Chicago Daily Tribune_, November 28, 1853. Mason to Brayman, Chicago, January 1854, Brayman papers, Chicago Historical Society. Mason to Frederick Schuchardt, trustee for I.C. mortgages, Chicago, November 25, 1854, IC-11N1.5. Mason, memorandum on completion of main line, December 29, 1854, IC-1M2.1. Johnson to Osborn, Chicago, June 2, 1855; September 27, 1856, IC-1J6.2.

[29]_Alton Daily Morning Courier_, June 21, 1852.

[30]_Ibid._, May 9, 1853. _Chicago Daily Tribune_, October 28, 1853.

[31]David A. Neal, Vice Pres., to Schuyler, St. Louis, November 15, 1852, IC-1N4.1.

[32]_Alton Daily Morning Courier_, January 8, 1853, reports wages of $1.00 to $1.25 and work available for 1,000 more men.

[33]Mason to Schuyler, La Salle, April 18, 1853, IC-1M3.1.

[34]_Ibid._

[35]Mason to Schuyler, Vandalia, April 27, 1853, IC-1M3.1.

[36]_Ibid._

[37]_Chicago Daily Tribune_, December 17, 1853.

[38]Lewis Broad, for Bailey Broad and Co., to pres. and directors of I.C., Chicago, May 31, 1854, IC-11N1.5.

[39]Mason to Burrall, Chicago, August 2, 1854, IC-1M3.1.

[40]Bross, Rail-Roads, History and Commerce, pp. 47-48.

[41]Alton Daily Morning Courier, May 9, 1853; sentence order reversed.

[42]In the spring of 1854, about 2,000 teams were assisting the 7,000 men at work on the road. Bross, Rail-Roads, History and Commerce, p. 44.

[43]The length of the working day varied with the season and from place to place. In the spring of 1853, Mason noted that different contractors were working their men 11, 11-1/2, 12, and even 12-1/2 hours. Mason to Schuyler, La Salle, April 18, 1853, IC-1M3.1. On the sixth division the work was being pushed day and night, two sets of hands being employed in twelve hour shifts. Bloomington Intelligencer, February 9, 1853.

[44]Burrall to Perkins, Chicago, September 6, 1854, IC-1B9.1. In 1856 Mason upbraided a contractor on the Chicago branch for laying only 2-1/4 miles of track in a week, but the blame really belonged to the sun, for the weather was so hot that the contractor's men refused to work at any price. Johnson to Osborn, Chicago, June 30, 1856, IC-1J6.2.

[45]Burrall to Perkins, Chicago, September 6, 1854, IC-1B9.1.

[46]Burrall to Jonathan Sturges, Director, Vandalia, May 9, 1854, IC-1B9.1.

[47]Bloomington Intelligencer, November 9, 1853.

[48]Lewis F. Ashley, Assistant Engineer, [to Brayman?], Jonesboro, January 25, 1853, Brayman

papers, Chicago Historical Society. Mason to Sturges, Chicago, November 12, 1854, IC-1M3.1.

[49]Milo Custer, "Asiatic Cholera in Central Illinois, 1834-1873," _Journal of the Illinois State Historical Society_, XXIII (April, 1930), 113-162.

[50]_Alton Daily Morning Courier_, August 2, 1852, copying _St. Louis Union_. _Bloomington Intelligencer_, August 4, 1852, quoted in Custer, "Asiatic Cholera," p. 152. The disease disappeared in three weeks, according to the _Alton Daily Morning Courier_, August 2, 1852, copying _Peru Democrat_.

[51]Ovan Ott to William R. Head, Chicago, March 1897, IC-2.91.

[52]Burrall to Sturges, Chicago, May 28, 1854, IC-1B9.1.

[53]Burrall to Sturges, Chicago, June 14, 1854, IC-1B9.1.

[54]Burrall to Sturges, Chicago, June 13, 1854, IC-1B9.1. Another outbreak at this time caused several deaths at a labor camp on the first division fourteen miles north of Cairo. _Cairo City Times_, June 14, 1854.

[55]Burrall to Sturges, Chicago, June 22, 1854, IC-1B9.1.

[56]Mason to Burrall, Chicago, July 10, 1854; July 11, 1854, IC-1M3.1. See also Bross, _Rail-Roads, History and Commerce_, p. 71.

[57]Mason to Burrall, Chicago, August 5, 1854, IC-1M3.1. At this time an outbreak of cholera killed thirty-five persons at Dixon, a town on the seventh division, but it is not clear that any of the victims were railroad laborers. _Dixon Telegraph_, August 3, 1854.

[58]_Chicago Daily Tribune_, May 23, 1853. When a somewhat similar accident claimed the life of Roswell Mason's son, the _Tribune_ was less flippant in

its comment. Ibid., March 13, 1855.

[59] Ibid., September 3, 1855. See also Mason to Burrall, Chicago, September 4, 1853, IC-1M3.1. Brayman to Burrall, Chicago September 1, 1853; September 4, 1853, IC-1B7.1.

[60] Chicago Daily Tribune, October 27, 1853.

[61] Alton Telegraph and Madison County Record, February 2, 1855. Cairo City Times, December 13, 1854. Dixon Telegraph, April 28, 1855.

[62] Erickson, American Industry and the European Immigrant, pp. 71-72.

[63] Lewis Broad, for Bailey Broad and Co., to pres. and directors of I.C., Chicago, May 31, 1854, IC-11N1.5.

[64] In the correspondence of I.C. officials there is little discussion of provisions for housing and feeding the men, as such matters were left to the local contractors. A newspaper reporter who visited a labor camp at La Salle noted the presence of a number of boarding house keepers and whisky sellers and described them as "a desperate and bloody set of men who are constantly breeding quarrels among the workmen, and who live by robbing them of their earnings." Chicago Daily Tribune, December 19, 1853.

[65] Mason to Schuyler, Vandalia, April 22, 1853, IC-1M3.1.

[66] Weekly Northwestern Gazette (Galena), April 28, 1853. Mason to Matthias B. Edgar, Treas., Chicago, October 21, 1854, IC-1M3.1.

[67] These general comments are based on contemporary newspapers, which presumably reflected community attitudes and concerns. See also Jane Martin Johns, Personal Recollections of Early Decatur, Abraham Lincoln, Richard J. Oglesby and the Civil War ([Decatur]: Decatur chapter of D.A.R., 1912), p. 35.

[68] Mason to Schuyler, Chicago, February 1, 1853,

IC-1M3.1. Alton Daily Morning Courier, June 17, 1853.

[69]Alton Daily Morning Courier, June 23, 1853.

[70]William F. Martin, quoted in Johns, Personal Recollections, pp. 36-38.

[71]Alton Daily Morning Courier, May 17, 1853, copying Decatur Gazette, May 13, 1853.

[72]Mason to pres. and board of directors, Chicago, January 1, 1854, IC-2.12. This letter was printed in Report of the Directors to the Stockholders of the Illinois Central Company, March 15, 1854 (New York: Geo. Scott Roe, 1854), pp. 13-19, but Mason's reference to whiskey as "this cursed stuff" was deleted.

[73]Chicago Daily Tribune, June 16, 1853, copying Ottawa Republican, July 2, 1853.

[74]Bloomington Intelligencer, June 16, 1852.

[75]DeWitt Courier (Clinton), June 16, 1855, copying Age of Steam (Vandalia), June 2, 1855.

[76]Alton Daily Morning Courier, April 17, 1854; May 4, 1854. Quotation from May 4 issue. La Salle had no less than seventy-five such "doggeries," about every eighth house in the entire town, according to the Ottowa Republican, June 10, 1854. The Republican did not censure the La Salle vigilantes but remarked, "They may consign enough [liquor] to the Illinois to make it navigable through the dry season, without exhausting the quantity brought to be sold" at Peru and La Salle. Ibid., April 29, 1854.

[77]Daniel H. Brush, Growing Up with Southern Illinois 1820 to 1861 (Chicago: Lakeside Press, 1944), p. 191. The sale of liquor was prohibited in Carbondale's founding ordinance. Ibid., pp. 174-77.

[78]Chicago Daily Tribune, December 17, 1853; December 19, 1853. Ottawa Republican, December 17, 1853. Alton Daily Morning Courier, December 19,

1853; December 20, 1853; December 21, 1853. P. B. Wyman to Mason, La Salle, December 16, 1853, IC-11N1.5. Brayman to J. A. Matteson, Governor of Illinois, Chicago, July 4, 1854, Brayman papers, Chicago Historical Society.

79 Alton Daily Morning Courier, October 8, 1852.

80 Brayman to Burrall, Chicago, December 16, 1853, IC-1B7.1.

81 Chicago Daily Tribune, December 17, 1853.

82 Alton Daily Morning Courier, December 21, 1853.

83 Chicago Daily Tribune, December 19, 1853.

84 Ibid., December 17, 1853.

85 Timothy B. Blackstone, Division Engineer, to Mason, La Salle, December 22, 1853, IC-11N1.5. Alton Daily Morning Courier, February 13, 1854. The first trial of the men accused of killing Story was inconclusive, but a second jury convicted the six who were sentenced to death. Alton Daily Morning Courier, February 23, 1854; April 21, 1854; April 25, 1854.

86 Chicago Daily Tribune, June 16, 1854.

87 Ibid., June 20, 1854. Farnsworth added that similar treatment should be accorded the non-Irish mobs that had murdered Elijah Lovejoy and Joseph Smith.

88 Brayman to Gov. Matteson, Chicago, July 4, 1854, Brayman papers, Chicago Historical Society. Mason did not share Brayman's view. He said, "I think there is strong doubt of the propriety of the Governor's clemency. . . . I am told the remark is not infrequently made at La Salle by the Irish that the Governor is on their side." Mason to Burrall, Chicago, August 6, 1854, IC-1M3.1.

89 Alton Telegraph and Madison County Record,

July 21, 1854; August 4, 1854.

[90]German laborers were more likely to acquire farms than were the Irish, according to the Chicago Tribune, June 21, 1854, but Gates, Illinois Central, p. 97, says that I.C. land office records indicate that many Irishmen did acquire farms. In the correspondence of John Newell, a division engineer in 1859-60, IC-1N6.1, there are many references to track laborers, most of whom have Irish names. It seems reasonable to infer that some of these men were holdovers from the construction period.

CHAPTER II

AN EMERGING INDUSTRIAL ENVIRONMENT

By the time the Illinois Central charter lines were complete, the permanent operations of the road were already underway. In the spring of 1853, the board of directors authorized Roswell Mason to set up a transportation department and to inaugurate freight and passenger service on the various sections of the line as soon as they were finished.[1] In May regular trains began running on the sixth division, traversing the sixty miles of prairie between La Salle and Bloomington. A. D. Abbott had the honor of serving as the first Illinois Central conductor of record, and he proved worthy of that distinction. An early customer said he was "every inch a gentleman, and by his pleasant, cheerful manner, and off-hand way of doing business gained the good opinion of his passengers. Even those whom he dislodged from an omnibus at the end of the route, to admit females and children, must honor his firmness and gallantry."[2] Abbott was joined by a good many fellow workers in the next three years, as train service was extended to other parts of the charter route. By 1856 the Illinois Central was in full operation and employed thousands of men in engine and train crews, at the stations along the line, on section gangs, and at the company's car shops and repair facilities.

Managers and Men

The corporate charter of the Illinois Central Railroad Company vested all of the lawful powers of the corporation in its board of directors and in such officers and agents as the board might appoint.[3] In practice, the directors exercised only a very general control over the operations of the road, through occasional instructions to the company president. The president coordinated the activities of the railroad's legal, financial, and operative departments, but he rarely gave orders which directly affected the company's employees. The great majority of decisions affecting the labor force were made by the officials of the so-called operative department, which was divided according to function into two parts, the engineering department and the transportation department.[4]

The transportation department was responsible for all of the running arrangements of the road. It was headed by the master of transportation. Beneath him were the division superintendents, originally two in number, each of whom was responsible for the operations of a portion of the line. The division superintendents were each aided by several assistant superintendents, who exercised direct control over trainmen (conductors, brakemen, and baggagemen) and station agents. Most station agents directed the activities of a number of laborers. Also included in the transportation department were the shops at which the company's locomotives and cars were serviced and repaired. These facilities were in charge of an official known as the master of machinery, who was equal in rank to the division superintendents. Beneath the master of machinery were the master mechanics of the various repair facilities. Each master mechanic gave orders to the enginemen (engineers and firemen) assigned to his district and to the several foremen who directed the work of machinists, boilermakers, blacksmiths, painters, carpenters, and other tradesmen in the local shops.

The remainder of the Illinois Central labor force was encompassed by the engineering department, which was responsible for all construction and maintenance work on the roadbed and on the depots, buildings, water towers, bridges, and fences along the lines. This department was headed by the chief engineer. Beneath him were four division engineers, each responsible for a portion of the lines. Under each division engineer were a half dozen or so supervisors, each in charge of a subdivision, usually some thirty to forty miles in length. The subdivisions were further split into several sections. A gang of laborers was assigned to each section, and each gang was directed by a foreman. The maintenance of bridges was the special responsibility of a separate part of the engineering department. The foremen of the traveling gangs which kept the bridges in repair reported directly to the superintendent of bridges, who was an immediate subordinate of the chief engineer.

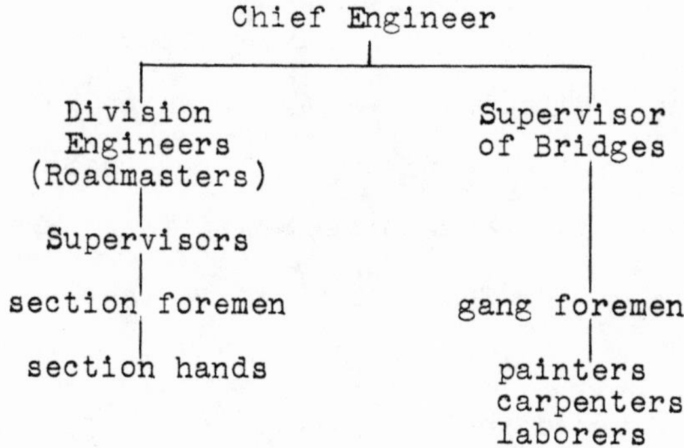

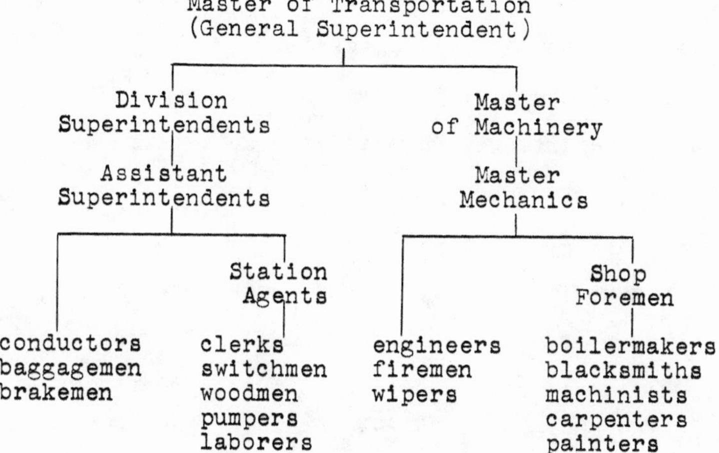

Fig. 2.--Illinois Central operative department, 1857

Although the company possessed a rather elaborate managerial hierarchy, the structure was not so clear-cut and rigid as it may appear. In both of the operating departments combined there were only about fifty officers above the level of station agents and gang foremen. Most of the principal officers were well acquainted with one another, and they conducted their business in a personal way. For example, it was not unheard of for the head of the transportation department to ignore the chain of subordinate officers and deal directly with the lowliest of station agents.[5]

The officers of the transportation and engineering departments directed the activities of many hundreds of employees. The greatest number of men employed in the year 1856 was 3,581, consisting of 44 officers, 134 station agents and clerks, 616 station laborers, 153 track foremen, 1,359 track laborers, 23 construction foremen, 266 construction laborers, 28 shop foremen, 633 shopmen, and 325 trainmen and enginemen.[6] An idea of the distribution of the work force may be gained by looking rather closely at the force employed on one part of the Illinois Central route: the 221-mile stretch which linked Wapella and Dunleith and which was known as the northern division (see Table 2).

On the northern division were situated some twenty-five stations, each of which was manned by an agent. Four of the stations were so small that the agent was the only person there, but in all other cases the agent had at least one subordinate to obey his instructions and do the less desirable work. Some of the larger stations--Freeport, Mendota, Amboy, and La Salle--had nine or ten men attached to them, and Dunleith and Galena had forces totalling seventeen and twenty men, respectively. At the larger depots there could be considerable division of labor; at Galena the work was divided among an agent, a clerk, a ticket seller, a baggage checker, a baggage handler, a yardman, a watchman, a switchman, and a dozen pumpers and general laborers. But at the smaller stations the agent had to serve as a Jack-of-all-trades, unless he had a laborer or two to attend to the rough work of hauling baggage and seeing to it that locomotives were provided with water and fuel wood. The wages of station employees

TABLE 2

SCHEDULE OF MEN EMPLOYED ON ILLINOIS CENTRAL LINE BETWEEN WAPELLA AND DUNLEITH IN JULY, 1855

Occupation	No.	Monthly Wage	Total
Transportation Department			
1. Officers and Clerks			
Master of Transportation . .	1	$83.33	$ 83.33
Paymaster . . .	1	83.33	83.33
Wood Agent . . .	1	60.00	60.00
Clerks	2	30.00-$40.00	70.00
2. Station Employees			
Agents	25	33.33- 75.00	1039.95
Clerks	11	35.00- 80.00	451.66
Warehouse and Yardmen . . .	5	35.00- 50.00	210.00
Watchmen	6	31.00- 35.00	201.00
Teamster	1	30.00	30.00
Woodmen	3	26.00	78.00
Switchmen . . .	5	27.00- 35.00	154.00
Baggagemen . . .	3	17.50- 33.33	84.16
Car Repairers .	2	31.00- 35.00	66.00
Pumpers	10	26.00- 40.00	297.00
Laborers	52	25.00- 27.00	1357.00
[not given] . .	3	[not given]	148.00
3. Roadside Pumpers . . .	7	27.00- 30.00	201.00
4. Trainmen			
Conductors . . .	13	60.00	780.00
Baggagemen . . .	4	35.00	140.00
Brakemen	24	30.00	720.00

TABLE 2--Continued

Occupation	No.	Monthly Wage	Total
5. Enginemen			
Engineers . . .	22	60.00- 65.00	1395.00
Firemen	20	35.00	700.00
Wipers	17	30.00	510.00
6. Shopmen			
Foremen	9	50.00-100.00	698.38
Workmen	97	[not given]	3844.00

Engineering Department

Occupation	No.	Monthly Wage	Total
1. Officers			
Roadmasters . .	2	100.00	200.00
Assistant Roadmasters .	2	50.00- 60.00	110.00
2. Section Men			
Foremen	40	[not given]	8225.00
Section Hands .	305	[not given]	
3. Ditching Train Crewmen . . .	45	[not given]	1285.00
4. Wood Train Crewmen . . .	22	[not given]	550.00
5. Track Raising Crewmen . . .	25	[not given]	645.00

Source: "Schedule of Men employed on the Ill. C. R. Road in July 1855," catalog no. 2.21, item 16a, Burlington Railroad Archives, Newberry Library.

varied considerably from place to place, although common laborers nearly always received $26.00 per month, or about $1.00 for each day of work. The range of wages of other station employees is shown in Table 2. Because some stations did not have water supplies adequate to meet the needs of the locomotives, roadside pumpers were occasionally placed between stations at points where ample water was available. There were four such locations on the line between Wapella and Dunleith.[7]

In the 1850's, there were normally four passenger trains per day on the northern division--one day train and one night train in each direction. There was also one regular freight train in each direction, and extra freights were run when necessary.[8] Every train was under the charge of a conductor, who supervised the work of several brakemen and baggagemen. Conductors were paid $60.00 per month, while their subordinates received $30.0C or $35.00. To move the trains, engineers and firemen ran locomotives either south from Dunleith to Amboy or north from Wapella to the same destination. At Amboy they normally were given a one-day layover before being assigned a run which took them out again to Dunleith or Wapella.[9] Each week the firemen and engineers usually made two round trips from Amboy, which meant that they manned their engines for a total of four days. During their two layover days they were expected to be at the Amboy shops performing any necessary maintenance work on their engines. However, they were spared the arduous task of scrubbing the locomotives clean of grease and grime.[10] That dirty job was left to a crew of engine wipers, who were usually young men anxious for promotion from wiper to fireman and--someday--from fireman to engineer. Their ambition is understandable, inasmuch as wipers were paid $30.00 and firemen $35.00, while engineers received the princely sum of $60.00 or $65.00 per month.

While the enginemen were expected to make minor repairs as well as perform maintenance work on their engines, all major work on locomotives and rolling stock was left to the skilled mechanics employed in the company shops. Small repair shops employing nine or ten men existed at Wapella and Dunleith, but most shop facilities for the northern division were concentrated at Amboy, where about seventy-five machinists, boilermakers, blacksmiths, painters, carpenters, and other mechanics were on the payroll. In the early years, these shop facilities were rather primitive, according to the recollection of a machinist who began work at Amboy in the spring of 1856. At that time all engine repairs were still being done right in the roundhouse, and an old locomotive was used to furnish the power necessary to run the shop machinery, which consisted of four laths, a drill press, and one small planer.[11]

All of the workmen in the shops, on the trains, and at the depots belonged to the transportation department. The remainder of the labor force consisted of what are nowadays called maintenance of way workers, and these individuals belonged to the engineering department. A gang of from four to ten such workers was assigned to each of the forty sections which comprised the line between Wapella and Dunleith. These section gangs tightened spikes, replaced ties, levelled ballast, and performed all other tasks necessary to keep the roadbed in good condition. The section hands were paid about $1.00 a day and were required to work long hours. "In the summer," wrote the chief engineer,

> the men should work eleven hours, arriving at their work by 6 o'clock and breaking off at the same hour in the evening, allowing one hour for dinner; but this hour must suffice for going to and returning from their work. In sickly season and intensely hot weather this arrangement should be somewhat changed.[12]

In addition to the regular section hands, large numbers of common laborers were employed during the fair weather months of the year for service on work trains which moved along the line performing specialized functions, such as distributing ballast or clearing ditches and culverts of refuse. In the winter these same laborers might sometimes secure temporary employment in snow shovelling gangs, which were sent out to free snowbound trains and make the lines traversable. Snow clearing was an exhausting job, sometimes requiring the unremitting toil of hundreds of men for days on end. In 1855 a newspaper reported that the Illinois Central road had been

> shovelled off some three or four times, the wind filling it up again so that no trace of work could be seen. . . . Let

> our readers imagine themselves 100 miles from anywhere, with nothing to eat but what was carried with them, no place to sleep except in the cars, and out from eight to twelve days with 500 men to provide [for] and they will have the true state of the case on the I.C.R.R.[13]

The labor force which manned the Illinois Central between Dunleith and Wapella was of course more or less duplicated on the southern portion of the main line and on the Chicago branch. However, at Chicago the company established far more extensive shop facilities than those that were maintained at Amboy on the northern division or at Centralia in the south. The Chicago shops were erected on the lake shore in that city in the mid-fifties. They employed between 250 and 300 men and were so well equipped that as early as 1862 they were able to build a complete locomotive.[14]

Hard Times

The late 1850's were difficult years for the Illinois Central company, which was ill-prepared to weather the storm that struck the American financial system only a year after the completion of the charter lines. When the failure of the Ohio Life Insurance and Trust Company triggered the great financial crisis of 1857, the Illinois Central company was compelled to make a temporary assignment of its assets in order to prevent creditors from seizing its property. It required strenuous efforts by President William H. Osborn to restore confidence in the corporation's ability to meet its obligations. But Osborn did succeed in ending the assignment and restoring the company to a sound financial basis by the close of 1858. The situation remained precarious, however, for a series of droughts and crop failures caused the railroad's traffic and earnings to decrease in 1858 and 1859. In these years, the net revenue did not equal so much as a third of the interest charges accruing during the period.[15] Naturally these vicissitudes had consequences for the work force of the Illinois Central, as officers of the road were required to take every possible step toward the reduction of operating expenses.

Retrenchment was the order of the day, and Master of Transportation James C. Clarke exercised considerable ingenuity in devising means for maintaining operations while at the same time reducing his labor force. In the spring of 1857, he reduced the number of men employed at several stations, despite the protests of the local agents who were compelled to make do with fewer men.[16] He ordered that no more than two brakemen should be assigned to any passenger train, the baggageman now being required to help set brakes when necessary.[17] The number of work trains transporting the labor gangs of the engineering department was reduced, and all of the men who had operated these trains were dismissed, except for engineers. From now on each work train was run by one engineer and one other man, a former engineer, who now performed the duties previously done by one conductor and one fireman. Instead of employing brakemen, as heretofore, Clarke ordered that "some good man be selected from the working party to do this duty when the train is running."[18] Even if he were a thoroughly good man, it seems unlikely that a carpenter, painter, or other member of the working party could have made a very reliable brakeman. Still, it was better than requiring the man serving as both conductor and fireman to run back and set brakes--in addition to managing the train and stoking the furnace.

While reducing his work force, Clarke tried "to avoid so far as possible making any compulsory discharges" by ordering that no new man should be hired whenever anyone left the service. But of course such vacancies did not occur frequently, and so Clarke ordered that the best men should be "culled out to be retained" should dismissals be necessary.[19] Clarke preferred to cut the pay of all of his men rather than dismiss some of them, but he found it necessary to do both. In the fall of 1857, he announced a pay cut of about 10 per cent for all employees. He also ordered the discharge of sixty-two station laborers, twelve signalmen and watchmen, eleven brakemen, and nine other employees.[21] And when Clarke saw the financial balance sheet for the year 1857, he bemoaned the fact that he had not taken earlier and more severe steps to diminish expenses. He wished he had retained only the force needed from day to day, instead of having worried about there being men available to handle an increase in traffic if such had arisen. "I am no prophet and cannot foretel [sic] what our business will be," he wrote to President Osborn, "but one thing I can tell, I shall never be caught in the same dilemma again."[22]

Clarke had hoped that he could rescind his

wage cut and perhaps rehire some men once the winter slack season was past. But when spring came he decided that business justified no general increase in wages nor expansion of the labor force.[23] He did raise the monthly pay of passenger conductors, freight conductors, baggagemen, and brakemen (to $66.00, $60.00, $40.00, and $35.00, respectively) but ordered that these men be paid only for time made, on a pro rata basis.[24] Clarke admonished his subordinates to continue to economize in every possible way, and he even urged them to look over their divisions and see if the labor force could not be reduced still further.[25] When the first six months of 1858 came to a close, Clarke found that despite his efforts the earnings of the transportation department had continued to decline. He sent President Osborn a gloomy projection of expenses for the rest of the year and promised to take drastic action:

> On the 21st day of August or 1st Sept. at latest, [he wrote] I shall make a general reduction in the pay of all men in the machinery and transportation departments of from 10 @ 20 per cent on the present wages, giving our employees a fair notice, and their own choice whether they will remain in the service or not-- Our large decrease in business and future prospects demand such a course.[26]

The actions of the master of transportation to reduce expenses in 1857 and 1858 were paralleled by those of the chief engineer, George B. McClellan. McClellan's job was made difficult by the relative scarcity of common laborers in Illinois, which prevented him from reducing the pay of his section hands in the spring and summer of 1857. At the same time that he wrote one of his division engineers to "pray be careful in keeping down expenditures," he was compelled to permit the same official to raise the wages of his section hands from $1.00 to $1.12-1/2 per day.[27] To another division engineer he gave a similar dispensation: "You are authorized to increase the wages as you think necessary--the men must be had."[28] McClellan found his situation frustrating but was powerless to alter it. He wrote President Osborn that he could not get enough men even after raising wages everywhere to $1.10 or $1.12-1/2. He had even considered bringing in men from Missouri but had found to his chagrin that at St. Louis employers were sending to Cincinnati for men and then failing to hold them, even with a pay of $1.30.[29] All that McClellan could do was to employ as small a force as he could get away with and avoid all maintenance work that was not essential to the safe operation of the road. He also tried to avoid increasing the pay of any of his subordinate offiders. "You will credit me the absolute necessity of keeping down the salaries," he wrote to one of them. "We cannot afford high pay with the present earnings of the road, or we will soon cut our own heads off."[30]

In August, McClellan and James Clarke made a joint effort to pare the Illinois Central labor force to the bone. Together the two executives rode a special engine from Chicago, stopping at each station to examine the books and see whether any reduction in expenses could be made. Their tour was not very successful, for both officers had been striving for some time to comply with William Osborn's reiterated directions to keep all costs to a minimum. McClellan wrote to the company treasurer that about all he and Clarke had accomplished was to amass a list of "good reasons for maintaining the present force."[31] Nothing more could be done to reduce labor costs until the coming of autumn.

When the harvest season had passed, thousands of agricultural workers swelled the pool of available laborers in Illinois. With men no longer scarce, it was no longer imperative to offer high wages to common laborers. In mid-September, McClellan ordered his division engineers to lower the pay of their section hands to $1.00 per day, and two months later he ordered a further cut, to $0.90 per day.[32] McClellan was reluctant to go any lower than that, in spite of pressure from President Osborn, who favored still more reduction. When Osborn suggested a cut to $0.80, McClellan replied that many of the men were being worked only four days a week, and "80 cents would make but a poor share for them."[33] McClellan evidently realized that his laborers would suffer severe hardship if a further reduction were imposed. He did not question the need to reduce costs but preferred to place any new burdens on shoulders better able to bear the load. He ordered a cut of about 10 per cent in the pay of painters, carpenters, and other skilled workers in the bridge gangs, and dismissed some men whose services were not needed in the winter season.[34]

He also lowered the pay of section foremen and division engineers, and he even suggested to President Osborn that his own salary be lowered until the earnings of the road improved--certainly an acid test of his sincerity.[35] McClellan showed still more concern for the common laborers of his department by ordering that track hands should not be dismissed for lack of work; instead, he ordered that half of each section gang should be worked on alternate days. Of course this policy cost the company nothing, and it was useful to keep superfluous men more or less on call so that they would be available when a larger force was needed in the spring.[36] Despite his sympathy for the men who suffered dismissal or wage reduction, McClellan never hesitated to do whatever he deemed necessary, and he did not always think of the effect his actions would have upon wage earners and their families. In January 1858, he casually remarked to William Osborn, "Nothing new on our road today--discharged some more laborers and carpenters."[37]

McClellan had hoped to partially restore wages once the business of the road recovered from its usual winter slump. But the earnings of the road remained low throughout 1858 and McClellan's subordinates had no difficulty in securing all the men they needed through the spring and summer without raising wages. There were minor shortages in some areas but these were easily remedied by recruiting men at Chicago and sending them wherever they were needed.[38] It did prove necessary to pay higher wages to some of the skilled workers in the bridge gangs. The supervisor of bridges was instructed to inquire what the local pay was for tradesmen in each area where a bridge gang was working, and then pay his own men at an equal rate "but not above it, if you can possibly avoid doing so, as it is really necessary for us [to] practice close economy during the present year."[39] Even during the harvest season there was no shortage of labor, partly because crops were poor that year in Illinois. After the harvest, there was such a surplus of laborers that McClellan decided at long last to further reduce the wages of section hands and of unskilled workers on gravel and ditching trains. Except at Cairo and a few other localities where the prevailing pay for day laborers was higher than was the norm in the state, McClellan ordered the wages of Illinois Central laborers lowered from 90 to 80 cents per day.[40]

Unfortunately, it is not possible to carry this general account of Illinois Central wage policies on into the 1860's. James Clarke resigned his position at the close of 1858, and the correspondence of his successor as master of transportation has not been preserved. George McClellan remained with the railroad until 1860, but his letters end with 1858. Some valuable letters that have survived are those sent out by John Newell, who was the division engineer responsible for the line between Wapella and Dunleith. Newell's papers begin at about the same time that McClellan's end, and they provide some additional information on labor in the engineering department.

Because wage policy was set by the chief engineer, Newell's letters have little to say on that subject. They do indicate that laborers continued to be in good supply in 1859 and 1860, and so it is unlikely that wages rose significantly in those years. In the spring of 1859, Newell ordered one of his supervisors to dismiss a man who demanded more money, while a year later he ordered another supervisor to pay a gang of laborers 80 cents a day "and if they earn it and it is best will pay them 90 cts." In July, 1861, laborers on a ditching train were still receiving 80 cents, and as late as January, 1862, Newell was still pressing his subordinates to hold expenses to the lowest practicable point.[41]

The most striking aspect of labor policy that emerges from Newell's letters is the total lack of job security for laborers on the railroad. Work gangs were assembled, enlarged, reduced, and abolished with astonishing frequency. If there was some ditching to be done, a gang was hastily assembled and put to work, and whenever the job was finished the men were instantly dismissed.[42] Even regular section crews were enlarged or reduced almost on the spur of the moment. In the fall of 1860, a third of the track hands on Newell's division were discharged, and during the winter of 1861-62, supervisors were instructed to work their track gangs only when necessary and only in good weather.[43] There is only one recorded instance in which Newell advised a supervisor not to dismiss some superfluous men, and in that case it was not concern for the men that prompted Newell's action, but rather his desire to have them on hand for some other work that was imminent. Moreover, Newell told the supervisor to adopt McClellan's policy of working two groups of men on alternate days, so that the retention of excess men was accomplished without cost to the company.[44]

The War Years

The coming of the Civil War in 1861 was a momentous event in the history of the Illinois Central Railroad. The outbreak of hostilities halted all shipments of grain and merchandise to points south of Cairo, thus adding to the financial woes of the company. Also, all normal freight and passenger service within Illinois suffered as a consequence of sudden and overwhelming demands upon the company to provide transportation for troops and military supplies. But as soon as these initial shocks had been absorbed, the railroad began to share in the prosperity born of government spending for war purposes. In Illinois both agriculture and manufacturing were so stimulated by military purchases that the Illinois Central soon was faced with the pleasant problem of having traffic demands far exceeding the capacity of its facilities. Moreover, the continued movement of soldiers and supplies proved a profitable business even at the reduced rates extended to the army. During the war years, both the gross revenue and the net earnings of the company more than doubled, so that in 1865 the Illinois Central began paying an annual dividend of 10 per cent on its stock.[45] Naturally the wartime economic conditions which so greatly affected the fortunes of the railroad company also had their consequences for the labor force of the Illinois Central.

Early in 1862, some of the Company's employees found themselves directly involved in the war effort, thanks to President Osborn's fervent devotion to the Union cause. In February, Osborn met with Thomas A. Scott, the former vice president of the Pennsylvania Railroad who was now serving as Assistant Secretary of War and was making an inspection tour of military facilities in the West. From Scott, Osborn learned that a fleet of a dozen ironclad gunboats and thirty-eight mortarboats was being equipped at Cairo for service against the Confederacy. However, work on these vessels was being so hindered by labor shortages that it appeared that only six gunboats and no mortarboats would be finished in time to provide naval support to General Ulysses S. Grant in his efforts to seize Fort Donelson, the Confederate stronghold on the Cumberland River. Osborn saw that he was in a position to render a great service to the Union cause, and he determined to do so at once. He ordered a partial suspension of work in the Illinois Central car shops at Chicago and dispatched Chief Engineer Leverett H. Clarke, four foremen, and fifty skilled workers to Cairo, where they took charge of the boat-building with such vigor that the task was completed in a matter of days.[47]

Unlike the Chicago shopmen, most Illinois Central employees could not contribute directly to the war effort without leaving the service of the company. Several hundred of them therefore decided to quit their jobs in order to volunteer for military service, in many cases following the example of company officers who resigned in order to assume military commands.[48] The passage of the federal militia act of 1862 providing for the drafting of 300,000 men spurred further enlistments by employees, because many of them felt that they would be drafted eventually and so they preferred to volunteer for service at once rather than wait and acquire the stigma of being a conscript.[49] President Osborn rejoiced at the pluck and resolution displayed by the 250 Illinois Central workers who volunteered for the army in a single week, but he feared that further depletion of the company's work force might cripple the operations of the road. He joined with the chief executives of several other railroads in appealing to Secretary of War Edwin M. Stanton to exempt skilled railroad employees from the draft. Osborn pointed out that the Illinois Central had employed 3,600 men before the war but that enlistments had reduced the work force to about 2,300. Now he feared that 600 or 700 employees would be drafted and that these conscripts would include many men with skills vital to the functioning of the railroad.[50] Stanton consented to remove from the draft rolls telegraphers and locomotive engineers, but he declined to issue blanket exemptions for any other groups of workers, such as conductors, brakemen, firemen, and skilled shop hands. However, he did issue a ruling that any railroad employee who happened to be drafted could be discharged from the army if his employer could convince government officials that the man's services were vital to the railroad.[51]

The manpower requirements of the military, together with the increased demand for labor by farmers and manufacturers, made it increasingly difficult for the Illinois Central to maintain an adequate labor force during the war. "Mechanics as well as laborers are becoming quite scarce," noted John Newell in the summer of 1862, and the following spring William Osborn wrote that labor shortages were hampering the work of the engineering department. Osborn said that the chief engineer did not have enough regular section hands to handle the work but was unable to hire extra men for special jobs "without paying them such an amount that it would make trouble among our own track men."[52] The tight labor market, coupled with the currency inflation resulting from government deficits, compelled the Illinois Central to raise the wages of virtually all of its employees during the war. A good illustration of this is provided by the Centralia shop rolls, which have survived intact for the years 1860 to 1870 (See Fig.3).[53]

In the summer of 1860, boilermakers, blacksmiths, machinists, and painters at Centralia were being paid a maximum of $1.80 to $1.95 per day. Carpenters received slightly less than that, while the comparatively unskilled men employed as car repairers and engine wipers earned $1.30 and $1.00 a day, respectively. These wage rates remained fairly steady until the summer of 1862, during which a strong upward trend set in. Maximum wages climbed to higher and higher levels as the war continued, until they reached unprecedented heights in January of 1865. Boilermakers were then being paid as much as $4.25 a day, which was more than double their prewar maximum. Compared to their maximum pay in 1860, the wages of carpenters were up 57 per cent, painters 71 per cent, machinists 74 per cent, and blacksmiths 94 per cent. Car repairers had not shared proportionately in the wage rise, their pay having gone up only 31 per cent, but engine wipers, tradionally the lowest paid shopmen, were receiving $2.00 a day, or exactly double their prewar wages.

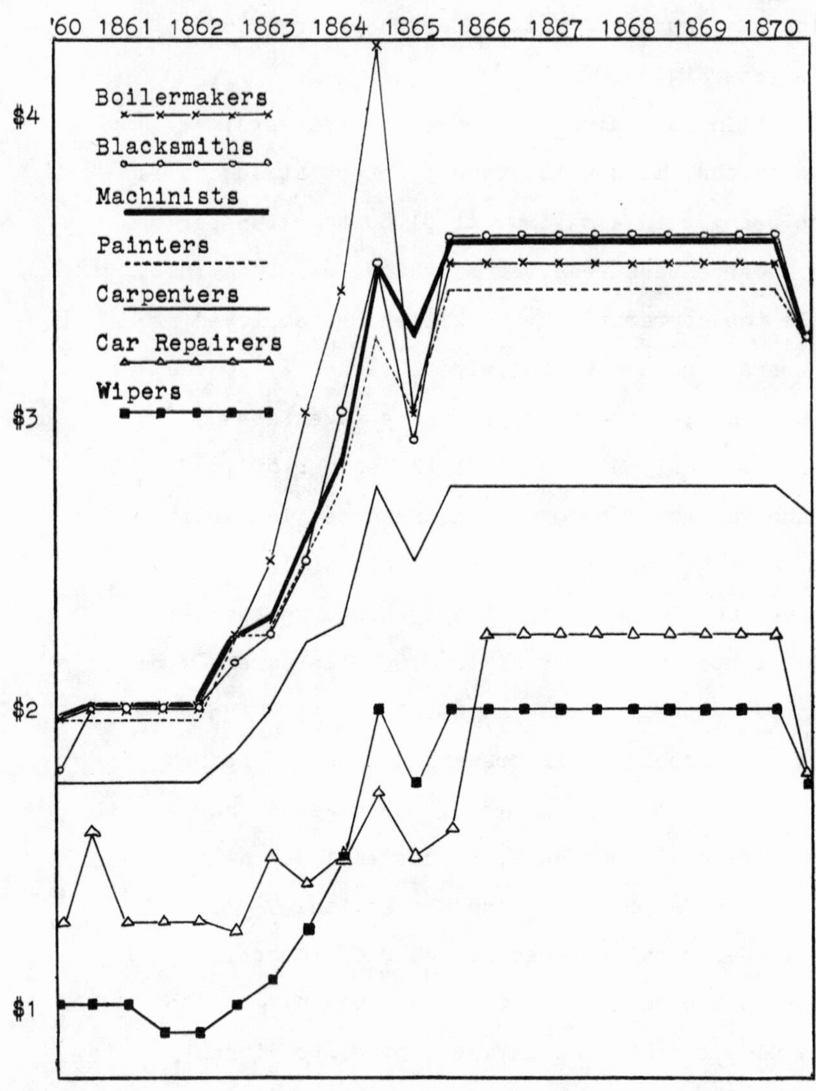

Fig. 3.--Maximum daily wages of Centralia shopmen

Other classes of railroad laborers also shared in the wartime wage increases. John M. Douglas, who succeeded William Osborn as president of the Illinois Central in mid-1865, estimated that the company's labor force as a whole had received wage increases averaging 75 per cent between December 1860 and December 1865. He calculated that in that period "the wages of Conductors, baggagemen and workmen advanced 16 to 33 per cent, while the wages of engineers, firemen, mechanics, and laborers, forming by far the larger number of our employees, . . . advanced 66 to 117 per cent."[54]

However, it should be emphasized that much of the increase in wages merely reflected wartime currency inflation and did not result in any real gain to the workers involved. For example, the average cost to the Illinois Central for the wages of engineers and firemen increased from $3.84 for each 100 miles of locomotive operation in 1861 to $5.65 for each 100 miles run in 1865 (See Table 3). Yet in these same years the value of U.S. paper currency depreciated to such an extent, relative to gold, that the value <u>in gold</u> of the amounts paid to

TABLE 3

PAYMENTS TO ENGINEERS AND FIREMEN PER MILE RUN
IN CURRENCY AND GOLD, 1861-1870

Year	Value in Currency of One Gold Dollar	Wages per Mile as Paid in Currency	Value in Gold of Wages Paid per Mile
1861	$1.000	$0.0384	$0.0384
1862	1.133	0.0385	0.0339
1863	1.425	0.0393	0.0270
1864	2.033	0.0556	0.0273
1865	1.573	0.0565	0.0359
1866	1.409	0.0578	0.0410
1867	1.382	0.0618	0.0447
1868	1.397	0.0611	0.0437
1869	1.330	0.0588	0.0442
1870	1.149	0.0595	0.0517

Source: Memorandum on wages, October 1896, IC-1F2.2.

the enginemen actually fell from $3.84 in 1861 to $3.59 in 1865.

An indication of the real value of wartime wages may be gained by considering changes in the cost of living during the war.[55] According to a study of consumer prices based on data from some forty cities of the United States, the average increase in the cost of consumer goods between 1860 and 1865 was: rent, 34 per cent; fuel and light, 59 per cent; food, 70 per cent; and clothing, 138 per cent. The same study reports that when each of these items is weighted according to its relative importance in the budget of a typical family, it appears that during the war the cost of living rose approximately 75 per cent. And that figure, be it noted, is precisely the amount by which President Douglas said that the wages of Illinois Central workers had risen in 1860-65. Thus, it is probable that during the Civil War the wage increase received by the average Illinois Central employee barely equalled the increase in his cost of living.

Of course, as Douglas noted, some employees received increases far above the average. Also, many employees must have experienced a rise in their total real income because the full employment economy of wartime afforded widespread opportunities for overtime work for shopmen, extra runs for enginemen and trainmen, and perhaps faster promotions for workers seeking higher paying jobs. But to raise his income by such means as these, a worker had to exert himself beyond the norm, and many men had to run as fast as they could just to stay where they were on the treadmill of currency inflation and rising prices.

When the war ended, the managers of the Illinois Central immediately began the conversion to peacetime operations, and they took steps which were of considerable importance to the company's labor force. "The service including running of trains &c has grown up partly with reference to gov[ernmen]t business and probably we have a larger force than is now required," wrote President Douglas. "We may be able to dispense with some things and reduce the price of labor, materials, &c. We agreed yesterday upon an order . . . to dispense with part of our force and advise employees that this is to be followed by a reduction in wages."[56]

A general wage cut was instituted on June 1, 1865. Evidently it was a severe one, judging from its effect on the Centralia shopmen (Figure 3). However, the cut was soon rescinded--at least so far as the shopmen were concerned--for by the following January nearly all of the Centralia men were earning wages equal or superior to those received prior to the cut. From 1865 until the end of the decade there was virtually no change in the maximum wages of the Centralia men. An old time book recording the pay of some Illinois Central engineers and firemen in the years 1867-69 indicates that these employees as well experienced no change in their pay rates during that period.[57] Thus it seems that the latter half of the decade was a time of wage stability on the Illinois Central. That stability probably came as a relief to both employer and employee after the hectic war years. Yet it is easy to picture at least one boilermaker dreaming of those glorious occasions when the paymaster's car pulled into Centralia, and the clerk counted out his monthly earnings at the incredible rate of $4.25 per day.

Controlling the Labor Force

The problem of controlling the Illinois Central's labor force was one of the earliest concerns of its managers. In fact it might be said that the railroad had some of its work rules before it had any workers, inasmuch as the company's charter specified that employees in the passenger service were to wear identifying badges on their caps, that freight and baggage cars were never to be placed behind passenger coaches when making up trains, and that a bell or whistle was to be sounded whenever a locomotive approached a crossing.[58] The company's officers were anxious that these rules be obeyed, since violations could result in lawsuits. The chief attorney of the road warned that "a slight deviation from the letter of the law" would almost surely result in a trial verdict against the company, for "juries are always with the citizen--against the corporation."[59]

Soon after the trains began running, Roswell Mason, in his newly-assumed role of master of transportation, worked out a fairly elaborate list of regulations, and he had the list printed on the back of the company's early timetables for the edification of employees. Most of Mason's rules were routine statements specifying the duties of each class of workman and are of interest only in that they show the primitive character of railroading at mid-century. Brakemen, for example, in addition to their nominal function, were required to trim the oil lamps and tend the pot-bellied stoves in passenger coaches, and whenever the train stopped to take on water they were expected to strike every car wheel with a hammer to test for cracks or flaws. Mason's list also included two general rules for employees: the use of alcohol or tobacco while at work was prohibited, and the habitual consumption of liquor, even if confined to an employee's off-duty hours, was "entirely discountenanced."[60]

Mason and other officers gave considerable thought to means for ensuring employee honesty, for well they knew that the railroad business offered many opportunities for petty thefts and embezzlements by workers. This was especially true of ticket clerks and passenger conductors, who handled numerous cash transactions. David Neal thought that a system might be introduced whereby a conductor would sell tickets to passengers on his train, and then the baggageman would go through the coaches, take up the tickets, and place them in a locked box, the key to which would be in the possession of a clerk in the city where the train ended its run. This system would prevent conductors from embezzling fares, since they would have to turn in cash for all the tickets collected by the baggageman and counted up by the clerk.[61] Mason thought it would be prudent to have some check upon the conductor, but he decided that Neal's proposal was impractical. Mason pointed out that a baggageman would not always be able to leave his regular post in order to go collect tickets. And while he supposed there was some safety in the fact that one man probably would not care to have another one know that he was dishonest, he still considered it entirely possible for the conductor and baggageman to connive together so as to render the plan useless.[62] A simpler means of preventing losses from embezzlement was proposed by William Osborn, who suggested that station agents and conductors be required to post bonds guaranteeing their honesty. This idea also proved impractical. A company attorney advised that many men holding such positions were young and not well known in their communities, so that in many cases they would be unable to furnish the required security. The attorney thought it better to rely upon frequent settlement of accounts and constant vigilance by company officers.[63] In essence, this common sense approach was the policy adopted by the company. Early in his career as master of transportation, James C. Clarke expressed his conviction that a close watch on station agents and the sending of twenty or thirty embezzlers to the penitentiary was all that was needed to guarantee the safety of company receipts.[64]

The vigilance of company officers was the chief means of preventing employee malfeasance, but the officers sometimes had the assistance of extra sets of eyes and ears. Early in 1855, the Illinois Central joined several other railroads in a contractual arrangement with Pinkerton and Company of Chicago. In return for liberal payments by the railroads, the Illinois Central's share being

$8,000 for one year, Allan Pinkerton agreed to set up an office at Chicago "devoted to the service and business of the railroads." It seems clear that the Illinois Central engaged the Pinkerton detectives for the purpose of apprehending thieves and embezzlers, although the wording of the contract was broad enough to encompass any type of investigative work. The contract stated specifically that Pinkerton would pass on to the railroads any information that he might acquire "concerning the habits or associations of the employees."[65]

Of the actual work of the Pinkertons for the Illinois Central, little evidence survives. In 1855 Mason called upon some "police detectives," probably Pinkerton and Company, to look into the problem of thefts from freight trains and to "keep their eyes upon some employees of the road who may be suspected of a want of integrity in their returns to the company."[66] A Pinkerton agent was sent to Amboy, where he posed as an ordinary worker seeking employment. The assistant superintendent at Amboy was told that he might recognize the agent by his assumed name, Samuel Harp, and by his garb, which consisted of a blue frock coat, a black and white checked vest, mixed pants, a low-crowned black felt hat, and some whiskers on his chin.[67] Aside from his angelic pseudonym and elegant haberdashery, nothing is known about this detective. Another occasion on which the Illinois Central called on the Pinkertons for help occurred several years later when the division superintendent at Chicago requested the services of "a smart detective to ferret out sundry small thefts of segars wines &c that have occurred along the line, and which it is feared are committed by some of our Employees," but again no information on the work of the detective has survived.[68] The Pinkertons' greatest success in the 1850's was their gathering of sufficient evidence to convict Oscar T. Caldwell, a conductor on the Burlington Railroad, of embezzling passenger fares. Illinois Central officials were delighted at this accomplishment, which they felt sure would provide a fine object lesson for all railroad workers.[69]

In the first few years of operations on the Illinois Central, Roswell Mason and other officers were still so preoccupied with construction problems that they exercised relatively little control over the company's growing labor force. In fact, a company director went so far as to assert that there was "little or no discipline among employees" on the road.[70] This lax situation began to change in 1855, when James C. Clarke was made a division superintendent with headquarters at Amboy. Clarke was admirably qualified for his job, for he had spent ten of his thirty years in the service of the Baltimore and Ohio Railroad. He had started out as a section hand and had subsequently worked as a fireman and then an engineer before entering the lower levels of management. Clarke had risen from the ranks by his own effort and ability and had commanded the respect of both officers and men on the B. & O.[71] It did not take him long to establish a similar reputation on the Illinois Central. As Clarke himself told the story in later years, he arrived at Amboy late one night and joined a group of workers seated around the stove in the depot building. Not knowing the identity of the new arrival, the men paid no attention to him and continued their talk, much of which concerned a fellow by the name of Clarke who they had heard was coming to straighten out affairs at Amboy. Some of the men boasted of their past success in hoodwinking company officers and told of their plans for making life miserable for their new superintendent.[72] Clarke listened closely to all of this conversation and acquired considerable information, which he soon put to use. "Mr. Clark [sic] appears to be straitening [sic] affairs at Amboy, that Prairie Sodom," wrote a company officer soon afterwards. "He has already discharged one Engineer for intoxication while on a Passenger train, and another for insubordination."[73] Clarke tightened discipline among all the employees on his division. In the Amboy shops, he saw to it that each employee worked a full ten hours every day. Each man's presence was recorded thrice daily and no one was paid for any time not actually worked.[74]

Clarke continued to add to his reputation as a disciplinarian after his appointment as master of transportation in October 1856. Many men resented his vigorous exercise of authority but were compelled to cooperate or else leave the service of the company. Several shopmen at Chicago quit soon after Clarke took charge of the transportation department, and within a month a number of engineers on the

Chicago branch left their jobs.[75] President Osborn wrote that Clarke was getting rid by inches of the old clique of men who had been accustomed to lax discipline. He praised Clarke's tough policies, for he believed that without them "the wheels would have stopped turning on the rails."[76]

Clarke's method of enforcing discipline was unsophisticated but effective. He simply fired anyone whose actions he considered undesirable. His most common grounds for dismissals was disobedience to company rules, especially if such disobedience had resulted in a collision or other mishap. Whenever a train accident occurred, an attempt was immediately made to find out what employees were at fault, and the culprits almost invariably were discharged at once. Clarke specifically ordered his subordinates "to dismiss from the service any men engaged upon trains . . . who disregard or neglect the rules or regulations."[77] Accidents were not infrequent, and neither were dismissals. Probably the most memorable accident of the ante-bellum period occurred in the fall of 1856, when a freight engineer ran his train off the end of an open drawbridge at Galena. An investigation showed that this disaster had resulted from the direct violation of rules involving signals and the requirement that every train come to a full stop before crossing the drawbridge. Consequently, Clarke ordered the dismissal of six men whose dereliction of duty had caused this spectacular accident.[78]

Violation of running rules was the most common reason for discharging men, but there were several other grounds upon which Clarke and his assistants saw fit to make discharges. These other grounds included being insubordinate to officers, failing to carry out orders, and indulging while on the job in such forbidden activities as drinking, gambling, and sleeping. Men also were dismissed for behavior off the job whenever that behavior tended to cause trouble for the company. Several men were dismissed for failing to pay private debts, resulting in the company's being bothered with garnishments on their wages. One station agent lost his job for indulging in what Clarke referred to as "immorral habits." Neighbors had complained that the agent was living with a woman at his station.[79]

Clarke's discipline policy might be described as strictly fair in the sense that all employees were treated alike. Certainly that was his own view of it. But the policy was also harsh in that the power to dismiss was an absolute prerogative of management, and it was exercised often enough to cause constant anxiety to employees concerned about job security. Obviously there was considerable room for abuse of this arbitrary power by incompetent or misguided officials. An attempt was made to prevent such abuses through procedures established in both the transportation and engineering departments in 1855. In the engineering department the general policy was instituted of limiting the power to discharge men to officials two ranks above the individuals involved. Thus a section foreman was forbidden to dismiss a track hand; he could only recommend to his own immediate superior, the supervisor of the subdivision, that the man be fired. Similarly, the foreman himself could not be dismissed by anyone below the rank of division engineer, and the supervisor could be dismissed only by the chief engineer.[80] In the transportation department a somewhat similar plan was introduced. Under it, such lower level employees as baggagemen, switchmen, firemen, and brakemen could be discharged only with the approval of the assistant superintendent, and the higher status conductors and engineers could be discharged only by order of the division superintendent.[81] The object of this new policy was defined as the creation of:

> a corps of active and intelligent operatives who, by feeling that they are identified with the company and are secure in their positions, so long as they discharge the duties of their offices with ability and zeal, will soon become convinced that their own welfare and advancement will be best promoted, by an implicit obedience of orders and an undivided attention to the interests of the Road.
>
> All reports of misconduct shall be promptly noticed, and all complaints of grievances meet with attentive consideration.[82]

The new procedures restricting the authority to make dismissals were a significant step toward a formal system of discipline on the Illinois Central. Although the road was small in comparison to the great interstate system into which it was to grow in later decades, its size was already sufficient to generate an apparent need for some bureaucratic innovation in this area.[83] But in most respects that need remained unsatisfied in the 'fifties and 'sixties. For example, the railroad naturally considered it desirable that no man dismissed by an officer of the company for cause should thereafter by re-employed by some other officer at another location. Yet no means was developed to prevent such occurrences, aside from the chance exchange of information among company officers. "I shall of course under all circumstances set my face against the employment of any man where my authority stands, who has been discreditably discharged from your division," promised one superintendent to another, but he could carry out this pledge only when he happened to learn that a job applicant had previously been discharged elsewhere on the Central road.[84] Aside from Roswell Mason's introduction of running rules and James Clarke's innovation respecting the power to make dismissals, the discipline procedures on the Illinois Central remained unsystematic and completely dependent upon the personal judgment of the officers of the operating department.

The management of employees did not consist solely of discipline and dismissals. Although these negative sanctions were of great importance, company officers knew that a carrot can sometimes be as effective as a stick. They tried to see that good conduct was rewarded just as surely as bad behavior was punished. Their chief means of recognizing exemplary performance by an employee was to promote him to a position of higher status and remuneration. Thus a young man accepting employment as a brakeman could hope someday to become the conductor of a freight train, and perhaps later on hold the same position in the passenger service. Or he might elect to start out as an engine wiper in the shops, in which case, if he performed his duties conscientiously, he would eventually be made a locomotive fireman, and while working in that capacity he would observe the actions of the engineer and thus serve an informal apprenticeship for that position. Vacancies in all but the lowest class of jobs were nearly always filled from within the ranks of the company labor force. These appointments were made solely at the discretion of company officers, there being no established qualifications for any job. The master of transportation himself sometimes took a personal hand in the promotion of employees, as is well illustrated by a note from James Clarke to an assistant superintendent:

> I shall appoint Thomas Wight station agent at Centralia;--this will leave his place to be filled on the passenger train.
>
> If you think John Manson fitted for conductor of passenger train I shall promote him to this position;--by so doing this will cause a vacancy in your freight conductors. I propose to fill this by promoting Manson's brakeman John or Frank I forget his first name, if you think he is a capable man and fit to fill the position.[85]

Promotion was the normal reward for faithful and diligent service to the company, but in a few cases of service above and beyond the call of duty, employees received special recognition. A shop foreman who had saved valuable property during an engine house fire received a personal letter from President Osborn and a check for $100. A locomotive fireman who, after a collision of two trains, had flagged down a third train and thereby prevented a further disaster was presented with a similar congratulatory letter along with a gold watch.[86]

In controlling the labor force of the 'fifties and 'sixties, the Illinois Central managers dealt with their men individually rather than collectively. As the bargaining power of an individual workman was negligible in comparison with that of his employer, there was no restraint upon the power of the managers to control the labor force in any manner desired. In a few instances some Illinois Central employees sought to band together for their mutual protection, but such organization was ephemeral and had no effect on management. "The Conductors' Union," founded by a group of Illinois Central men at Amboy in the spring of 1868 is of historical interest in that it was the first well authenticated example of organization among conductors on any American railroad, but it is doubtful that company officers were aware of, much less influenced by, this early labor union.[87] There were a few minor strikes by labor gangs in the engineering department, but these collective efforts were spontaneous and short-lived. Company officers dealt with them either by granting a moderate wage increase or by replacing the men who had ceased work with new men.[88] The only major work stoppage on the Illinois Central prior to the 1870's occurred in May 1867, when shopmen and other employees at Chicago, Amboy, and Centralia joined with thousands of Illinois workingmen in an unsuccessful effort to secure an eight-hour day. The Illinois Central followed other employers in refusing to reduce the standard day of ten hours and was able to carry on its business without serious interruption until the strike collapsed.[89] Generally Illinois Central workers exerted collective influence on their employer only briefly and in isolated instances. In discipline as in all other areas of the work environment there was no countervailing force to temper the power of management over the work force.

Accidents and Compensation

Railroading was an exceptionally dangerous occupation throughout most of the nineteenth century, largely as a consequence of crude, unreliable equipment and the general absence of safety devices. The fact that in the 1850's and '60's the Illinois Central was considered a well built and well equipped road only serves to emphasize the primitive state of railroad technology. Such lifesaving innovations as block signals, automatic couplers, and air brakes were unknown. When an engineer wished to slow his train, he used the locomotive whistle to signal to that effect and then waited while the brakemen climbed out onto the cars and screwed down the brakes by hand. The cars were joined together by a simple link-and-pin device, which meant that a brakeman had to lean out between the cars and drop a metal pin into position whenever a coupling was desired. Sometimes the pin did not fall into place of its own accord, and when that happened the brakeman had to tease it a bit from beneath, which ticklish operation could cost him a finger or two. If a brakeman lost his grip or footing for even a moment, the consequences could be terrible. Signalling devices were primitive, and engineers were simply instructed to watch out for misplaced or "wild" trains, something much easier said than done. A train stopped on the line was required to send out flagmen to warn other trains, but this did not always give an approaching engine time enough to stop. Collisions were common, and the simple, box-like construction of cars and coaches gave them a tendency to smash together or "telescope" whenever a collision or derailment occurred.[90]

Newspapers of the 1850's were filled with accounts of railway accidents, usually replete with gory details of injuries and deaths. In fact, losss of life on the rails was so common an occurrence that the Chicago Tribune included the category "Killed on Railroad" within the list of diseases for which it published mortality statistics.[91] The first major Illinois Central accident to be reported in the Tribune was itself a good illustration of the hazardous nature of railroad work. This mishap occurred on January 27, 1853, on a steep grade about thirty miles south of Chicago. A conductor by the name of Low was coupling two parts of a southbound train when one section of the train started to roll into the other, and Low was crushed between the two. He was extricated immediately and placed in a car, and the engineer tried to push the train toward the nearest source of aid, which was uphill toward Chicago. Unfortunately, his locomotive lacked sufficient force to make the grade, and so the engineer tried to back up half a mile in order to get a running start. But as he did so, one of the train's coupling pins gave way, so that when he came back up the grade at full steam he ran into several detached cars which were rolling down the slope. This collision caused further injury to Mr. Low, who was in one of the detached cars, and it nearly claimed the life of a brakeman who was on the collision end of the detached section, trying frantically to screw on the brakes. Fortunately the force of the collision was not sufficient to break the coupling irons on the cars which crashed together; otherwise the brakeman would have been crushed between them.[92]

The newspapers reported only those accidents that were bloody or otherwise interesting and thus are of little help in determining exactly how many accidents occurred on the Illinois Central in its early years. Perhaps some idea of their frequency may be gained from the fact that President Osborn's assistant at Chicago told him of the occurrence of at least ten train accidents in the latter half of 1855.[93] Train accidents were by no means the only cause of injuries to railroad employees, but there exist no data on which to base a discussion of personal injuries in the repair shops, at local stations, and among the work gangs and section crews of the engineering department.

Within the judicial norms of the mid-nineteenth century, the Illinois Central Railroad seldom had any legal obligation toward employees injured in the company's service. No employer was liable for damages to an injured employee if it could be shown that the victim's own carelessness had played any part in causing the accident; the slightest "contributory negligence" by the worker could release his employer from all liability. The employer was also judged blameless if the actions of another employee--a "fellow servant"--had caused the injury. Finally, it was assumed under the law that any worker in accepting a job thereby took upon himself the normal risks inherent in his occupation. For example, it was well known that a brakeman might slip and fall while engaged in his normal activities, and so such a fall was considered an "assumed risk" for which he could not hold his employer liable. These legal doctrines limiting the liability of employers were all well established by the time the Illinois Central began its operations in 1853.[94] Consequently, when a former brakeman ventured to write James C. Clarke a note suggesting that the company pay him damages in consideration of his having had a foot cut off by the driving wheel of a locomotive, Clarke replied briskly that the company was "not bound for damages to employees on the Road . . . and especially when accidents occur to those employees from the fact of their being out of their proper posts at the time and consequent upon their own carelessness or recklessness."[95] When an engineer threatened to sue the company for damages as a result of his being injured in a derailment, one of Clarke's subordinates was of the opinion "that it would be well to let him test the question of liability if he was disposed to do so, believing that the company would have nothing to fear from the result," inasmuch as the injured party's own negligence had contributed to the accident.[96]

Although company officers had little to fear so far as legal responsibility was concerned, they nevertheless displayed considerable interest in the welfare of injured employees. There was no set policy regarding aid to accident victims, but assistance often was given, each case being judged on its own merits by company officers. We have already mentioned Clarke's strong statement to an injured brakeman that the company was not bound for damages. Clarke did indeed make this statement, but he added to it a promise to pay the injured man's doctor bill and to allow him half pay during his convalescence.[97] In this particular case Clarke's generosity was prompted by a letter from a local officer who told him that the injured brakeman was "a poor boy without friends or money." The officer said he "had had him cared for as well as possible[,] and the Co. will probably have the Bills to pay."[98] Employees in the engineering department also were given aid when officials considered them needy and worthy of help. George McClellan ordered a division engineer to "pay Loftus (the man hurt on Engine 47) say $30 per month during the time he was disabled, or as much less as will satisfy him if you think him deserving--how would $20 per month answer?"[99] Even the lowest ranking laborers received financial help when injured. When Peter Coffin, a member of a ditching gang, suffered a broken leg in a train accident, McClellan authorized the payment of his

$35 medical bill, even though the company already had paid his board bill of $28.43 and given him a check for $7.60.[100] In another case, a laborer by the name of Hennissy had a doctor bill paid by the company, although he received no help in paying for the team which had driven him to the doctor, since in the opinion of his division engineer the hiring of the team was an unnecessary extravagance.[101] When another laborer was "hurt on a hand car while at work on the section," the same division engineer told the local supervisor, "If the man is faithful and steady and intends continuing on the section you can allow him time enough while he is laid up to pay his board."[102]

Efforts were made to provide employment for men whose injuries resulted in permanent disabilities rendering them unfit for their former occupations. When the brakeman on the paymaster's car suffered a permanent wrist injury, McClellan wrote to officials of the transportation department in an effort to provide the man with a new situation. "He is honest and intelligent so far as I know," wrote the chief engineer, "and I would be glad if you can give him some place as flagman or other position in which his disabled wrist will not interfere with the performance of his duties."[103] In another instance of this sort, Division Superintendent John Newell ordered a supervisor to make a crossing watchman of Bryan McKinney, a laborer who had been injured by a stick of wood thrown off an engine.[104] Whenever disabled men were given jobs they were made to understand that the company would not guarantee to continue to employ them permanently. President John Douglas stressed this point in a letter which he wrote to a company attorney who was arranging a financial settlement with an accident victim in 1868. He said:

> We cannot promise to provide [the injured party] with a situation and cannot assume any obligation to do so. Such is the necessity of discipline and so uncertain as to whether an employee will discharge his duty to the satisfaction of the company that we can only employ men who hold their places so long as our interests are subserved; and can not permit the tenure by which places are held to be dependent to any extent upon antecedent obligations.
>
> I shall be very happy if we can find it to our interest to accommodate this unfortunate man but can not connect that consideration in any way with this settlement.[105]

In cases of need, charitable assistance sometimes was rendered to the families of men who lost their lives in the company's service. When a clerk was run over and killed by a train, leaving a wife and child in destitute circumstances, McClellan shipped the man's remains to Baltimore at company expense and also paid the widow's fare to that city. He also recommended to President Osborn that the company give the widow $300 to enable her to start a boardinghouse.[106] In another case, the company gave a widow the same amount of money, contingent upon her signing a statement releasing the Illinois Central from all further liability in the death of her husband, a track supervisor who had been run over and killed as a result of losing his footing while uncoupling some cars. Before making this donation, McClellan had his division engineer ascertain the financial situation in which the dead man had left his family.[107]

During the 1860's the completely informal, personalized accident compensation procedures of the early years were supplemented by a systematic insurance program for Illinois Central employees. Several private insurance companies tried to persuade the railroad managers to enter into an arrangement whereby the employees would be encouraged to purchase accident insurance, but their efforts were blocked by President John Douglas, who frowned on the idea.

> I do not regard these companies with favor [wrote Douglas]. They approach Railroad employees generally with offers of stock, and to say nothing of the tendency of this so far as the employees are concerned, I do not believe their insurances can be relied upon by the public.
>
> One or two might possibly do some good, but they are springing up every where, and many of them are likely to prove failures.
>
> I believe I would have nothing to do with them.[108]

Instead of cooperating with an outside insurance company, the Illinois Central organized its own insurance program, known as the Illinois Central Relief Club.[109]

The I.C. Relief Club was a compulsory insurance plan supported by deductions from wages. Every month the paymaster withheld an amount equal to one-half of one per cent of the earnings of each employee. These funds were then used to provide pecuniary relief to sick and injured men, to pay funeral expenses in case of death, and to make small contributions for the temporary assistance of needy relatives of deceased men. The chief surgeon of the railroad served as medical advisor to the club, while a company secretary handled its regular business, acting under orders from its board of managers, which consisted entirely of ladies, being the wives of the principal officers of the railroad. The plan was carried on for approximately four years, amidst much complaint and fault-finding by employees, many of whom considered it a hardship to be required to contribute, even in so small a degree, to the insurance fund. Finally some employees held meetings and appointed committees to protest against the compulsory nature of the program. The company thereupon made the plan voluntary, and the resultant drop in membership soon led to its decline. The club lingered on for a few years with a declining membership and treasury and then quietly faded out of existence.[110]

***

The rise of modern industry was already beginning its transformation of American society by the 1850's and '60's, and railroading was at the heart of this transformation. As the railroads tied the nation together economically they tended to make workingmen's wages increasingly dependent on national economic conditions and less sensitive to local variations. Hence the great impact of the Panic of 1857 and of the Civil War upon the earnings of Illinois Central employees. Another effect of industrialism that was much in evidence from the earliest days on the Illinois Central was the danger inherent in the use of heavy, powerful, and fast-moving machinery. The railroad equipment of the early years was fast and powerful but in a primitive state of technological development. In the absence of safety devices, accidents and injuries occurred with shocking frequency, and injured men seldom had any legal claim upon their employer.

Industrialization brought the rise of giant enterprise, and even at its beginning the Illinois Central had many of the qualities peculiar to a big business. The ownership of the company was largely separate from its management, its property was spread over a wide area, many of its operations were reduced to a timed schedule, and it employed a large and heterogeneous labor force. These big business characteristics created a need for bureaucratic structure and for formal procedures, although in the early years that need was only dimly perceived and partially realized.

The managers of the Illinois Central created a managerial heirarchy and tried, less successfully, to establish a mechanism for furnishing aid to sick and injured men. The managers also took their first steps toward a formal system of employee discipline replete with written rules and systematic procedures. In the absence of organization and collective action by the workers, the power of the employer over the labor force was unrestricted. That power could be and often was used harshly. But its impact was mitigated by the personal relationships linking the managers and the employees. The Illinois Central was a big business, but it was not yet so big as to thoroughly separate managers from men. The master of transportation could still take a personal interest in the promotion of a brakeman, or the chief engineer seek out suitable employment for a disabled section hand.

This sense of community between officers and workmen would be difficult to maintain through later decades, as the Illinois Central grew into a giant transportation system stretching from the Great Lakes to the Gulf of Mexico. The pressures of the industrial environment threatened to snap that bond as though it were a defective pin in an old-fashioned coupler. And when their personal relationships with management officials ceased to shield them from the harsher features of their job environment, the railroad workers would experience more fully the nature of workingclass life in an industrial age.

[1]Minutes of the Board of Directors, March 16, 1853, *IC-+3.1.

[2]*Alton Daily Morning Courier*, September 2, 1853.

[3]An Act to Incorporate the Illinois Central Railroad Company, February 10, 1851, section 5.

[4]The following description is based upon an outline of the departmental organization in George B. McClellan, Chief Engineer, to William H. Osborn, Pres., Chicago, October 29, 1857, IC-1M2.1.

[5]An example is James C. Clarke, Master of Transportation, to F. Fisher, Agent, Chicago, May 11, 1858, IC-1C5.1.

[6]I.C.R.R., *Report to the Stockholders*, March 18, 1857, IC-+2.1.

[7]The following paragraph is based upon "Schedule of men employed on the Ill. C. R. Road in July 1855," catalog no. 2.21, item 16a, Burlington Railroad Archives, Newberry Library. This hand-written notebook listing employees on the line between Wapella and Dunleith was prepared by John Van Nortwick, I.C. Division Superintendent in the 1850's, and later president of the Chicago Burlington and Quincy Railroad.

[8]Statement of J. B. Adams, former machinist (and subsequently roundhouse foreman and master mechanic), Amboy, April 1897, IC-2.91.

[9]When spending the night at Dunleith, enginemen were compelled to sleep on their locomotives. No better facilities were available until late 1856, when Osborn ordered "a stall of the Engine house fitted up with bunks &c." Joseph Kirkland, Auditor, to J. Newton Perkins, Treas., Chicago, November 17, 1856, IC-1K3.1.

[10]Statement of J. B. Adams, Amboy, April 1897, IC-2.91. The maintenance work included "pack-

ing pistons and valve Stems and setting out their cylinder packing and Packing the Driving and Truck Box Cellars if necessary."

[11] Ibid.

[12] McClellan to J. F. Ashley, John Newell, and Leverett H. Clarke, Division Engineers, Chicago, March 27, 1857, IC-1M2.1.

[13] Cairo City Times, February 7, 1855. A vivid account of the struggle against snow on the Chicago branch appears in the Kankakee Gazette, February 10, 1855.

[14] They were known as the Weldon shops and were the company's principal repair shops down to the 1890's. They are described in the Chicago Daily Tribune, June 2, 1854. The building of the first locomotive at Weldon is mentioned in Corliss, Main Line of Mid-America, p. 67.

[15] Brownson, History of the Illinois Central Railroad to 1870, pp. 66, 116-130.

[16] R. Keeler, Agent, to John C. Jacobs, Division Supt., La Salle, April 28, 1857, IC-1J2.1, reluctantly agrees to reduce his force from seven men to four. A. J. West, Agent, to Jacobs, Tonica, April 28, 1857, IC-1J2.1, resigns his post as a result of having his force cut to a single man.

[17] Silas Bent, Assistant to Master of Transportation, to Phineas Pease, Assistant Supt., Chicago, May 6, 1857, IC-1C5.1.

[18] McClellan to Ashley, Chicago, August 8, 1857, IC-1M2.1.

[19] Bent to Pease, Chicago, April 12, 1857, IC-1C5.1.

[20] James Clarke to Jacobs, Chicago, November 23, 1857, IC-1C5.1.

[21]Pay cuts are ordered in James Clarke to B. R. Abbott, Agent at Cairo, Chicago, November 23, 1857, IC-1C5.1; Clarke to A. Mitchell, Assistant Supt., Chicago, November 23, 1857, IC-1C5.1; Clarke to Henry Wilson, General Wood Agent, Chicago, November 23, 1857, IC-1C5.1; Clarke to Pease, Chicago, November 23, 1857, IC-1C5.1. Dismissals are mentioned in Clarke to William F. Biddle, Assistant Engineer, Chicago, October 15, 1857, IC-1C5.1.

[22]Clarke to Osborn, Chicago, January 2, 1858, IC-1C5.3.

[23]Clarke to Pease, Chicago, April 21, 1858, IC-1C5.1.

[24]Clarke to Pease, Chicago, April 7, 1858, IC-1C5.1.

[25]Clarke to Mitchell, Chicago, May 8, 1858, IC-1C5.1.

[26]Clarke to Osborn, Chicago, July 31, 1858, IC-1C5.1.

[27]McClellan to Newell, Chicago, April 26, 1857, IC-1M2.1.

[28]McClellan to Leverett Clarke, Chicago, April 27, 1857, IC-1M2.1.

[29]McClellan to Osborn, Chicago, April 28, 1857, IC-1M2.1.

[30]McClellan to Ashley, Chicago, May 13, 1857, IC-1M2.1.

[31]McClellan to Perkins, Mattoon, August 31, 1857, IC-1M2.2.

[32]Biddle to Ashley, Leverett Clarke, and Newell, Chicago, September 14, 1857, IC-1M2.1. McClellan to Osborn, Chicago, November 24, 1857, IC-1M2.1.

[33]McClellan to Osborn, Chicago, November 24, 1857, IC-1M2.1.

[34]McClellan to Ashley, Newell, Leverett Clarke, and J. M. Kellog, Division Engineers, Chicago, November 20, 1857; November 24, 1857, IC-1M2.1.

[35]McClellan to Ashley, Newell, Leverett Clarke, and Kellogg, Chicago, November 27, 1857, IC-1M2.1. McClellan to Osborn, Chicago, November 17, 1857, IC-1M2.1. The salary of the supervisor of bridges also was reduced. McClellan to J. A. Shepherd, Supervisor of Bridges, Chicago, November 28, 1857, IC-1M2.1.

[36]McClellan to Kellogg and Leverett Clarke, Chicago, November 20, 1857, IC-1M2.1.

[37]McClellan to Osborn, Chicago, January 4, 1858, IC-1M2.2.

[38]McClellan to Ashley, Chicago, March 24, 1858, IC-1M2.1. Biddle to Ashley, Chicago, May 3, 1858, IC-1M2.1.

[39]Biddle to Shepherd, Chicago, May 3, 1858, IC-1M2.1.

[40]McClellan to Ashley, Newell, Leverett Clarke, and Kellogg, Chicago, August 11, 1858, IC-1M2.1, announces reduction effective September 1. See also McClellan to Leverett Clarke, Chicago, August 19, 1858, IC-1M2.1.

[41]Newell to M. A. Stafford, Supervisor, Amboy, April 1, 1859, IC-1N6.1. Newell to Peter Rockwell, Supervisor, Amboy, May 29, 1860, IC-1N6.1. Newell to Leverett Clarke, Amboy, July 31, 1861, IC-1N6.1. Newell to S. M. Churchill, Supervisor, Amboy, January 7, 1862, IC-1N6.1.

[42]A few examples are those discussed in Newell to James Y. Kennedy, Supervisor, Amboy,

June 16, 1860, IC-1N6.1; Newell to Stafford, Amboy, June 18, 1860, IC-1N6.1; Newell to Kennedy, Amboy, December 2, 1861, IC-1N6.1. Many letters from Newell to Leverett Clarke, who succeeded McClellan as chief engineer, mention other instances of this sort.

[43] Newell to Leverett Clarke, Amboy, October 10, 1860, IC-1N6.1. Newell to Stafford, Kennedy, Churchill, Rockwell, C. E. Willis, and Charles McCoy, Supervisors, Amboy, October 10, 1860, IC-1N6.1. Newell to Churchill, Amboy, January 7, 1862, IC-1N6.1.

[44] Newell to Churchill, Amboy, April 30, 1861, IC-1N6.1.

[45] Brownson, History of the Illinois Central Railroad to 1870, pp. 66-67, 146.

[46] Samuel R. Kamm, The Civil War Career of Thomas A. Scott (Philadelphia: University of Pennsylvania, 1940), p. 101.

[47] Osborn to Thomas E. Walker, Director, Chicago, February 16, 1862; February 17, 1862, IC-106.2.

[48] An impressive number of former Illinois Central officers rose to positions of great responsibility in the Union army. George McClellan is, of course, the outstanding example. Corliss, Main Line of Mid-America, p. 129.

[49] "Our men have a perfect fever for enlisting. . . . I have spent the whole day with some of our best men on this drafting issue--they hate the idea and prefer to enlist." Osborn to Walker, Chicago, August 6, 1862, IC-106.2.

[50] Osborn to Stanton, Chicago, August 6, 1862; August 8, 1862, IC-106.2. Osborn to P. H. Watson, Asst. Secretary of War, Chicago, August 5, 1862, IC-11N1.5. The appeals to Stanton by officers of several other railroads are printed in U.S. War Department, The War of the Rebellion: A Compilation of the Official Records of the Union and Confederate Armies, 3rd series, II (Washing-

ton: Government Printing Office, 1899), 309, 310, 315, 322-24, 326, 337.

[51]War of the Rebellion, 3rd series, II, 294, 358.

[52]Newell to Leverett Clarke, August 22, 1862, IC-1N6.1. Osborn to A. H. Danforth and Co., Chicago, April 22, 1863, IC-106.1.

[53]The following paragraph, and also the chart appearing as Figure 3, are based upon the Centralia shop rolls, July 1860-November 1870, IC-+3.9. These payrolls include some men stationed at Cairo and Du Quoin, but most of the work force was employed in the main shops at Centralia. The chart gives the maximum wages paid to men in various occupations in January and June of each year, except for 1860 and 1870. For 1860 the chart shows the wages paid in July, and for 1870 it shows the wages paid during June and November. It should be noted that the chart shows maximum wages. Most workmen earned somewhat less than the amounts shown. Minimum wages are not shown in Figure 3 because it is not possible to separate the lowest wages paid to regular employees from those earned by helpers, apprentices, and temporary workers.

[54]John M. Douglas, Pres., to C. D. Bowen, chairman of committee of [Chicago] Board of Trade, Chicago, February 3, 1866, IC-1D7.1.

[55]The consumer price index cited here was compiled by Ethel D. Hoover. It appears in Historical Statistics of the U.S., pp. 110, 127.

[56]Douglas to Osborn, Chicago, May 17, 1865, IC-1D7.1.

[57]Engineers' and Firemen's Time Book, Dubuque, Iowa, October 1867-February 1868; May-October 1869, IC-3.9. The Illinois Central acquired control of the Dubuque and Sioux City Railroad on October 1, 1867.

[58]An Act to Incorporate the Illinois Central Railroad Company, sections 12-13.

[59]Memorandum on suits pending, October 31, 1854, Mason Brayman papers, Chicago Historical Society.

[60]An undated but early list of proposed rules drawn up by Mason is located in file 2.3, Burlington Archives, Newberry Library. The same file contains a shorter list drafted by David Neal. A few rules proposed by George Watson, a division superintendent, are in Watson to Mason, Ewington, March 28, 1854, file 1.2, Burlington Archives, Newberry Library. Mason drew on all of these early lists in working out the regulations which were placed in effect on May 18, 1854. This list was printed in the Cairo City Times, October 16, 1854, and appears on the reverse side of early timetables, examples of which are located in IC-+3.8 and in the Broadsides Collection, Chicago Historical Society.

[61]The plan is described in Neal's undated list of proposed rules, file 2.3, Burlington Archives, Newberry Library.

[62]Mason to William P. Burrall, Treas., Chicago, June 12, 1853, IC-1M3.1.

[63]E[benezer] Lane to Osborn, Chicago, April 24, 1856, IC-1L2.1.

[64]Clarke discovered embezzlements by station agents at Centralia and Ashley in 1858. His reactions are made clear in Bent to Osborn, Chicago, April 17, 1858; April 22, 1858, IC-11N1.5; Clarke to Osborn, Chicago, April 22, 1858, IC-1C5.3; and Clarke to Pease, Chicago, May 21, 1858, IC-1C5.1.

[65]Contract between Illinois Central Railroad Company and Pinkerton and Company, February 1, 1855, IC-2.32.

[66]Benjamin F. Johnson, Asst. to Pres., to Osborn, Chicago, September 15, 1855, IC-1J6.1.

[67]Pinkerton and Company to Van Nortwick, Chicago, September 17, 1855, photostatic copy in file 2.21, Burlington Archives, Newberry Library.

[68]McClellan to Allan Pinkerton, Chicago, December 5, 1858, IC-1M2.1. McClellan also inquired about the possibility of having Pinkerton furnish "a special depot police" to the Illinois Central. George Power, Secretary to Vice Pres., to Pinkerton, Chicago, November 22, 1858, IC-1M2.1.

[69]Caldwell's conviction produced a profound sensation among the class of workers "composed of about one third loafer, one third gambler and one third Railroad man," according to Benjamin Johnson. Johnson to Osborn, Chicago, November 27, 1855, IC-1J6.1.

[70]John N. A. Griswold, Director, to Perkins, Chicago, December 25, 1854, IC-1G7.1. Griswold hoped the Illinois state legislature might be persuaded to assist the railroads by enacting a law "regulating Rail Road employes [and] making any disobedience of order by which accidents are caused a penal offense." He added, "We have taken measures to keep the members [of the legislature] in good humor by issuing invitations to them to ride over and examine the road during the session free of charge."

[71]Clarke's career on the B. & O. is summarized in Ackerman, Historical Sketch, pp. 134-35.

[72]Ibid.

[73]Johnson to Perkins, Chicago, December 28, 1855, IC-1J6.2.

[74]Johnson to Osborn, Chicago, January 23, 1856, IC-1J6.2.

[75]Johnson to Osborn, Chicago, October 15, 1856, IC-1J6.2.

[76]Osborn to Perkins, Chicago, November 20, 1856, IC-106.2. According to Osborn, some men resented Clarke so much that they sabotaged locomotives on the Chicago branch. Osborn reported that Clarke went "to Urbana to spend a week upon the Road," and after that there were no more reports of sabotage. Osborn to Perkins, Chicago,

December 12, 1856, IC-1O6.2.

[77]James Clarke to Pease, Chicago, January 16, 1857, IC-1C5.1.

[78]Johnson to Perkins, Chicago, September 5, 1856, IC-1J6.2.

[79]The out-going letters of James Clarke, IC-1C5.1, and McClellan, IC-1M2.1, contain numerous references to the dismissal of employees on these varied grounds.

[80]McClellan to Ashley, Chicago, March 27, 1857, IC-1M2.1. "A fault or neglect of duty on the part of any employee will be at once reported by his immediate superior to the officer next in rank above him, who will act according to the authority given in this letter."

[81]Bent to Asst. Supts. Berry, Pease, and Mitchell, Chicago, March 26, 1857, IC-1C5.1.

[82]*Ibid*. The statement probably originated with James Clarke.

[83]The charter lines were extensive enough to lead to misunderstandings and friction between employees on different parts of the road. When a division superintendent complained that engineers from another division were causing a disturbance by trying to tell his own engineers "what they will do, and what they will not do," James Clarke ordered that there be "no party feeling . . . upon this Road to the detriment of its interests, or to the disturbance of its harmony. Every man upon it, from the highest to the lowest, is employed by the Ill. Central R. R. Co. to give his time, services, and attention to the success of the *whole* Road and no one will be suffered to create discord with impunity upon it." Pease to Jacobs, Centralia, March 9, 1857, IC-1J2. 1. James Clarke to Pease, Chicago, March 2, 1857, IC-1C5.1.

[84]Bent to Jacobs, Chicago, March 23, 1857, IC-1J2.1. See also Bent to James Clarke, Chicago, June 19, 1857, IC-1C5.1.

[85]Clarke to Mitchell, Chicago, April 24, 1858, IC-1C5.1.

[86]Osborn to John Sweeney, Chicago, February 21, 1861, IC-106.1. Bent to John Whiting, fireman, Chicago, May 5, 1857, IC-1C5.1.

[87]Edwin C. Robbins, Railway Conductors: A Study in Organized Labor, Studies in History, Economics, and Public Law, Vol. LXI, No. 1, whole no. 148 (New York: Columbia University Press, 1914), p. 15. A similar organization was founded among employees of the Burlington Railroad, and on July 6, 1868, the two groups met at Mendota, Illinois, and combined into one organization. Other lodges were added, forming the nucleus of the national union later known as the Order of Railway Conductors of America.

[88]Track gangs in the vicinity of La Salle, Galena, and Freeport successfully struck for a raise from 80 cents to 90 cents per day in June 1862, a time of labor scarcity. Newell to Leverett Clarke, Amboy, June 10, 1862; June 19, 1862; June 26, 1862, IC-1N6.1. A similar effort by men at Urbana in 1858 had been a failure. The strikers were dismissed and new men hired. "If the Urbana men give any trouble, in the way of interfering with the new men," ordered the chief engineer, "resort at once to such legal measures as may be applicable--whether for assault and battery, trespass, conspiracy or what not." McClellan to Leverett Clarke, Chicago, September 10, 1858, IC-1M2.1.

[89]The state legislature, under pressure from the Grand Eight-hour League of Illinois, had passed a law making eight hours the standard working day in Illinois as of May 1, 1867. The law was ineffective in that it did not apply to any employee who agreed with his employer to work for more than eight hours. The Illinois Central joined other Chicago railroads in posting a notice in its shops that the work day would continue to be ten hours. Douglas to Osborn, Chicago, May 2, 1867, IC-1D7.1, describes the effect of the strike on the I.C. Marvin H. Hughitt, General Supt., to F. Rankin,

Chicago, May 13, 1867, IC-1D7.1, reports a large number of men back at work at Amboy as of that date. The background and events of this strike are described in Paul V. Black, "May Day in the Middle West: The Illinois Eight-hour Movement, 1866-67," unpublished paper submitted to Professor Allan G. Bogue, History 641, University of Wisconsin, 1968.

[90]The dangers inherent in primitive railroad equipment are discussed at length in Charles Francis Adams Jr., Notes on Railroad Accidents (New York: G. P. Putnam's Sons, 1879). See also Robert B. Shaw, Down Brakes: A History of Railway Accidents, Safety Precautions and Operating Practices in the United States of America (London: P. R. Macmillan Limited, 1961). Illinois Central equipment of the early years is described in Corliss, Main Line of Mid-America, pp. 70-80.

[91]Chicago Daily Tribune, 1853-54, passim.

[92]Ibid., January 27, 1853.

[93]Johnson to Osborn, Chicago, July 6, July 13, September 8, September 11, September 15, November 1, November 2, November 14, December 11, 1855, IC-1J6.1. December 1856 must have been a record month for mishaps; Osborn mentioned that there were nine engines off the track at one time just on the the line between Wapella and Dunleith. Osborn to Perkins, Chicago, December 31, 1856, IC-106.2.

[94]U.S. Department of Labor, Growth of Labor Law in the United States (Washington: Government Printing Office, 1967), pp. 137-38.

[95]James Clarke to Milton Brown, Chicago, February 7, 1857, IC-1C5.1.

[96]Van Nortwick to James Clarke, Batavia, March 7, 1856, file 2.21, Burlington Archives, Newberry Library.

[97]James Clarke to Brown, Chicago, February 7, 1857, IC-1C5.1. Clarke also said the company might see fit to extend further pecuniary relief later on.

[98]C. M. Smith to Clarke, Decatur, October 25, 1856, IC-1J2.1.

[99]McClellan to Newell, Chicago, April 20, 1858, IC-1M2.1.

[100]Newell to Leverett Clarke, Chief Engineer, Amboy, October 18, 1859; February 27, 1860; March 3, 1860, IC-1N6.1. Newell to S. A. Mitchell, Agent at Elery, Amboy, November 11, 1859, IC-1N6.1. Newell to Dr. N. W. Abbott, Amboy, February 28, 1860; March 2, 1860, IC-1N6.1.

[101]Newell to J. R. Booth, Amboy, August 23, 1860, IC-1N6.1.

[102]Newell to O. E. Willis, Amboy, April 16, 1859, IC-1N6.1.

[103]McClellan to W. R. Arthur, Division Supt., Chicago, January 4, 1859, IC-1M2.1. *Cf*. McClellan to Jacobs, Chicago, January 4, 1859, IC-1M2.1; Phillips to Newell and Ashley, Chicago, January 31, 1859, IC-1M2.1.

[104]Newell to Churchill, Amboy, March 9, 1869, IC-1N6.1. McKinney must have been a laborer as his wage seems to have been 80 cents per day. He was given half wages from February 8 to April 30, and the total amount given him was $28.80--probably seventy-two days at 40 cents a day. Newell to Leverett Clarke, Amboy, January 24, 1862, IC-1N6.1. A month later, McKinney was doing well at his new job as flagman at a crossing in Galena. He was unable to do any heavy work but was keeping the crossing clean and nearby ditches clear. Newell to Leverett Clarke, Amboy, April 5, 1862, IC-1N6.1.

[105]Douglas to R. H. McClellan, attorney, Chicago, June 4, 1868, IC-1D7.1.

[106]George McClellan to Osborn, Chicago, May 11, 1858; October 6, 1858, IC-1M2.1.

[107]McClellan to Leverett Clarke, Chicago, June 16, 1857, IC-1M2.1. McClellan [to Osborn?], Chicago, November 6, 1867, IC-1M2.1. McClellan to

Mrs. E[mma] R. Leffingwell, Chicago, April 3, 1858, IC-1M2.1. Release of claim by Emma Leffingwell, widow of Frederick O. Leffingwell, November 13, 1858, IC-3.92. Forty years later a son of the deceased employee tried to obtain a job on the I.C. W. H. Leffingwell to Stuyvesant Fish, Pres., Brooklyn, N.Y., n.d. [received February 19, 1898], IC-1F2.2.

[108]Douglas to Osborn, Chicago, April 10, 1865, IC-1D7.1.

[109]Only two pieces of contemporaneous material survive as evidence of the existence of this club in the 1860's: a card certifying that a conductor, A. J. McDonough, belonged to it in 1865 (photostatic copy in IC-3.6), and a letter, Mrs. J. J. Hayes, Treasurer I.C. Relief Club [and doubtless the wife of Master Mechanic Samuel J. Hayes of the Weldon shops], to Lynde A. Catlin, Secretary (of I.C.R.R.), Weldon, April 3, 1866, IC-11N1.5, acknowledging the receipt of $19.95 "due the association." Fortunately the operations of the club are described in Edward T. Jeffery, General Manager, to James C. Clarke, Pres., Chicago, June 8, 1888, IC-1F2.2. In the 1860's, Jeffery had been secretary of the club and had handled most of its business, or so he said in 1888.

[110]This description is based entirely upon Jeffery's letter of 1888, cited in the preceding note.

CHAPTER III

DEPRESSION, DRIFT, AND REBELLION

After the turbulence of the Civil War era there ensued a decade of relative quiescence on the Illinois Central. The managers of the road seemed to succumb to a kind of battle fatigue, for their policies in the immediate postwar years were generally conservative and even timid in nature. At a time when other railroad executives were extending their lines and invading new territory, the officers of the Illinois Central did little to expand the business of their road or even to protect its existing traffic from inroads by competing lines. In one exceptional instance they did guarantee to their enterprise a continued flow of traffic from the west by acquiring control of the Dubuque and Sioux City Railroad, which spanned the state of Iowa. But within Illinois they failed to shield the Illinois Central from the aggressive competition of the eastern trunk lines, which cut freight rates and drained away traffic. The Illinois Central's freight revenues, which had reached as high as $6,310,000 in 1869, declined in both 1870 and 1871 and dipped to $5,866,000 in 1872. In the same years, passenger revenues fell from $2,103,000 to $1,759,000. Although the company continued to pay an annual dividend of $10 a share on its stock until 1873, it had to draw on reserve funds in order to do so, for the earnings of the road totalled only $7.47 a share in 1872 and $8.45 in 1873.[1] As if these troubles were not enough, the company was soon faced with the additional problem of coping with the effects of a nationwide depression.

Depression Wage Policy

Outside the devastated areas of the South the United States enjoyed prosperous times in the years just after the Civil War. However, these good times came to an abrupt close on September 18, 1873, when the failure of the banking house of Jay Cooke and Company revealed the precarious condition of a financial market swollen by speculative investments in railroad and other securities. Thousands of investors threw their stocks onto the market, and the resulting collapse of security prices led to the failure of hundreds of banks and businesses.

When the Panic of 1873 struck, the Illinois Central's managers took swift action to curtail expenditures. On October 15, William Osborn recommended that the company follow the lead of several eastern railroads in imposing a wage cut of 10 or 20 per cent.[2] John Newell, who had become president in 1871, met with the chief executives of other railways terminating at Chicago in order to discuss cooperation among the roads on a policy of wage reductions. The executives kept one another informed of their respective actions in the next several weeks. On the Illinois Central, the superintendent of machinery imposed a 10 per cent reduction in the pay of all shopmen effective November 1, and President Newell recommended to the chief engineer that the pay of section hands be reduced wherever possible to a maximum of $1.25 a day. Newell also ordered the general superintendent of the transportation department to take up the question of wage cuts among freight handlers and other employees and to cooperate with other roads in making any reductions proposed by them.[3]

As the depression deepened during the next few years, further pay cuts were imposed on most classes of employees. In 1876 the work day in the company shops was reduced from ten to eight hours, so that the shopmen suffered another decline in their earnings even though their hourly wages were not changed.[4] James Clarke, who had re-entered the service of the Illinois Central with the title of General Manager, took strong measures to lower expenditures in the summer of 1876. Clarke had learned from his experience in the depression of the 'fifties that half-way measures would not do the job. On September 1, 1876, he ordered a reduction in the salaries of all officers and men of the transportation department who were employed on a monthly basis. The cut ranged from 5 per cent for the lowest paid men to 25 per cent for the highest paid officers.[5] Clarke also introduced a new pay schedule for engineers and firemen, under which they were paid on a mileage basis rather than at a monthly salary.[6] The new schedule reduced the earnings of the enginemen, although not to so great a degree as Clarke would have liked. "I did not succeed in getting this matter to the point I desired," he said, "but I have broken the ice and disrupted all the old arrangements. The next turn I have at it, I hope to reach bottom." Nevertheless, he estimated that the new schedule would save the company some $36,000 to $40,000 in a year's time.[7] In the fall of 1876, Vice President William K. Ackerman estimated that in the preceding ninety days Clarke had lowered the pay of officers, clerks, engineers, firemen, and track hands to such an extent as to provide an annual saving of $100,000.[8] Statistics bore him out, for in September 1876 the cost to the Illinois Central for the wages and salaries of employees was $8,000 less than it had been in the corresponding month of 1875, in spite of the fact that the company's labor force had increased approximately 5 per cent during the intervening year (see Table 4). Yet the wage cuts were not enough to overcome the effects of declining freight and passenger revenues, which fell each year from 1873 until 1878. Consequently, the company's annual dividend, which had been 10 per cent from 1865 to 1873, was lowered to 8 per cent in 1874 and 1875, 4 per cent in 1876, and 6 per cent for the remainder of the decade.[9]

Because business conditions remained depressed through the winter of 1876-77 and on into the folowing spring, company officials took additional

TABLE 4

COMPARATIVE STATEMENT OF FORCE EMPLOYED
ON THE ILLINOIS CENTRAL RAILROAD
IN SEPTEMBER 1875 AND 1876

Branch of Service	September 1875		September 1876	
	No.	Pay	No.	Pay
General Offices	142	$ 17,504	140	$ 13,905
Transportation Department				
Chicago Div.	577	30,590	532	27,665
Northern Div.	328	17,028	333	15,713
Iowa Division	320	14,418	285	13,337
Road Department				
Division 1	401	15,030	388	13,119
Division 2	214	11,066	351	13,643
Division 3	493	19,071	573	20,759
Division 4	442	17,495	635	25,792
Machinery Department	1,671	83,820	1,574	74,241
Telegraph	81	1,892	91	1,686
Total	4,669	$227,915	4,902	$219,860

Source: William K. Ackerman, Vice Pres., to Lewis V. F. Randolph, Treasurer, Chicago, October 24, 1876, IC-1D7.1.

steps to reduce costs. These measures included a reorganization of the road department, which eliminated a number of jobs.[10] In April the officers of the transportation department arranged for a series of meetings at which they tried to convince a committee representing the company's locomotive engineers that they should submit to a reduction in pay. The officers succeeded in persuading the engineers to agree to take on the job of moving their locomotives in and out of the roundhouses, a duty which in the past had been carried out by engine hostlers, whose wages had cost the railroad about $3,000 a year. But the engineers refused to accept any lowering of their wages. Many of them belonged to the Brotherhood of Locomotive Engineers, and the collective strength which they obtained through this union was sufficient to restrain company officers from imposing a reduction arbitrarily. William Ackerman grudgingly conceded that since he could not secure the cooperation of other Chicago railroads in forcing a cut, it would be best to wait "until some other period when business [was] dull."[11]

Because retail prices in the United States declined by nearly 20 per cent in the years 1873-79, it would seem that the real earnings of most Illinois

Central employees did not fall despite the wage cuts imposed during the depression. But probably the total real income of most men was lowered because of shortened working hours, and it need hardly be said that for those men who were compelled to join the swelling army of the unemployed, these were years of desperation.[12]

Working Conditions: Section Hands and Shopmen

The working environment of Illinois Central employees changed little in the 1870's. Although the company curtailed the pay of its employees, it was careful to pay them promptly the amounts which they earned, even when doing so strained the immediate resources of the company. When an operating deficit one month put the company behind in its payments to the men, Ackerman tried to rectify the situation as soon as possible. Speaking regretfully of the failure to pay the monthly rolls punctually, he said:

> This always causes great dissatisfaction to Employees. The fact that we have for so many years paid our Rolls promptly is one reason why we have always been able to pacify Engineers, Firemen and Shopmen when some of the more contentious have

> been disposed to get up a strike; differences of opinion between officers and employees that cost the Ohio and Missi[ssippi] and the I[ndianapolis] B[loomington and] W[estern] many thousands of dollars, we have been able to reconcile speedily because the men felt that they were dealing with a reliable paymaster.[13]

Several months later, Ackerman had adjusted matters to his and the employees' complete satisfaction. "We started the Paymaster out about five days earlier last month," he wrote, "and I think it a good plan to continue this in the future, for if the men are paid promptly they work better, and are better satisfied in every respect."[14]

Very little record survives of the experience of the Illinois Central's maintenance of way workers during the 'seventies. Certainly they suffered both wage cuts and reduced employment during the depression years, but detailed information is lacking. There is evidence that late in 1876 track laborers were being paid 10 to 11 cents an hour and that they were working ten hours a day, or at least they did so when work was available.[15] The nature of their toil differed little from what it had been in the 'fifties and 'sixties, except that the task of keeping the tracks free of snow blockage in the winter months was rendered somewhat less rigorous as a result of the introduction of large coal-burning locomotives. These heavy engines could plough their way through all but the deepest drifts, and even in bitter cold they seldom failed to keep up steam, as had often been the case with the frail wood-burners of the ante-bellum years. But a really severe snowstorm could still create problems, especially on the Iowa lines. In the winter of 1875, it required a week of shoveling by hundreds of men to clear the track between Fort Dodge and Dubuque following one such storm. At one point in that ordeal, the shovelers refused to work through a particularly windy afternoon, for they were soaked to the skin and had had practically no rest for five days.[16]

When Chief Engineer Leverett Clarke resigned his position in the spring of 1877, company officers seized upon this opportunity to alter the administrative structure under which the road workers were managed. The old engineering department was abolished, and all of its employees were placed within the jurisdiction of the transportation department. Division superintendents now assumed the responsibilities formerly exercised by division engineers, and beneath each superintendent a number of roadmasters took charge of the maintenance work on several sections of line. This consolidation was made in order to reduce costs by eliminating a number of salaried officers at a time when business was slow and minimal maintenance work was being done. It had no immediate effect on the former engineering department employees, except that obviously it ended such minor differences as had existed between the labor policies of the two departments now combined into one.[17]

For the tradesmen employed in the Illinois Central repair shops, the 'seventies were lean years. Following the Panic of 1873, their wages were reduced to their lowest level since the first years of the Civil War, and they were not increased during the remainder of the decade. At the Centralia shops in the winter of 1878, boilermakers were paid 24 to 30 cents per hour, blacksmiths 22-1/2 to 28 cents, machinists 20 to 28 cents, painters 28 cents, carpenters 19 to 23 cents, and engine wipers 13 to 14 cents.[18] Even more serious than the reductions in pay were the imposition of cuts in the work force and short-time for the men kept on the job. "All our shops are running on 8 hours time with a reduced force, and we are daily watching each item of expenditure," reported Ackerman to Osborn in the fall of 1876. During the winter of 1878-79, so little work was done in the shops at Centralia that the mayor of that community wrote to Ackerman for assurance that the Illinois Central did not intend to close the shops at that point. Ackerman replied that the company had no such intention, but, he said, "We have been obliged to make very large reductions in our forces at all points, and even here in Chicago, for more than a year past. We have been obliged to run our Shops 8 hours a day, for only 5 days in the week, and that too with a largely reduced force."[19]

Of course this departure from the ten-hour day and six day week of the 1860's reduced by one-third the take-home pay of the shopmen. Nevertheless, some of them came to like the forty hour work week and were reluctant to give it up when, in 1879, the company proposed a return to the old standard. The men's reluctance doubtless was increased by the company's announcement that hourly wages would be somewhat reduced at the same time that the ten-hour day was restored. "This plan would yield the men more money, but they would be obliged to work two hours additional," explained Ackerman. "For instance a man receiving 20 cents per hour and working eight hours per day, would get $1.60 per day; and we thought of increasing the number of hours to ten, and paying 18 cents per hour, which would yield him $1.80 a day." The announcement of this plan brought Ackerman a letter from William B. Creech, a molder at the Chicago car shops, who wrote on behalf of his fellow shopmen to protest against the idea. Ackerman received the letter in good humor. In fact, he passed it on to the company treasurer, along with a note expressing, if a bit superciliously, his own sympathy toward the stand taken by the shopmen:

> The men, as a general thing, we learn, prefer to work but eight hours a day. The subject under discussion has inspired Mr. Creech to break forth in song. Knowing you to be of a poetical turn of mind, I thought you would enjoy reading a copy of the letter. Personally I am an eight hour man, and I believe that on an average, a workman will give us better work in eight hours than he can in ten, either in summer or winter. On account of the introduction of labor saving machinery, our great study has been in the past two years to employ the largest number of men that we can at the reduced number of hours. As all are paid <u>by the hour</u>, it makes no particular difference to us.[20]

In 1878 Superintendent of Machinery Samuel J. Hayes and General Superintendent Edward T. Jeffery introduced a list of sixteen rules governing the employees of the machinery department. The list provides some idea of what a normal work day was like for the shopmen of the 1870's. When the shops were operating on their normal schedule of ten hours a day, six days a week, the men were expected to be on the job ready for work when the whistle sounded at 7:00 A.M. They then labored from 7:00 until noon, took an hour's break for dinner, and then worked from 1:00 until 6:00 P.M. On Saturdays they were allowed to leave an hour early but were required to clean up and put away their tools after the quitting time of 5:00 P.M. The early closing on Saturdays cost the company little, for nearly all of the shop workers were paid by the hour and only for time actually worked. When men were required to work beyond the regular hours or on Sundays, they were allowed time-and-a-half, but of course such overtime work was a rarity in the depression years. While on the job, shopmen were forbidden to receive visitors, to spend time on anything but company work, and to read or smoke.

Alcoholic beverages were banned from the shops and anyone using them to excess, even off the job, was liable for dismissal. The shop workers also were enjoined to keep their tools and machines in good order and neat in appearance, to refrain from filching tools or materials, and to give utmost attention to the prevention of fires.[21]

The rules introduced by Hayes and Jeffery said nothing about shop apprentices, but a policy on that matter was adopted on the suggestion of President Ackerman in October, 1878. At his request, the rule was established of subjecting apprentices to a three-month trial period, during which they were paid about 50 cents per day. Unless they showed sufficient mechanical skill and application to their work, they were not retained beyond the ninety-day trial.[22] Ackerman seldom took so direct an interest in the management of machinery department employees as he did on this matter of apprentices, but there was at least one occasion on which he did make it his business to investigate the treatment of some shopmen.

An anonymous letter addressed to the stockholders of the Illinois Central company was brought to

Ackerman's attention in the summer of 1877. The letter alleged that shop employees at Waterloo, Iowa, were being victimized by several company officers. It charged that Superintendent of Machinery Samuel Hayes, Assistant Superintendent Edward Jeffery, and Master Mechanic T. W. Place had bought up land in Waterloo prior to the erection of the shops there, and that subsequently they had sold house lots to company mechanics for three or four times their value, it being "partly obligatory" for the shopmen to buy lots "in order to retain their situations." The letter also claimed that the foreman of the machine shop kept a boardinghouse and a store, which employees were compelled to patronize.[23] Although he naturally gave little credence to the statements of an anonymous accuser, Ackerman immediately began a thorough investigation of the charges. He required the machinery department officers to explain their dealings in Waterloo property, and he then checked their testimony against county real estate records. He also ordered that the machine shop foreman at Waterloo be notified at once either to quit the company's service or else close out his store, for, said Ackerman, "it would be an easy matter for a man to get the impression that he was required to deal at this store, and any man having the boldness to deal elsewhere might be made a subject for dismissal."[24] Ackerman eventually concluded that there was no real substance to the charges that company officers had coerced shopmen into buying land at inflated prices. "The real estate transactions referred to were very insignificant," he found. "What few lots were sold to our own men were sold at reasonable prices, and in one instance, where a workman could not make his remaining payments for a lot, the money that he had paid was returned to him."[25] Ackerman notified the superintendent of machinery that he had investigated the charges fully, was convinced that there was "little or no foundation for the same," and that he had dismissed the subject from further consideration.[26]

Working Conditions: Trainmen and Enginemen

We have seen that the Illinois Central's maintenance of way workers as well as its shopmen experienced little change in their working environment during the 'seventies. The same held true for the conductors, baggagemen, and brakemen in the train service. The trainmen shared in the wage cuts and work reduction of the depression, but there was no significant change in the conditions under which they worked. The trainmen continued to be paid, as they always had been, on a monthly basis. Whenever they were detained four hours beyond the scheduled time for a run they received a half day's extra compensation, and if detained for eight hours they received a full day's extra pay.[27]

The job of the railway brakemen continued to be as hazardous and uncomfortable as it had been in earlier decades. The father of a young man who began working as a brakeman in the fall of 1879 wrote President Ackerman, with whom he was acquainted, that his son had experienced some protracted trips during his first two months on the railroad. One run had taken seventeen hours. But, said the proud parent, "I am gratified to hear from my son that upon his second payment he received full pay as a brakeman. . . . He writes full of courage and neither _dunckings_ [_sic_] nor _cold_ seem to have impaired his vigor. When I was at Chicago he gave me, from memory, every distance, switch and spur on the road."[28]

One class of employees that did experience some significant change in its job environment during the 'seventies was the men in engine service. The locomotive engineers and firemen of the Illinois Central were required not only to accept a wage reduction such as was imposed on all of the company's employees, but also to adjust to an entirely new system of wage payment, which amounted to a kind of piece-work system. They also had to cope with a major innovation involving the arrangement of engine runs. For the engineers, both of these developments involved an affront to their professional pride, as we shall see in a moment. There is a certain irony in the fact that the locomotive engineers, the only Illinois Central employees with a significant degree of collective strength, should also be the one class of employees most adversely affected by management innovations in the 1870's.

On July 1, 1876, General Manager James C. Clarke introduced a new system for determining the wages of engineers and firemen.[29] Heretofore the enginemen had been paid a fixed sum per month, less deductions for any days not worked. For passenger engineers and firemen, a trip over the division to which they were assigned constituted one day's work. The same was true for enginemen in freight service, except that if they ran four trips in one week and spent two days working on their engines in the shops, they were allowed six days' time. If they ran six trips in one week, they were credited with eight days' time toward their monthly quota of working days.[30] All of this was now changed. Under Clarke's new system, each regular locomotive run was assigned a specific monetary value, and this amount was paid to each engineman every time he made that run. The fixed amount was generally equal to about 3-1/4 cents per mile, and 100 miles was viewed as the normal day's run for an engineer.[31] Under the old system, engine crewmen who were delayed four or more hours beyond schedule time for a trip had been allowed overtime pay in the same manner as trainmen. But now, Clarke declared, "This rule is abolished and each claim for over time, or extra compensation, rests entirely on its own merits."[32]

Under the new system, the engineers were divided into three classes according to the length of time they had been employed by the Illinois Central--whether for five, ten, or fifteen years--and it was the policy of the company to allow the most senior class of men to make full time each month.[33] The classification of the engineers led to some disputes, especially since oftentimes there was not enough work to permit men outside of the senior group to make full time. Clarke personally ruled on half a dozen such cases which were appealed to him after the superintendent of machinery had made decisions unsatisfactory to the men involved.[34] One such case concerned an engineer named Davenport, who was employed on the Iowa lines. Some of Davenport's fellow engineers protested against his being placed among the senior engineers, because he had once testified in a court case that the type of engine they were required to run was unsafe. Clarke evidently saw nothing wrong with taking this utterly irrelevant accusation into account, although he did rule that Davenport should be classed among the senior engineers until the superintendent of machinery could obtain a copy of the court testimony allegedly made by the engineer. In a second case, Clarke ruled that although Dennis Canney "seems to be a meritorious man and while we regret exceedingly that we have not work for all our engineers, so that they may make full time and earn a fair compensation, I respectfully recommend to the Supt. of Machinery to let Mr. Canney fall back into the junior class and do the best he can for him in common with those of that class."[35] In a third case, Clarke ruled that J. H. Pollard of the Iowa division should be placed in the senior class even though his career as an engineer had been interrupted for a time while he served as a roundhouse foreman. Clarke forcefully declared that he would not allow the question of seniority to impinge upon management prerogatives:

> While it is the wish and intention of the managers of this line to deal fairly and impartially with all the men in its service, at the same time it must be distinctly understood that the superior officers . . . have the right and authority to make such details of men as in their judgment the interest of the Co. may require; and the fact of a man being detailed for any specific service must not be permitted to work injury to him. . . . Any other course than this would be a premium to inefficient and undeserving men.[36]

Clarke believed that "all our good men, whose opinions are worth having will acquiesce in the decision of the various cases." But he insisted that while each employee would "as far as possible . . . have equal and even-handed justice done to him," still, "the officers of the company, with the facts laid before them, must be the judges to mete out such justice."[37]

Another problem created by the new system was that of determining the pay to be given enginemen for making special runs not listed on the wage schedule. Local master mechanics tried to deal with such cases in common sense fashion. Again, some of their decisions were appealed all the way up to the general manager. In one such case Clarke wrote directly to C. J. Justus, an engineer at Waterloo, to explain why he was not overruling the decision of Master Mechanic T. W. Place. "If you will look at the Schedule," wrote Clarke to Justus, "you will see that in allowing you this time [$7.00 for a round trip from Fort Dodge to Remsen], Mr. Place took a similar run to see what it paid, and as the pay for a round run is not so much in any case as a straight run of a given number of miles, I do not think you have any reason to complain."[38] The willingness of Clarke and other officers to consider individual complaints and grievances undoubtedly helped to blunt the enginemen's resentment of the new wage system. But no corresponding procedure could be used to make the engineers amenable to another important innovation in their job environment: the introduction of continuous engine runs.

From the earliest days of the Illinois Central, locomotive engineers had been assigned to specific engines. They were held responsible not only for the proper running of their locomotives but also for seeing to it that they were kept clean and in good mechanical condition. Most engineers took great pride in the condition and appearance of their locomotives and spent many hours in the shops packing moving parts with grease, adjusting the headlamp, polishing brasswork, and superintending additonal cleaning by firemen and engine wipers. The engineers came to know the idiosyncrasies of their own locomotives and to regard them with both pride and affection. Often they gave them pet names and spoke of them as though they were compounded of flesh and blood rather than brass and iron. It was, therefore, an affront to the pride and feelings of the locomotive engineers when James C. Clarke proposed to introduce a new system in which this attachment of man to machine would be no more.[39]

In the summer of 1876, Clarke sent Assistant Master of Machinery Edward T. Jeffery on a trip to the East to inspect a new system for running locomotives which had been introduced on the New York Central, the Pennsylvania, and the Philadelphia and Reading Railroads.[40] On these lines, locomotives were being run continuously over long distances, stopping occasionally to change engine crews, but omitting the long layovers which had been unavoidable when each locomotive was consigned to a specific engineer. Jeffery compiled a full report on this innovation as it was practiced on the eastern roads. He concluded that its adoption had led to reduced costs because of the much more efficient use of engine power which it made possible. But he also found that the new arrangement was not without its disadvantages. There was, he said, a tendency for engineers to overwork their engines and to use excessive amounts of fuel. And since under the new system the maintenance work formerly done by the engineers was now performed by other men, the locomotives tended to suffer from less meticulous upkeep. In addition, the men hired to do the cleaning and repairs formerly attended to by the enginemen entailed added expense to their employer, although Jeffery noted that this difficulty might be surmounted by reducing the pay of the engineers.[41]

Despite Jeffery's rather equivocal conclusions, Clarke decided to introduce the system of continuous engine runs on the Illinois Central, first on the Chicago branch, then over the rest of the charter route, and finally on the Iowa lines. "Our own experience," he wrote, "will, after all, be worth more to us than any information, which we can gain through any other course."[42] Clarke first applied the new arrangement only to the passenger service. In mid-September of 1876, he began running passenger trains straight through from Centralia to Chicago, eliminating the former stopover at Champaign. Within a few weeks he extended the experiment to other parts of the line. Engines now ran continuously from Centralia to Chicago, from Centralia to Amboy, and from Amboy to Waterloo. Once the new system was working smoothly and reserve engines had been strategically placed for use in case of accidents or breakdowns,

Clarke also applied the plan to the Illinois Central freight service. Clarke hoped that continuous running would save the company money by reducing the quantity of capital invested in motive power and also by making the machinery department of the road more efficient as a result of the consolidation of shop facilities. He pointed out to William Osborn that by making Chicago, Centralia, Amboy, and Waterloo the headquarters for engine runs, he was able to eliminate nearly all necessity for maintaining repair facilities at Champaign, Cairo, Wapella, Dunleith, Dubuque, and Fort Dodge.[43]

In introducing the new system, Clarke displayed the thoroughness and tenacity that always characterized his policy once he had decided upon a course of action. He was determined to give continuous running an exhaustive test even if it took a year to do it, and he would allow no one to thwart him in that purpose. To his division superintendents, he wrote:

> It is probably to be expected that some indirect opposition may be offered by subordinates, as it is an innovation upon the old rules and customs. This is to be looked for to some extent, and necessary allowance made for it. . . . [But] if we find in our service employees disposed to stand in the way of this matter, they must be removed from the service.[44]

In testing the new system, Clarke might shrug off or squelch the opposition of disgruntled employees, but he could not ignore or combat what soon became a strong case against the economy of the scheme. As the months went by, it became increasingly clear that continuous running did not save the company much money, especially as it applied to the operation of freight trains.[45] "Statistics begin to show that continuous runs for engines on some parts of our line are not a success," reported William Ackerman. "If the Engines were certain of a full load all the way through, as on the 'New York Central,' the case would be different. The Superintendent of Machinery gives it as his opinion that, where a Company has a full complement of equipment, it does not pay to overwork engines on long hauls."[46]

In his zeal for efficiency and economy, Clarke had attempted an innovation that was not suitable for the Illinois Central of the late 'seventies. In these depression years, traffic was light and so the road had sufficient locomotives to meet all of its needs without resorting to the system of continuous runs. And so, in the spring of 1877, all freight operations were returned to the old system of short trips and layovers, and the number of continuously running passenger engines was severely curtailed.[47] Not until heavy traffic demands strained the resources of the railroad in the following decade would it prove worthwhile, in fact mandatory, for the Illinois Central to give the plan a second trial.

Rise of the Brotherhood of Locomotive Engineers

In introducing continuous engine runs as also in changing the procedure for computing the pay of enginemen, Clarke and other officials had taken steps which were opposed by the engineers in the service of the road. The fact that the railroad managers were able to proceed with these innovations in spite of their unpopularity among the engineers is a measure of the inability of the latter group to determine management policy. But that is not to say that the engineers could not influence management decisions to a limited extent. There is in fact ample evidence that during the 1870's it became clear to Illinois Central officials that they had to handle that class of employees carefully because of the growing strength of their labor union, the Brotherhood of Locomotive Engineers. In a strictly formal sense, the railroad officers did not recognize the existence of this labor organization. They did not sign contracts with it. They did not enter into negotiations with it. They did not even listen to spokesmen for the Brotherhood. But they were willing to give a hearing to any and all Illinois Central employees, either individually or through their chosen spokesmen, at any time. And when they listened to representatives of the engineers in the service of the company, they were, in actuality, generally listening to men actively identified with the Brotherhood. Certainly the company officers were well aware of the potential for collective action which the Brotherhood organization gave to the engineers, and that awareness colored their policies to a measurable degree.

As early as 1871, President John Newell agreed to meet with a committee of engineers which wished to present certain grievances involving the pay of themselves and their fellows. In his subsequent discussion with the committeemen, Newell assented to at least one of their requests: that engineers making the run between Chicago and Champaign be allowed extra compensation in consideration of their having to cover a greater distance and do more work than the men assigned to other sections of the road.[48] The fact that on the very day of his meeting with the committee Newell sent a complimentary pass over the Illinois Central lines to Charles G. Wilson, national president of the B.L.E., suggests that Newell knew perfectly well that in meeting with the committee he was dealing, however indirectly, with the Brotherhood organization.[49] But he did not have to admit it. He could say quite honestly that he was merely talking with some of his employees and that it was no concern of his what fraternal affiliations they might or might not have.

As general manager of the Illinois Central, James C. Clarke pursued a two-faced policy toward the Brotherhood. On the surface he sought to cultivate good relations with the organization. When he lowered the pay of his engineers in 1876, he wrote the national head of the B.L.E. to explain his action, stressing that "all officers and employees, as well as locomotive engineers, have to bear the burdens of decreased compensation, the first two classes to a greater degree than the latter." Clarke claimed that despite the cut the Illinois Central still paid its engineers better than most railroads did, and he asserted that the men recognized that necessity had dictated the reduction of their wages.

> For intelligence, ability and morality [Clarke went on,] we have as good a class of locomotive engineers as any railroad in the United States, and it is the policy and intention of this company to deal justly and liberally with this class of employees; and it will be only when justice to all will make it necessary, that they will be called on, with all others, to share reduced compensation and if necessary increased labors to produce results. The large majority of these men have always been ready and willing to bear their full share.[50]

When the president of the Brotherhood, in an address to the national convention of the union, stressed the merits of conciliation and conservatism, Clarke seized upon the occasion to further cultivate good relations with that official. "Without intending in any way to flatter you," wrote Clarke, in an obvious attempt at flattery, "I have no hesitation in saying that, if the members of the organization live up to and are governed by the sound doctrine and good advice contained in that address, it will not only advance their personal and individual interest, but [also] will strongly commend their organization to the confidence of their employers."[51]

However, in his correspondence with other railroad officials, Clarke revealed a less than cordial attitude toward the Brotherhood of Locomotive Engineers. He made it quite clear that he resented the fact that the allegiance of Illinois Central employees to the Brotherhood made it difficult for the company to trim their wages unless other railroads followed suit. After introducing the new system of paying engineers by the trip, Clarke wrote, "This class of employees is still paid too high, but has to be handled very carefully to avoid strikes. When our neighbors take some action in this branch, we will be able to reduce still further."[52] Clarke thought that "it would be a good thing, if all the railroads of note in Illinois would make about twenty-five engineers per year, so as to produce a surplus of this grade of employees."[53] It was lucky for the enginemen that Clarke did not succeed in getting the officers of other railroads to cooperate with him either in reducing wages or in creating excessive numbers of engineers.

Clarke's negative attitude toward the Brotherhood was shared by Vice President William K. Ackerman. In 1877, Ackerman was unable to persuade the company's engineers to accept another wage cut, which he believed necessary at the time, and he dared not force it upon them because of the danger of a strike. "The brotherhood," he remarked ruefully, "is stronger in the West, I believe, than it is in the East."[54] Ackerman ordered General Superintendent Edward Jeffery to confer with the superintendents of other lines in hopes of securing their cooperation in forcing a wage cut, but again this effort was unsuccessful.[55] Ackerman took a keen interest in the attempt by President Franklin B. Gowen of the Philadelphia and Reading Railroad to compel the engineers on that line to quit the B.L.E., and he thought that it would prove "a benefit to the whole R.R. interest" if Gowen were successful.[56] Just how anxious Ackerman was to counteract the Brotherhood is indicated by his remarkable suggestion on how that organization might be combatted:

> All the companies in the west could combine and offer the Engineers the same or even better advantages than they now obtain in their own associations. If the men of the first class could be assured of a life appointment, some consideration in case of sickness, and a gratuity to their families in case of sudden death, it would take from them their present feeling of insecurity and restlessness--and it would also give the men in the second something to look forward to.[57]

Ackerman promised to "present this matter in a more definite form at some future time," but he apparently changed his mind, for he never mentioned the proposal later on.[58] This is understandable, for Ackerman was a careful, methodical person, not at all the sort of man who would be likely to carry through so bold an innovation as he had proposed. Had Ackerman's deep insight into the psychology of the engineers been coupled with James Clarke's vigor and decisiveness, the Illinois Central might well have pioneered in a policy of welfare capitalism that was decades ahead of its time.[59] Instead, the company adopted less imaginative means for avoiding trouble from its employees. In the fall of 1878, for example, Ackerman suggested to Jeffery that it would be well to hire as firemen (and therefore future engineers) some young men "who have sufficient intelligence to reason with" and to "cull out some of the inferior men, who are likely to give us trouble in case of a strike."[60]

Discipline Policy

From such fragmentary evidence as is available, it appears that disciplinary procedures on the Illinois Central changed very little during the 'seventies. While he was serving as general manager, James Clarke pursued the same hard-headed policy that he had introduced to the road some twenty years before. After a train accident in 1875, he urged the general superintendent to advise the division superintendents and trainmasters that careless men should be dismissed from the service. And, he said, "I think it would be well for you to require Div[isio]n Sup[erintenden]ts to investigate fully and closely all accidents which occur, by suspending all parties implicated, until a thorough investigation is had."[61] After another accident a few weeks later, Clarke ordered the dismissal of all employees in any way connected with the incident.[62] Two conductors and an engineer were fired, although Clarke later permitted them to be reinstated, in consideration of their past records and service.[63]

In 1877, Clarke resigned as general manager of the Illinois Central in order to take charge of certain railroad lines south of Cairo in which the I.C. had acquired a dominent financial interest. As manager of the southern lines, he was soon pushing for "a rigid observance of discipline" and complaining that there was "not enough snap" among the employees.[64] He ordered the dismissal of anyone caught drinking on duty and suggested that any employees who were habitual tipplers should be replaced with sober men.[65] He also continued his policy of dismissing all workers whose negligence contributed to accidents. After a collision resulting from a misunderstanding of telegraphed orders, he reiterated this rule, which he considered essential to the safe operation of a railroad. "Any employee unfit by reason of judgment, habits, or character to hold the position he occupies" should be dismissed immediately, he said. "We must have no more such damned outrageous things as this occurring on our line."[66]

When Clarke took charge of the southern lines, General Superintendent Edward Jeffery became the chief official in charge of discipline on the Illinois Central proper. Jeffery did not introduce any major changes in policy or procedures, except that he tended to be somewhat less severe than Clarke in his treatment of negligent employees. After investigating a collision of a train and a handcar, which had resulted in the death of a bridge carpenter, Jeffery concluded that the accident had resulted from the combined carelessness of a bridge supervisor, a yardmaster, and a locomotive engineer. But Jeffery dealt leniently with the culpable employees. "I consider the blame to be so evenly divided between [sic] the three men mentioned, that I don't see how we could consistently discharge one from the service without discharging the other two," he said. "I shall write a letter to each of the men severely reprimanding him for their [sic] parts in the transaction."[67] It is difficult to imagine James Clarke resolving the matter in quite this way.

In the correspondence of D. W. Parker, the division superintendent in charge of the Iowa lines in the 'seventies, there is record of a novel method of discipline: the deduction from employees' wages of damages resulting from their carelessness. Perhaps this idea originated with James Clarke, who as early as 1874 had ordered a trainmaster to deduct the cost of damaged goods from the wages of some freight handlers who had been reckless in loading them.[68] At any rate, the policy was common practice in Iowa in the late 'seventies. Between June and October of 1878, at least sixteen employees were assessed for damages. A switchman who allowed some cars to run off a switch in the Sioux City yard was charged $9.88 for the cost of repairs. A conductor and a brakeman forfeited $30.87 and $18.53, respectively, as a result of the collision of two sections of their train, which had broken apart. Engineer Coburn was assessed $15.00 for allowing his engine to run into a cow, while conductor Dowand had to pay for a replacement when he lost his ticket punch. Perhaps the unkindest cut of all was borne by switchman D. W. Knight, who was charged $6.20 for a broken urinal caused by rough switching.[69]

Accident Compensation

The policy of donating financial aid to accident victims continued to prevail during the 1870's, although the practice seems to have been far less common than was the case in earlier decades. In 1871, President Newell received a plea for help from a brakeman whose leg had been crushed in a coupling accident. After sustaining this injury, the victim had suffered the further misfortune of losing all of his personal property in the great Chicago fire. His leg had required five operations, and he had been left penniless and without employment. "Now whether or not I have any legal claim or not on your Company," he wrote, "it seems to me that the claim of humanity ought to induce you to do something for me." Newell evidently agreed, for at the top of the man's letter he wrote "$100-$150," doubtless a notation as to what he thought would be an appropriate donation.[70]

General Manager James Clarke looked with a jaundiced eye on requests for aid to accident victims, for he was nearly always of the opinion that the accident had resulted from the carelessness or disobedience of the injured party. But he did permit donations if lower officials recommended them. When engineer Anderson's locomotive overturned near Dunleith in 1874, Clarke allowed him half pay while laid up, since this was recommended by the master mechanic, the division superintendent, and the superintendent of machinery. Clarke made this concession even though he considered it quite clear that Anderson had run his engine at excessive speed "and was not using the judgment, which his duties required."[71] When engineer Spangler and fireman Cross asked for help following another mishap, Clarke denied that the company owed them anything, as he was convinced that they had run their engine at a reckless speed. "I suppose they have both been in the service long enough to know that when a man does not work for this co., he is not paid," was his testy reaction to Spangler's request for $80.00 per month during his convalescence. Nevertheless, Clarke permitted both men to apply to the master of machinery for donations "on account of their former good conduct."[72]

When company officials feared that an injured man might have a valid legal claim against the railroad, they sometimes were willing to donate considerable sums of money in order to avoid a lawsuit. Thus General Superintendent Mitchell authorized the payment of $1,000 to engineer Ed Davis, who had been injured in a derailment caused by a broken rail, a circumstance for which the company probably would have been adjudged negligent and legally liable for damages had the case come before a court. But Mitchell refused a request for a larger sum from the brother of fireman O'Connor, who had been killed in the same accident. Mitchell told the brother of the dead man "that it had been the custom for the company to meet surgical and burial expenses[,] and in case family or parents were in need [it] made small donations." When the brother made a demand for $4,000, said Mitchell, "I answered that it would not be accepted."[73] In another case in which the company might well have been legally liable to an employee, James Clarke allowed engineer T. L. Parkinson $800 as full payment "of all claims of every kind and character resulting from the explosion of engine 113," of which Parkinson had been engineer.[74] Unless they felt sure that contributory negligence, the fellow servant rule, or the doctrine of assumed risk would cause the judge to direct a verdict in favor of the company, Illinois Central officials were anxious to settle employee injury cases out of court, for they could never be sure what damages a jury might award to the pitiful victim of an accident. As one means of preventing suits, Clarke ordered his division superintendents never to employ any minor who could not furnish a certificate from his parents consenting to his employment and absolving the company of all claims for damages or injuries that might be sustained by the child.[75]

When accident victims requested continued employment from the railroad, some attempt usually was made to find them a suitable situation, but no guarantee of a job was ever made part of a damage settlement. Clarke provided engineer Parkinson with a job as night foreman at the Centralia engine house but warned him that he could not promise him continued employment for any set length of time.[76] On another occasion, William Ackerman tried to find a position for A. H. Joynt, a station agent who had been run over by a wagon and as a result had been so crippled that he was compelled to quit his job after fourteen years in the company's service.[77] "I don't think the Ill C RR owes me a cent," Joynt had written to Ackerman, "but while in their service I got so terribly injured as renders me unfit for manual labor and will no doubt shorten my life and I hope this letter will meet with recognition and not be resigned to the wastebasket after a hasty perusal."[78]

Because of his lack of enthusiasm for company aid to injured employees, James Clarke was favorably disposed toward the efforts of private companies to sell accident insurance to Illinois Central workers. He encouraged Superintendent of Machinery Samuel Hayes to allow an agent of the Travelers Insurance Company of Hartford, Connecticut, to visit the company's shops and canvass among the men "as the means of affording employees an opportunity of securing some relief in cases of accident, for which the company would not be responsible to them." Clarke praised the Travelers company as "an institution which has been in successful operation for some years, and which, from the promptness with which it has made its payments to injured parties, who were insured with it, is commended to the confidence of the public."[79] Apparently a considerable number of employees did take out policies, for a few months later Clarke told the Illinois Central paymaster that he might, if he wished, make an arrangement whereby he would collect premiums on behalf of the insurance company. The men who had taken out policies would give the paymaster a legal order authorizing him to withhold from their wages the amount of their insurance premiums. Clarke told the paymaster that any arrangement he might make with the insurance company would be all right with the Illinois Central, "as it will be in your individual capacity and not as an officer of the company."[80] Apparently this plan was never instituted, however, or else it was soon abandoned, for in 1877 William Ackerman wrote an agent of the Travelers company that he would not allow the introduction of a proposed insurance plan on the grounds that it would be too distracting to the Illinois Central paymaster. "As our paymaster travels over 1300 miles of road monthly[,] paying off some 6000 men," wrote Ackerman, "I do not see how he can attend to your business, without running the risk of making mistakes in his own."[81]

In 1877, Ackerman proclaimed himself very much interested in a company-sponsored insurance system which had just been introduced on the Philadelphia and Reading Railroad.[82] The Reading company had set aside a total of $25,000 to support a life and accident insurance system for its train hands, primarily as a means of enticing men away from their attachment to the Brotherhood of Locomotive Engineers. Ackerman was having his own troubles with the Brotherhood at this time, which is probably the reason that he was so intrigued by the Reading plan. There is no evidence that Ackerman seriously considered introducing any comparable system on the Illinois Central. But it is likely that he gave at least tacit encouragement to an effort which was made in 1878 to organize a voluntary life insurance association among Illinois Central employees.

The origins of the "Illinois Central Rail-Road Mutual Benefit Association" are obscure. No doubt this scheme was encouraged if not actually instigated by company officers, but it functioned as an entirely autonomous organization, financially independent and open to all persons between twenty-one and sixty years of age who were in ordinary good health, who were not addicted to habitual drunkenness, and who were employed on the Illinois Central Railroad or any sleeping car company, freight line, or express company running in connection with that railroad. According to its by-laws, the association consisted of three divisions, each furnishing a different amount of life insurance protection to its members. Whenever a member of "division A" died, his survivors were supposed to receive a sum equal to 50 cents for every member then belonging to the division. Each member of division A paid an entrance fee of 50 cents, and afterwards he was assessed a sum ranging from 45 to 90 cents, depending on his age, each time a member of the division died. "Division B" worked the same way, except that the entrance fee was $1.00, assessments ranged from 90 cents to $1.80, and a death benefit equal to $1.00 per member was paid to the survivors of any member who died. "Division C" had an entrance fee of $2.00, assessments of from $1.80 to $3.60, and a death benefit equal to $2.00 for each member. Since under the by-laws each division could enroll as many as 1,000 members, it was theoretically possible for them to pay death benefits of as much as $500, $1,000, and $2,000, respectively.[83] In practice, however, the plan never really got off the ground, and the benefits paid did not approach such sums. In 1883, an Illinois Central officer wrote that the membership of the association had never increased materially since its organization and that the death benefits which it paid were "so small that the employés along the line do not think it worth while to become members."[84]

Four Days in July: The Strike of 1877

During the summer of 1877 the American railroad industry was battered by an unprecedented wave of strikes and riots, which paralyzed transportation at dozens of points from Baltimore to St. Louis and which resulted in the destruction of millions of dollars worth of property and the deaths of scores of persons. The disturbances began with a strike by employees of the Baltimore and Ohio Railroad who refused to accept a wage cut which took effect on July 16. Three days later, some train crews on the Pennsylvania system ceased work in protest against an increase in the size of trains and in the length of engine runs, as well as in delayed response to a wage cut which had been imposed early in June. In the following week, stoppages occurred also on the Reading, Erie, New York Central, Wabash and other railroads. Mob violence and incendiarism broke out at Pittsburgh and other cities, and state and even federal troops were pressed into service to restore order.[85]

The first indication that the Illinois Central was to become involved in these disturbances came at 8:15 A.M. on Tuesday, July 24, when a crowd of men visited the company's Chicago freight yard and compelled employees to cease work in the yard and at the freighthouse. That same morning a committee of yard switchmen called on General Superintendent Joseph Tucker to ask for an increase in their wages, which had been reduced three weeks before. Tucker promised to consider their request, and the men appeared to be mollified by his response. Vice President William Ackerman shared Tucker's view that the request of the switchmen was not unreasonable. "These men," Ackerman reported to William Osborn, "have been cut twice within about a year and, perhaps, have more reason to complain than some of the others." He continued:

> The total of this force employed, with helpers, is 16. They are few in number, but very important in the service, making up, as they do, all the freight trains that go out, as well as switching to and from the elevators and stock yard. They originally got $70.00 per month, and the helpers $60.00 per month. On the 1st

> of September, 1876, the first were cut down to $66.50 and the latter to $57.00. On the first of the present month, the last reduction made, the switchmen were informed that they would receive $60.00 and the helpers $52.00. When matters are calmed down, . . . if the middle figure will induce the men to return to work, it might be policy to make the concession.[86]

But events quickly outran the conciliatory gestures of Ackerman and Tucker. The crowd of outsiders who had made the men quit work in the freight yard would not allow the switchmen to resume their duties.[87] Meanwhile, similar crowds of men had halted most work on other railroads at Chicago. Faced with this situation, Ackerman telegraphed to the governor of Illinois an appeal for state protection against the actions of a lawless mob which, he said, imperilled the property of the company and the lives of its employees.[88] Late that night, Ackerman ordered the Chicago yard cleared of rolling stock, sending the cars forty miles down the line. At about 3:00 A.M. the last of several trains removing the cars was attacked by a body of men who fired several shots into the caboose, boarded the train, pulled coupling pins in order to force it to a halt, and then compelled the engineer to return it to the freight yard.

The next day an unruly crowd of men, about

200 in number, again prevented work at the freight yard. Another crowd visited the Illinois Central machine shops and car shops, compelling the 400 hands employed at those facilities to stop work. Meanwhile, word reached Chicago that mobs composed largely of men on strike against other railroads were refusing to permit freight trains to run through Mattoon, Effingham, Carbondale, and Decatur. With its line interrupted at these four points, the Illinois Central was forced to discontinue all freight service, except in Iowa and on the line between Centralia and Cairo.[90]

Not until Thursday did the tide begin to turn against the fomenters of the disorders at Chicago. That afternoon some 500 troops arrived to reinforce the Chicago police force and local volunteer companies in their efforts to restore order. That same day Ackerman obtained from the mayor of the city a requisition for 100 muskets, 200 rounds of ammunition, and a small cannon, all of which was put at the disposal of about 100 Illinois Central employees who had answered an appeal by Ackerman for volunteers to guard the company's freighthouse, car shops, roundhouse, and other property.[91] The volunteer guards, many of whom were veterans of the Civil War, were placed under the command of James Noquet, a draftsman in the engineering department.[92] Ackerman chose Noquet as commander because once while serving in the army of France he had led troops against a mob in Paris.[93] Thursday afternoon passed by in relative tranquility, except that a crowd of people threw stones through the windows of one in-bound passenger train. By evening General Superintendent Jeffery considered the situation so much improved that he decided to attempt to resume work at the company shops the following morning. However, Ackerman reported that the excitement in the city was still intense, with so many contradictory rumors flying about that he dared not predict whether or not it would be safe to reopen the shops.[94]

Friday at 7:00 A.M. the screech of a steam whistle announced the reopening of the Illinois Central shops at Chicago. Of the approximately 400 men normally employed at these facilities, eighty-seven reported for work at the car shops and forty more at the machine shops. Ackerman pronounced himself satisfied with this turnout, for some sixty men had been excused on account of having been up all night serving as guards, and many others had not heard of the resumption of work or else had remained at home in order to look to the safety of their families.[95] Other branches of the service resumed operations that same day. Shippers were notified that out-bound goods would be accepted at the freighthouse, as the freight handlers and yard crews were again at work.[96] In the afternoon word was received that the blockade of the line had been lifted at the several points where freight trains had been halted since Wednesday. At Decatur it had been necessary for the governor to send in troops in order to compel the strikers and their sympathizers to allow the trains to pass. By evening Ackerman could telegraph to Osborn that all trains were moving and that the troubles appeared to be entirely at an end. The next morning he dispatched a short message confirming that the line was open at every point and the company's business resumed in all its branches.[97]

In assessing the significance of the 1877 disturbances so far as the employees of the Illinois Central were concerned, it is essential to bear in mind that during the troubled days of July none of these workers actually went out on strike against their employer. On the contrary, Ackerman reported again and again that the employees were unwilling participants in the work stoppage: "There has been no actual strike by any of our men, and I think they all would have continued work, if the outside mob had let them alone."[98] "There has been no strike. . . . Our men express a willingness to go to work this morning if they could have protection."[99] "Our men have acted nobly throughout."[100] "I am sure you have as devoted men in your service as any Railroad Co. in the country."[101] "Our men all remained true to us."[102] The interruption of work on the Illinois Central at Chicago and other points had in every case been forced upon the employees by crowds of outsiders, whom Ackerman described as a mixture of striking employees of other railroads, simple plunderers, and "Communists."[103] Of course Ackerman really had no way of knowing who made up the mobs that created the disorders. It seems likely that they were mostly unemployed men, who acted without any objective other than that of venting their rage against the suffering which they and their families had endured in the depression years. It is quite possible that they included considerable numbers of former Illinois Central employees who had lost their jobs as a consequence of the depression, although there is no evidence on this point.

Because the Illinois Central's workers had not willfully taken part in the disorders, their employer harbored no ill feelings toward them. In fact, Ackerman ordered that all employees should be allowed full pay for the time of the work stoppage, and at his suggestion the Illinois Central board of directors adopted a resolution recognizing the "loyalty and good sense shown by the company's employees in all Departments during a period of great excitement and trial" and endorsing the contents of a circular in which Ackerman had expressed his "thanks and commendation" to the men. Inasmuch as no demands had been made upon the company, no concessions had been made by it in order to bring about the resumption of work. Thus the troubles of 1877 had no immediate consequences, good or bad, for the men of the Illinois Central.[104]

But in the long run these events did have an

effect upon the labor force, in that they influenced the later attitudes and policies of Ackerman and other officials. For one thing, they taught the importance of maintaining good morale among the employees, for it was the loyalty of its workers that had allowed the company to weather the storm of 1877 without serious damage to its physical properties. In the 1880's, Ackerman was to show considerable interest in promoting welfare measures for the benefit of employees, as we shall see. Also, the riots made the railroad officers at least somewhat less hostile toward the Brotherhood of Locomotive Engineers. During the troubles, Ackerman said, "Our engineers have proven themselves plucky in this emergency and shown a good disposition towards us."[105] Naturally this did not mean that henceforth Ackerman was a devoted friend of the Brotherhood. But never again did he toy with plans for destroying that organization, as he had in 1876.

Finally, it is clear that the 1877 troubles had an important effect upon the wage policy of the Illinois Central, and, indeed, upon that of most of the nation's railroads and other major industrial employers. Never again would the employers impose wage cuts without far more soul-searching than had prevailed in the depression of 1873-77. The July rebellion had shown that there was a breaking point beyond which men could not be pressed. Thus the strikes of 1877 tended to put a floor under the wages of American workingmen, so that the earnings of the industrial labor force displayed a remarkable stability throughout the remainder of the nineteenth century.[106] Seventeen years after the July revolt, the managers of the Illinois Central still had not forgotten this lesson of 1877. When a general wage cut was suggested as a means of reducing expenditures following the Panic of 1893, the company's general superintendent reminded his superiors of the events of 1877 and warned them that the men would not be disposed to take the word of the company for the necessity of a wage reduction. He said that a careful effort would have to be made to convince them of that necessity, if "strikes and trouble" were to be avoided.[107]

***

The 1870's saw no great transformation of the labor policies of the Illinois Central Railroad.

Disciplinary procedures were not altered significantly, nor were any important welfare programs initiated. For the typical employee, working conditions differed little from what they had been in the Civil War decade, except that the good times of the immediate postwar period gave way to four years of lowered wages and narrowed opportunities for employment, following the Panic of 1873. In the 'seventies, only the locomotive engineer experienced a basic change in his job environment, through James Clarke's introduction of payment by the trip and his experimentation with continuous engine runs. These innovations undermined the prestige and independent spirit which had always characterized the locomotive engineer, for now he was paid on a piece-work basis and was forced to give up "his" locomotive--the iron monster which had been the tangible proof of his skill, pride, and importance. Clearly the engineer had become less of a free agent and more of a cog in the industrial machine.

The changed status of the engineer was one result of the constant drive for efficiency that was characteristic of the industrial environment and which was especially stimulated by the financial exigencies of the depression years. The same zeal for economy that led James Clarke to alter the working environment of the engineers and to reduce the wages of all employees also made him more reluctant to grant donations to accident victims than he and other officials had been in earlier years. Although Clarke and other officers continued to affirm their interest in the fair treatment of all employees, their relations with the labor force were increasingly formal and distant. The sense of community between managers and men was on the decline. Certainly the troubles of 1877 proved that the workers still felt a strong sense of loyalty to their employer, but the rising influence of the Brotherhood of Locomotive Engineers showed that their commitment to the company was not absolute. William Ackerman might insist that he dealt with his men only as employees and never as union members, but it is clear that he was greatly concerned with the power of the Brotherhood and that his actions were influenced by that awareness.

The Illinois Central was becoming a huge industrial enterprise. Its tracks stretched across

Iowa, and soon it would formally absorb the southern lines which it already controlled. Its managers faced the mounting pressures of industrialism, and little by little they learned to cope with them. They learned valuable lessons not only in times of crisis, as in July of 1877, but also from the countless undramatic incidents which occurred every day of every year. Progress toward a modern industrial environment came slowly in the 'seventies. But, inevitably, it came.

[1]Lewis E. Severson, "Some Phases of the History of the Illinois Central Railroad Company since 1870" (unpublished Ph.D. thesis, University of Chicago, 1930), pp. 10-13, 26-31, 187-88, 273, 290.

[2]William H. Osborn, Director, to John Newell, Pres., New York, October 15, 1873, IC-1N6.3.

[3]Newell to A. Mitchell, General Supt., Chicago, October 23, 1873, IC-1N6.1. See also Newell to Leverett H. Clarke, Chief Engineer, Chicago, October 28, 1873; October 29, 1873, IC-1N6.1. Timothy B. Blackstone, Pres. of Chicago and Alton Railroad, to Newell, Chicago, October 28, 1873, IC-1N6.3.

[4]James C. Clarke, General Manager, to D. Roby, Chicago, June 17, 1876, IC-1C5.2. William K. Ackerman, Vice Pres., to Osborn, Chicago, September 15, 1876, IC-1D7.1.

[5]James Clarke, memorandum on reductions in fixed salaries, Chicago, August 24, 1876, IC-1F2.2.

[6]James Clarke to Roby, Chicago, June 17, 1876, IC-1C5.2.

[7]James Clarke to J. C. McMullin, [General Supt. of Chicago and Alton Railroad], Chicago, July 5, 1876, IC-1C5.2. See also James Clarke to Lewis V. F Randolph, Treas., Chicago, October 14, 1876, IC-1C5.2.

[8]Ackerman to Randolph, Chicago, September 27, 1876, IC-1D7.1.

[9]Severson, "Some Phases," pp. 255, 273, 290.

[10]James Clarke to Ackerman, Chicago, April 16, 1877, IC-1C5.2. Ackerman to Osborn, Chicago, April 28, 1877, IC-1A2.1.

[11]Ackerman to Osborn, Chicago, April 28, 1877, IC-1A2.1. Ackerman to James Clarke, Chicago, June 7, 1877, IC-1A2.1. Quotation from Ackerman to Clarke.

[12]U.S. Bureau of the Census, _Historical Statistics of the U.S._, p. 127.

[13]Ackerman to Randolph, Chicago, February 20, 1877, IC-1D7.1.

[14]Ackerman to Randolph, Chicago, August 27, 1877, IC-1A2.1.

[15]James Clarke to W. C. Quincy, Chicago, December 11, 1876, IC-1C5.2.

[16]See series of seventeen telegrams from Joseph F. Tucker, General Supt., to James Clarke, dispatched from various points along the Iowa lines, March 17-24, 1875, IC-1D7.2.

[17]James Clarke to Ackerman, Chicago, April 16, 1877, IC-1C5.2.

[18]Centralia shop rolls, November 1878-January 1879, IC-+3.9.

[19]Ackerman to Osborn, Chicago, September 15, 1876, IC-1D7.1. Ackerman to M. B. Sadler, Mayor of Centralia, Chicago, January 27, 1879, IC-1A2.1. See also Ackerman to Osborn, New Orleans, February 24, 1879, IC-1A2.1.

[20]Ackerman to Randolph, Chicago, May 14, 1879, IC-1A2.1.

[21]I.C.R.R., _Rules for the Government of Persons Employed in the Machinery Department to Take Effect June 1, 1878_ (n.p., n.d.), broadside in IC-11M2.2.

[22]Ackerman to Edward T. Jeffery, General Superintendent, Chicago, October 3, 1878, IC-1A2.1, suggests this rule. Ackerman to H. T. Chance, Chicago, October 7, 1878, IC-1A2.1, mentions that it has been adopted.

[23]"A citizen of Waterloo who is very much interested" to I.C. stockholders, Waterloo, May 1877, IC-1A2.4. From internal evidence it seems likely that the writer was a disgruntled machinist who had been laid off in a cut-back in the work force at Waterloo.

[24]Ackerman to Samuel J. Hayes, Supt. of Machinery, Chicago, July 18, 1877, IC-1A2.1.

[25]Ackerman to Lynde A. Catlin, Secretary, Chicago, August 8, 1877, IC-1A2.1.

[26]Ackerman to Hayes, Chicago, August 7, 1877, IC-1A2.1.

[27]Ackerman to W. E. Mason, Chicago, March 31, 1879, IC-1A2.1.

[28]Henry B. Carrington to Ackerman, Hartford, Conn., December 20, 1879, IC-1A2.4.

[29]James Clarke to Roby, Chicago, June 17, 1876, IC-1C5.2.

[30]Newell to Blackstone, Chicago, July 8, 1873, IC-1N6.1.

[31]I.C.R.R., Schedule of Wages of Locomotive Engineers and Firemen, 1885 (Amboy: Journal Book and Job Office, 1885), catalog no. 33 1880 3.1, Burlington Archives, Newberry Library, gives the pay rates adopted in 1876 together with later revisions.

[32]James Clarke to Randolph, Chicago, October 14, 1876, IC-1C5.2.

[33]I.C.R.R., Schedule of Wages of Locomotive Engineers and Firemen, 1885.

[34]James Clarke to Tucker, Chicago, April 25, 1877, IC-1C5.2.

[35]Ibid. [36]Ibid. [37]Ibid.

[38]James Clarke to C. J. Justice, engineer, Chicago, October 16, 1876, IC-1C5.2.

[39]Carleton J. Corliss, "Old Gals of the Illinois Central," Railroad Stories, XVIII (November, 1935), 40-43, discusses the naming of early engines.

[40]James Clarke to Jeffery, Chicago, August 24, 1876, IC-1C5.2. Clarke to G. Clinton Gardner, Gen-

eral Supt. of Pennsylvania Railroad, Chicago, August 24, 1876, IC-1C5.2. Clarke to J. Tillinghast, General Supt. of New York Central Railroad, Chicago, August 24, 1876, IC-1C5.2.

[41]Jeffery to James Clarke, Chicago, September 8, 1876, IC-2.14. See also Ackerman to Osborn, Chicago, September 18, 1876, IC-1D7.1.

[42]James Clarke to Osborn, Chicago, September 9, 1876, IC-1C5.2.

[43]James Clarke to Osborn, Chicago, September 26, 1876, IC-1C5.2.

[44]James Clarke to C. A. Beck, J. C. Jacobs, and D. W. Parker, Division Supts., Chicago, October 30, 1876, IC-1C5.2.

[45]Tucker to Ackerman, Chicago, March 12, 1877, IC-1A2.4.

[46]Ackerman to Osborn, Chicago, March 13, 1877, IC-1D7.1.

[47]Tucker to Ackerman, Chicago, March 13, 1877; March 16, 1877, IC-1A2.4.

[48]Newell to Hayes, Chicago, April 28, 1871, IC-1N6.1.

[49]Newell to Charles G. Wilson, Grand Chief Engineer of B.L.E., Chicago, April 28, 1871, IC-1N6.1, presents an annual pass over the I.C. and its leased lines.

[50]James Clarke to P. M. Arthur, Grand Chief Engineer of B.L.E., Chicago, September 5, 1876, IC-1C5.2.

[51]James Clarke to Arthur, Chicago, November 16, 1876, IC-1C5.2. Clarke enclosed five dollars for a subscription to the monthly journal of the B.L.E.

[52]James Clarke to Randolph, Chicago, October 14, 1876, IC-1C5.2.

[53]James Clarke to McMullin, July 5, 1876, IC-1C5.2.

[54]Ackerman to James Clarke, Chicago, June 7, 1877, IC-1A2.1. In reply, Clarke agreed that the Brotherhood was stronger in the West than in the East, and he said he had long been of the opinion "that the only way for the railroads to protect themselves would be by concert of action and combination." Clarke to Ackerman, New Orleans, June 13, 1877, IC-1A2.4.

[55]Ackerman to Clarke, Chicago, June 7, 1877, IC-1A2.1.

[56]Ackerman to Randolph, Chicago, April 27, 1877, IC-1A2.1.

[57]Ackerman to Osborn, Chicago, April 28, 1877, IC-1A2.1.

[58]Ibid.

[59]On the contrast in temperament between Ackerman and Clarke, see Corliss, Main Line of Mid-America, pp. 210-11.

[60]Ackerman to Jeffery, Chicago, October 3, 1878, IC-1A2.1.

[61]James Clarke to Tucker, Chicago, February 2, 1875, IC-1C5.2.

[62]James Clarke to Beck, Chicago, February 24, 1875, IC-1C5.2.

[63]James Clarke to Beck, Chicago, April 1875, IC-1C5.2.

[64]James Clarke, Vice President and General Manager of Chicago, St. Louis, and New Orleans Railroad, to L. T. Brien, Asst. General Manager, Chicago, May 17, 1878, IC-1C5.2.

[65]James Clarke to N. Greener, J. White, and E. Anderson, Master Mechanics, Chicago, December 5, 1878, IC-1C5.2. James Clarke to R. N. Colquhon,

Mann, and McKinley, Supts., Chicago, December 5, 1878, IC-1C5.2.

66 James Clarke to Brien, Chicago, December 25, 1878, IC-1C5.2.

67 Jeffery to Ackerman, Chicago, May 18, 1877, IC-1A2.4.

68 Clarke to C. C. Berry, Trainmaster, Chicago, November 25, 1874, IC-1C5.2.

69 Parker to H. DeWolf, Asst. Treas., Dubuque, June 12, 1878; July 26, 1878; August 13, 1878; August 30, 1878; October 10, 1878; October 29, 1878, IC-1P2.1. Parker to T. W. Place, Master Mechanic, Dubuque, August 12, 1878, IC-1P2.1. Parker to W. P. Johnson, General Passenger Agent, Dubuque, October 8, 1878, IC-1P2.1.

70 S. H. Grannis to John Newell, Detroit, December 28, 1871, IC-1N6.1.

71 James Clarke to Tucker, Chicago, June 30, 1875, IC-1C5.2. See also Clarke to J. Anderson, Chicago, June 30, 1875, IC-1C5.2, informing him of the donation.

72 James Clarke to Jacobs, Chicago, December 4, 1876. See also Clarke to Hayes, Chicago, November 21, 1876, IC-1C5.2.

73 Mitchell to Newell, Chicago, June 14, 1873, IC-1N6.3.

74 James Clarke to T. L. Parkinson, Chicago, July 14, 1876; August 5, 1876, IC-1C5.2. Quotation from July 14 letter.

75 James Clarke to Tucker, Chicago, February 27, 1875, IC-1C5.2.

76 James Clarke to Parkinson, Chicago, August 5, 1876, IC-1C5.2.

77 Ackerman to Jacobs, Chicago, May 16, 1878, IC-1A2.1. Jacobs to Ackerman, Amboy, May 17, 1878,

IC-1A2.4. Jacobs promised to keep Joynt in mind in case anything should turn up.

[78]A. H. Joynt to Ackerman, Normal, May 14, 1878, IC-1A2.4.

[79]James Clarke to Hayes, Chicago, March 13, 1875, IC-1C5.2.

[80]James Clarke to C. H. Comstock, Paymaster, Chicago, July 14, 1875, IC-1C5.2.

[81]Ackerman to Charles N. Hammon, agent for Travelers Insurance Co., Chicago, December 18, 1877, IC-1A2.1. See also Ackerman to Randolph, Chicago, December 18, 1877, IC-1A2.1.

[82]Ackerman to James Clarke, Chicago, June 7, 1877, IC-1A2.1. See also Ackerman to J. E. Wooten, General Manager of Philadelphia and Reading Railroad, Chicago, June 8, 1877, IC-1A2.1, requesting information on the Reading plan.

[83]Illinois Central Railroad Mutual Benefit Association, Articles of Incorporation and By-laws (Chicago: J. S. Thompson and Co., printers, 1878), IC-2.22. A circular letter supporting the plan said, "You are earnestly requested to give the organization the benefit of your support--it being desired to unite, as far as possible, the employes of the Illinois Central Railroad in the bonds of brotherhood." Printed circular letter from Franklin Fairman, Secretary of I.C.R.R. Mutual Benefit Association, Chicago, n.d.; enclosed with William J. Mauriac, Asst. Auditor, to Stuyvesant Fish, Vice Pres., Chicago, September 5, 1883, IC-1F2.2.

[84]Mauriac to Fish, Chicago, September 5, 1883, IC-1F2.2.

[85]Robert V. Bruce, 1877: Year of Violence (New York and Indianapolis: Bobbs-Merrill Co., 1959), pp. 34-42, and passim.

[86]Ackerman to Osborn, Chicago, July 24, 1877, IC-1A2.1.

[87]Ackerman believed that the switchmen "all would have continued to work, if the outside men had let them alone, but, of course they have become somewhat restless by outside influence since they quit work." Ibid.

[88]Ackerman to Shelby M. Cullom, Governor of Illinois (and, ex officio, Director of the I.C.), Chicago, July 24, 1877, IC-1A2.1.

[89]Ackerman to Osborn, Chicago, July 24, 1877; July 25, 1877, IC-1A2.1. Ackerman to Cullom, Chicago, July 25, 1877, IC-1A2.1.

[90]Ackerman to Osborn, Chicago, July 25, 1877, IC-1A2.1. Ackerman to Cullom, Chicago, July 25, 1877, IC-1A2.1. Ackerman to B. Thayer, Chicago, July 25, 1877, IC-1A2.1. Ackerman to James Clarke, Chicago, July 25, 1877, IC-1A2.1. Ackerman to Osborn, Chicago, July 26, 1877, IC-1A2.1.

[91]At first the men were provided only with printed badges and improvised clubs made of sledge handles of "just the right length." Ackerman to Osborn, Chicago, July 26, 1877, IC-1A2.1.

[92]Ackerman to James Noquet, Chicago, July 26, 1877, IC-1A2.1.

[93]Ackerman, Historical Sketch, p. 110.

[94]Ackerman to Osborn, Chicago, July 26, 1877, IC-1A2.1.

[95]Ackerman to Osborn, Chicago, July 27, 1877, IC-1A2.1.

[96]Ackerman to Cullom, Chicago, July 27, 1877, IC-1A2.1. Ackerman to Randolph, Chicago, July 27, 1877, IC-1A2.1.

[97]Ackerman to Osborn, Chicago, July 27, 1877; July 28, 1877, IC-1A2.1.

[98]Ackerman to Osborn, Chicago, July 24, 1877, IC-1A2.1.

[99]Ackerman to Cullom, Chicago, July 25, 1877, IC-1A2.1.

[100]Ackerman to Osborn, Chicago, July 26, 1877, IC-1A2.1.

[101]*Ibid*.

[102]Ackerman to Osborn, Chicago, July 27, 1877, IC-1A2.1.

[103]Ackerman to Osborn, Chicago, July 24, 1877; July 27, 1877, IC-1A2.1.

[104]Ackerman to Jeffery, Chicago, August 28, 1877, IC-1A2.1, mentions the allowance of full pay for July. For the resolution by the board see Minutes of the Board of Directors, August 9, 1877, *IC-+3.1.

[105]Ackerman to Osborn, Chicago, July 24, 1877, IC-1A2.1.

[106]This point is stressed by Bruce, *1877: Year of Violence*, in his discussion of the aftermath of the strikes, pp. 301-21.

[107]James Fentress, General Solicitor, to Stuyvesant Fish, Pres., Chicago, February 5, 1894, IC-1F2.2, reporting remarks of General Supt. Albert W. Sullivan. Sullivan's views apparently had their effect, for no general wage cut was imposed during the depression of the 'nineties.

CHAPTER IV

TOWARD MATURE LABOR POLICIES

After 1877 the Illinois Central entered upon a period of vigorous activity, a renaissance in sharp contrast to the drift and drudgery of the postwar decade. Ten years of timidity now gave way to a time of energetic management and remarkable growth. Within five years the company increased its trackage in Illinois by some 240 miles by constructing new roadbed and purchasing existing feeder lines. Then, on January 1, 1883, the Illinois Central formally absorbed the 500-mile railroad line from Cairo to New Orleans which it had controlled for several years. James Clarke, who had been general manager of the southern road, now was named president of the parent company, and under his forceful leadership the Illinois Central undertook still further expansion. Between 1886 and 1888 the company purchased additional trackage within Illinois and also constructed a number of important subsidiary lines. The latter included a 233-mile link between Chicago and Freeport, along with branches to Madison and Dodgeville, Wisconsin; a feeder line in Iowa joining Manchester to Cedar Rapids; and branches from Cherokee, Iowa, to Onawa, Iowa, and Sioux Falls, South Dakota. A symbolic capstone to this series of accomplishments was added with the opening of the great Cairo bridge in the fall of 1889. This engineering marvel, then the longest railroad bridge spanning any river anywhere, joined all of the Illinois Central lines into an unbroken network of steel from Lake Michigan to the Gulf of Mexico.[1]

As the Illinois Central was metamorphosed into a great trans-American railway system, its internal workings changed. A business grown large and complex required formal and sophisticated managerial techniques in all areas, including labor policy. Thus the trend toward rationalized labor management which had emerged slowly in the years prior to 1877 now moved at a faster pace, as company officials introduced more systematic procedures for controlling their labor force. Company officials also began to show increased sophistication in their dealings with labor unions and to toy with schemes for promoting the welfare of employees by such divers means as furnishing more regular employment, subsidizing a system of relief for accident victims, and underwriting Y.M.C.A. work among railroad men. Although these plans were effected only to a very limited extent, they showed that the railroad managers were groping their way toward the new attitudes and policies that were demanded by changing industrial conditions.

Striving for Employment Stability

In discussing the Illinois Central labor force of the nineteenth century, it is all too easy to dwell upon the dramatic reductions that occurred in times of depression and to lose sight of the fact that even in good years most railroad workers never felt assured of steady employment. Their insecurity stemmed from the fact that the size of the labor force was continually adjusted to traffic demands, which were--quite literally--as variable as the weather. For example, in February 1877,

General Manager Edward Jeffery wrote:

> The winter traffic has necessitated the employment of a large force of train men, but the present soft condition of country roads is causing a sensible decrease in business and we are now beginning to reduce the number of our train employees. In doing so, however, we endeavor to retain the best of the men for the coming fall and winter work.[2]

In the years 1880-82, a relatively prosperous period and one for which some uniquely complete statistics have survived, the number of men employed in all three of the principal branches of the railroad labor force varied considerably from month to month in accordance with seasonal fluctuations in traffic demands (see Table 5). The force employed in the transportation department generally declined during the spring and early summer and then rose sharply in the fall, when the hauling of agricultural products swelled toward its seasonal crest. The same situation generally prevailed also in the machinery department, where it is possible to distinguish enginemen from shopmen and to see that both groups experienced considerable seasonal unemployment (see Fig. 4).

Serious as it was, the fluctuation that

TABLE 5

ILLINOIS CENTRAL WORK FORCE, 1880-82

Month	No. of Men in Select Branches				Total Work Force[a]
	Transportation Dept.	Road Dept.	Machinery Dept.		
			Enginemen	Shopmen	
1880					
Jan.	1423	1157	1729		4575
Feb.	1425	1132	1676		4501
Mar.	1358	1027	1652		4311
April	1317	1285	400	1186	4461
May	1352	1461	410	1171	4666
June	1376	1551	404	1144	4747
July	1403	1493	430	1138	4742
Aug.	1419	1700	445	1148	4985
Sept.	1500	1879	466	1223	5345
Oct.	1583	1952	475	1281	5675
Nov.	1631	1875	523	1406	5881
Dec.	1692	1313	594	1514	5410
1881					
Jan.	1674	1229	2113		5313
Feb.	1657	1267	2161		5381

TABLE 5--Continued

Month	No. of Men in Select Branches				Total Work Force[a]
	Transportation Dept.	Road Dept.	Machinery Dept.		
			Enginemen	Shopmen	
Mar.	1663	1671	2159		5790
April	1603	1416	500	1622	5610
May	1565	1781	490	1435	5466
June	1552	1533	477	1394	5511
July	1512	1828	463	1293	5392
Aug.	1545	1828	458	1263	5649
Sept.	1575	1716	467	1331	5604
Oct.	1627	1714	476	1361	5554
Nov.	1625	1690	517	1383	5596
Dec.	1636	1433	486	1373	5206
1882					
Jan.	1609	1077	482	1353	4843
Feb.	1598	1015	471	1345	4771
Mar.	1565	1061	468	1409	4812
April	1541	1561	459	1398	5263
May	1532	1780	446	1337	5397

TABLE 5--Continued

Month	No. of Men in Select Branches				Total Work Force[a]
	Transportation Dept.	Road Dept.	Machinery Dept.		
			Enginemen	Shopmen	
June	1510	2031	445	1315	5585
July	1571	2063	502	1339	5756
Aug.	1616	2224	487	1366	5971
Sept.	1640	2890	497	1384	6601
Oct.	1676	3070	501	1419	6955
Nov.	1725	3172	496	1482	7160
Dec.	1743	1923	522	1545	6032

[a]Total work force includes office staff, telegraphers, outside agents, and company surgeons, as well as employees of the transportation, road, and machinery departments.

Source: Comparative Statement of Force Employed, January 1880--December 1882, IC-3.9.

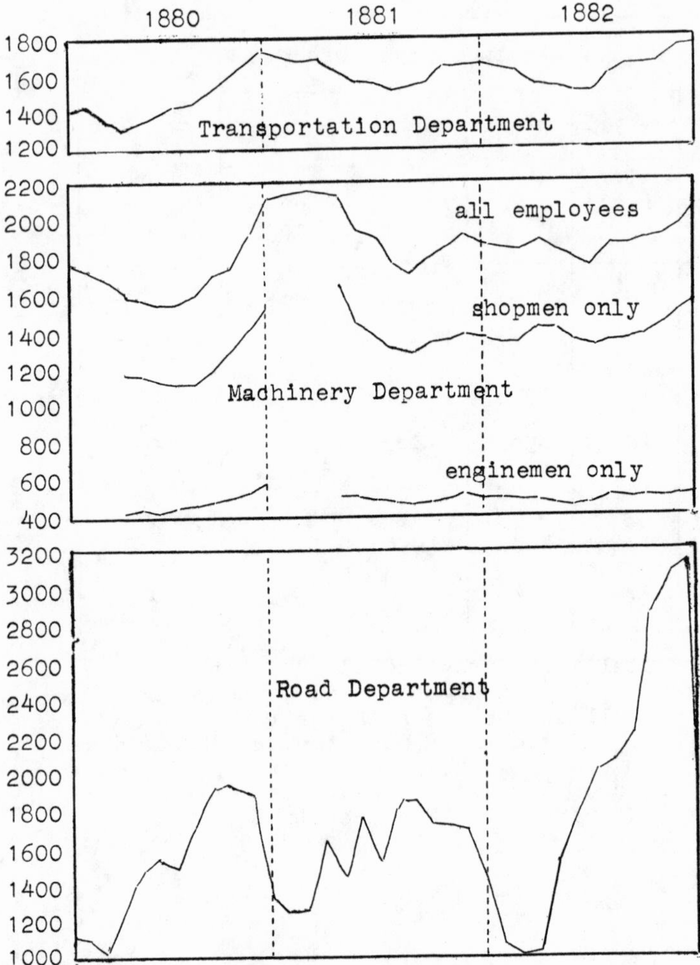

Fig. 4.--Number of men employed in Transportation, Machinery, and Road Departments, 1880-82.

occurred in the transportation and machinery departments was very mild compared with that which prevailed in the road department. Each year the work force of the road department rose unsteadily from March through November and then dropped precipitately as maintenance of way work was cut back severely in response both to light traffic demands and to weather conditions unfavorable for outdoor work. In one extreme case, the number of men employed in the road department was lowered from 3,172 in November 1882 to 1,923 the following month--a reduction of almost 40 per cent.

At least one Illinois Central official believed that something should be done to give more regular employment to maintenance of way workers. In 1885 Vice President Stuyvesant Fish suggested to President James Clarke that construction and maintenance work be mapped out four or five years ahead so that it could be accomplished more systematically. "The annual expenditures have varied enormously," Fish said. "It stands to reason that the company would have obtained more for its money if these expenditures had been made at a normal rate, year by year, and a force, or at least the staff necessary for the organization of a force of men[,] kept constantly upon this work." If such a policy were adopted, Fish went on, men would be willing to work for lower wages in consideration of having constant employment, and they could be trained to do more efficient work.[3] Fish may have been motivated in part by a desire to shield road workers from the burden of unstable employment, but if so he knew better than to mention such an intent when he presented his idea to James Clarke, who would have had little use for such sentimentality, even though he himself had once been a section laborer. As a matter of fact, Clarke was not impressed even by Fish's purely economic arguments. He answered Fish's letter with the terse comment that a five year program could not be carried through, since "what may be a good thing to do in 1885 may not be a good thing in 1886."[4] Nevertheless, Fish continued to advocate long-range planning, and a year later he succeeded in persuading Clarke to at least discuss the matter with General Manager Edward Jeffery.[5]

The absorption of the lines south of Cairo in 1883 had a significant effect upon the Illinois Central labor force, not only because it added thousands of names to the company payroll but also because it introduced into the ranks for the first time a large number of non-white employees. The performance of black workers had favorably impressed James Clarke during his years as manager of the southern lines. Clarke had come to believe that there was "no better laborer than the negro to be found among any race in the world," that Negroes "are now a valuable laboring population, and each year, as they acquire education, they will become better citizens," and that "they should be justly dealt with and treated with the respect due all honest laborers."[6] But alas, Clarke coupled his admiration for Negroes with the assumption that men of that race were "peculiarly fitted for labor in semi-tropical climates, and by nature cheerful, obedient, kind, imitative, and contented."[7] After 1883 something on the order of 1,000 black workers were employed on the Illinois Central lines in Kentucky, Tennessee, Mississippi, and Louisiana; but everywhere they were restricted to such jobs as fireman, brakeman, or shop laborer, with no possibility of promotion to engineer, conductor, or skilled tradesman.[8] Because Clarke assumed that Negroes were equipped biologically only for unskilled occupations, he saw no contradiction between the fact that Negroes were limited to lower level jobs and his own assertion that on the Illinois Central there was "no prejudice against the black man."[9] Within the narrow sphere to which Clarke believed that Negroes were confined by their own innate inferiority he wished them well. He said:

> They should be taught that freedom means honesty, intelligence, sobriety and virtue, to keep out of the hands of political demagogues. They should learn frugality and economy, secure their own homes from the savings of their labors. They are citizens entitled to all the rights among which are to elevate themselves to a higher standard[.] [They should] avoid rum mills, avoid all combinations and associations except such as tend to make them better men and women, and these are homestead, charitable, beneficial and religious societies. I was a former slave owner. I have great sympathy and respect for the colored race and shall be glad to see them happy prosperous and contented.[10]

But Clarke employed black workers not out of sympathy but for sound business reasons. If the price were right, he would exploit any source of labor. "I should have no hesitation in using Convict Labor," he told Stuyvesant Fish in 1886, ". . . if it should be found we can utilize this labor at lesser rates than we now have to pay for Free Labor."[11]

Holding the Line on Wages

Clarke must have been pleased with the wage situation on his railroad in the 1880's, for the pay of most employees increased very little during the decade. In the company shops the maximum pay per hour of blacksmiths, machinists, carpenters, and tinners did not change at all between 1880 and 1890 and the maximum hourly wages of boilermakers, painters, and molders varied up or down by only a cent in the same period (see Fig. 5)[12] The pay of engineers and firemen also remained stable throughout the decade. At an 1885 conference between company officers and a committee representing the engineers on the road, the pay of engineers assigned to construction trains and other irregular service was raised to $3.75 a day and it was agreed that henceforth men assigned to regular

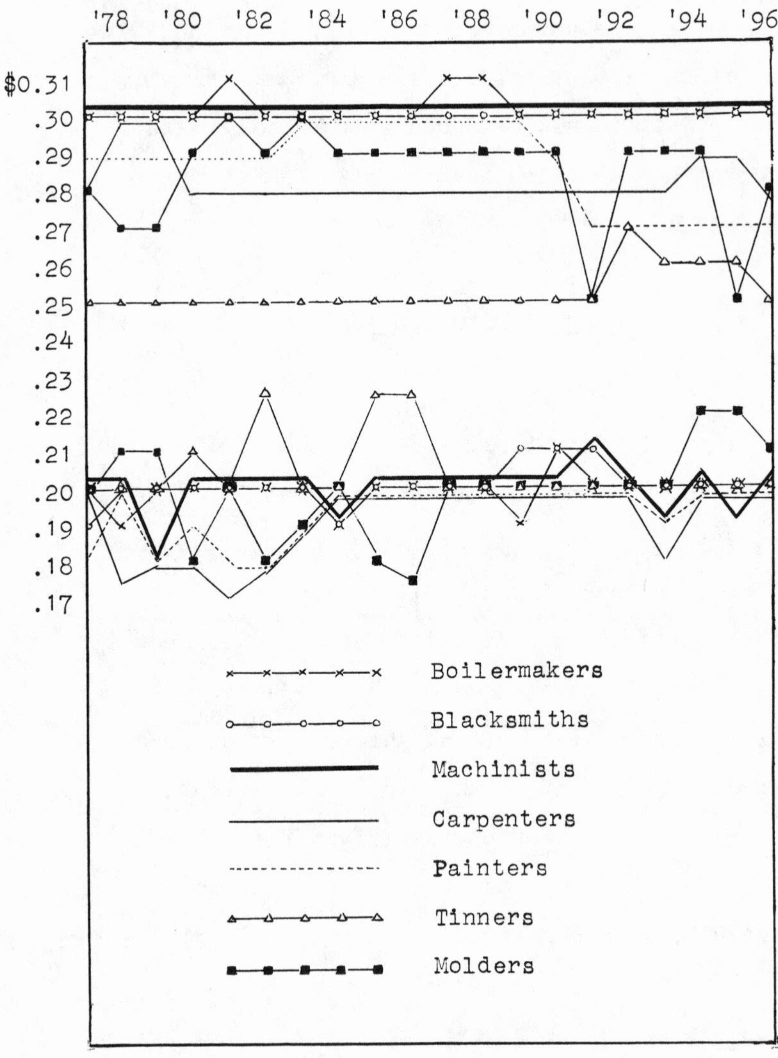

Fig. 5.--Maximum and minimum hourly wages of Illinois Central shopmen, 1877-96.

runs would receive overtime pay at the rate of 37-1/2 cents an hour whenever they were delayed two hours or more beyond scheduled time. But the standard pay allowed for each of the regular freight and passenger runs remained as originally adopted in 1876.[13] According to figures compiled by officials of another railroad, the average income in 1880 of Illinois Central passenger engineers was $1,322, while that of freight engineers was $1,129. Firemen in passenger service earned an average of $678 that year, while those in freight service had an income of $600.[14]

Company records of the 1880's contain no material relating to the pay of conductors and brakemen, which probably indicates that the wages of these trainmen did not change during those years. The records do contain many references to the wages paid to road department employees, and from these it is clear that the pay of those workers varied considerably over time and from place to place according to the condition of local labor markets. In 1880 the company found it necessary to pay section laborers $1.25 a day in the vicinity of Cairo, even after it had been decided to hire Negroes for service on section gangs because of the scarcity of white laborers.[15] At the same time, workers were in such short supply in Iowa that the railroad had trouble obtaining men at $1.25 because other roads were paying $1.50 and even $1.75 a day.[16] In 1887 the superintendent responsible for the lines within Illinois mentioned 11 cents an hour as his "standard pay" for road workers but noted that on sections north of Freeport it was necessary to pay from 11-1/2 to 12-1/2 cents an hour in order to obtain men.[17] The fluctuation in the pay of maintenance of way workers is understandable if it is remembered that these employees were unskilled day laborers drawn from a pool of available men whose numbers constantly rose or fell according to the immediate needs of local employers.

Now the fact that in the 1880's most Illinois Central workers experienced either no change or else a slight increase in their wage rates probably meant that considering the decade as a whole they experienced an increase in their real earnings, for after 1882 the cost of living in the United

States slowly declined until into the 1890's. But that extended period of falling prices was preceded by three years of rising living costs, from 1880 to 1882.[18] This rise in the cost of living during the first few years of the decade may explain why there was much agitation for wage increases among several classes of employees at that time. At any rate, in 1881 Illinois Central officials encountered petitions, strike threats, or actual strikes by freight handlers, shopmen, switchmen, engineers, firemen, and brakemen. Yet in each instance the railroad managers succeeded in resisting the demands of employees for increased compensation.

In April 1881 the men employed in the freighthouse at Chicago asked for an increase of 20 per cent in their wages.[19] When the Illinois Central rejected this demand, the freight handlers went out on strike. Apparently they soon reconsidered their position, however, for within a few days President William Ackerman reported that the strike had entirely subsided.[20] In the meantime, Ackerman learned that the workmen employed at the

Chicago car works were preparing to petition for an increase in their wages. Ackerman quickly squelched that activity by discharging eighty of the men employed at the car shops. He had been planning to cut the work force there anyway and so found it easy to take this step, which he said "came in very opportunely."[21] A few weeks later, Ackerman wrote that he had also reduced the force at the Welden locomotive shops "for the purpose of curtailing expenses and also for the purpose of breaking the force of a proposed strike."[22]

No sooner had Ackerman rebuffed the demands of the freight handlers and shopmen than he encountered a wage demand from the switchmen in the Chicago yards. On April 28 the switchmen of all the railroads entering Chicago served notice upon their employers that they would strike unless they were granted a wage increase by May 2. Ackerman complained that the switchmen could offer "no sufficient excuse for this, as their wages are already high enough," but he feared that one or more of the railroads might "yield to the clamor of the men," in which case the other companies would be compelled to follow suit.[23] Although a meeting of officials from several roads held on April 29 in the offices of General Manager Jeffery of the Illinois Central failed to produce any agreement for mutual action, the various companies all stood firm against the demands of the switchmen when they walked off the job on May 2.[24]

Ackerman was determined that the Illinois Central would not yield. "If we do not overcome this movement," he wrote, "it will doubtless be followed by a strike on the part of the Engineers and Firemen."[25] Some switchmen did not participate in the strike, and with the aid of these experienced men Edward Jeffery was able to move some trains at Chicago despite what he referred to as the "bull-dozing" of the "stinking switchmen."[26] In this way the effectiveness of the strike was undermined, and within two weeks most of the strikers gave up and returned to work. "Our troubles with the switchmen are at an end," reported Ackerman on May 16. "We have all the men that we need and have won the day." Ackerman added that he hoped that the failure of the switchmen's strike would prevent a threatened walkout by the company's brakemen. And apparently it did, for the brakemen remained on the job.[27]

After beating back the wage demands made in 1881, the Illinois Central enjoyed several years of freedom from such pressures.[28] Not until the spring of 1886 was there another major outbreak of labor unrest. The 1886 troubles stemmed primarily from a demand by the Chicago freight handlers that their work day be reduced from ten to eight hours without any reduction in their daily wage, or else that their pay for a ten hour day be raised from $1.50 to $1.75.[29] The freight handlers struck for about a week, but they did not succeed in disrupting the company's business. When the strike began, Edward Jeffery organized a group of forty clerks from the railroad's Chicago offices to handle perishable freight, and then he imported 125 laborers from along the line south of the city to replace the freight handlers.[30] On May 10 the freight handlers returned to work--except for a dozen men whom the company refused to take back.[31] In the midst of the freight handlers' strike there was also a brief work stoppage at the Chicago car works. As soon as Jeffery heard of the latter difficulty, he spoke to the men at the car shops for about an hour and succeeded in convincing them that the company could not and would not make any concession to them. Jeffery pointed out that the men's wages were the same as they had been ten years before, while the cost of living had dropped considerably. He also said that the company was building cars only in order to keep the men employed during the summer months.[32] And he was not bluffing, for a few days earlier James Clarke had decided that both the car works and the machine shops at Chicago would be closed for three months if the men went out on strike.[33]

Other Chicago railroads experienced similar labor difficulties at this same time, and the various companies cooperated in resisting the widespread agitation for wage increases and the eight-hour day. Jeffery kept in touch with the managers of other companies and he served as chairman at a series of meetings attended by the managers of a score of roads. He reported to Stuyvesant Fish that all of the railroad managers agreed that no concession should be made to any class of employees of any company, lest a climate of unrest "spread like wild fire through all the laboring classes and excite rather than allay the present disturbances."[34] After the strikes and other troubles had come to an end, James Clarke noted with satisfaction that not one of the twenty-one railroads serving Chicago had yielded to employee demands for shorter hours or increased pay. For the first time all of the Chicago roads had acted in concert in a successful resistance to the demands of labor.[35]

In the aftermath of the strikes of May 1886, the Illinois Central continued to cooperate with the other railroads by joining in certain steps calculated to forestall future labor troubles. In July the Illinois Central contributed $15,000 towards the establishment of a military post near Chicago.[36] Some other railroads and various other large industrial employers gave similar support to this project, which had been instigated by sleeping-car magnate George Pullman even before the May labor troubles.[37] James Clarke suspected that Pullman promoted this venture merely so that he could sell land for the fort at a big price, but Stuyvesant

Fish considered the Pullman project worthwhile in view of the large amount of property which the Illinois Central owned at Chicago and "the enormous loss which the stoppage of trains for a few days even would entail." Most members of the Illinois Central board of directors evidently found Fish's argument persuasive, for they authorized the subscription in spite of President Clarke's skepticism.[39]

While Clarke frowned on the Pullman plan, he gave enthusiastic support to another cooperative effort among Chicago railroads which was underway at the same time. This latter project consisted in a massive lobbying campaign by which the managers of the Chicago roads hoped to bring about the enactment of a law making it a criminal offense for anyone to obstruct the operations of any railroad engaged in interstate commerce. Such a statute would have prohibited most railroad strikes, and that is exactly what the managers had in mind. "We are asking railroads all over [the] US to bring influence to bear on US congressmen to get [the] I[nterstate] C[ommerce] act amended to outlaw strikes," wrote Clarke in describing the project to Stuyvesant Fish.

Clarke personally served on a committee responsible for drumming up support for the anti-strike law among the managers of railroads located east of the Mississippi and south of the Ohio.[40] He wrote to dozens of railroad managers urging them to promote the plan, and most of them agreed to get in touch with their Congressmen and to ask local business groups to pass resolutions endorsing the idea.[41] Nevertheless, in spite of all the pressure exerted by Clarke and his allies, the United States Senate voted by a large majority not to amend the Interstate Commerce Act so as to prohibit railroad strikes.[42] Consequently the Illinois Central and other railroads could not look to the federal government for automatic assistance in resisting labor demands. Yet certainly it is apparent that in the 1880's the railroads, individually and collectively, were quite capable of taking care of themselves.

Rationalizing Personnel Management

In the 1880's Illinois Central officers took giant steps in the direction of more systematic management and discipline of employees. For example, we know from earlier chapters that the company always followed the policy of hiring young men for low level jobs while filling higher positions by promotion from within the ranks. Such practices continued to prevail in the 'eighties.[43] But now for the first time there is evidence that at least some promotions were based not simply upon the judgement of company officials, but rather upon the results of formal testing. Among William Ackerman's papers is a "partial list of questions asked in examination of a fireman for position of locomotive engineer" issued by the superintendent of machinery in 1881. The list includes thirty questions, such as:

> What is atmospheric pressure?
>
> What is vacuum?
>
> How does inner bracing strengthen a boiler?
>
> How does a safety valve work?

According to a complaining letter received by Ackerman, the technical knowledge required to answer these questions was so great that one applicant for a job was unable to pass the examination even though he had previously worked for thirteen years as an engineer on a British railway![44]

Another step toward more formal employment practices was taken in the summer of 1880 when the chief medical officer of the Illinois Central tested the eyesight and color perception of many of the company's train service employees. Apparently Edward Jeffery was the chief sponsor of this innovation, for Superintending Surgeon John E. Owens congratulated him on being "the first in Illinois and the West to strive to eliminate such new sources of danger on railroads as are to be found under the head of visual defects."[45] In August, Owens reported to Jeffery that he had examined 967 employees, mostly enginemen, trainmen, and switchmen, and that of these forty-nine had been found to suffer from color blindness, while twenty-nine had defective vision.[46]

Still another indication of formal personnel management appears in a description by Edward Jeffery of the system for purchasing and distributing supplies which was in effect in 1888.

According to Jeffery, every time an engineer took on a load of coal for his locomotive he was issued a ticket, which he later turned in for forwarding to the division superintendent. A careful account was kept of the miles run and the tons of coal consumed each month by every locomotive, and each engineer was held rigidly accountable for the economical operation of his machine. Whenever a locomotive used more coal per mile than did the average engine of the same class, the engineer assigned to it learned of his bad performance via a letter direct from the superintendent of machinery.[47] However, this close control was not possible when heavy traffic demands compelled company officers to assign more than one engine crew to a particular locomotive. For instance, in September 1887, Jeffery reported that because of the worst shortage of motive power that he had ever seen in his thirty-one years with the Illinois Central, he had for more than a month past abandoned all idea of keeping engineers with their regular engines and instead had run the engines almost continually, changing enginemen after every trip.[48]

But Jeffery had not changed his opinion of continuous running in the ten years since the Illinois Central had given up its experiments with that system. "It is a very unsatisfactory way of handling men and motive power," he wrote in 1888. "The engines do not get the attention they ought to have . . . and the men do not take interest in engines the same as when they are regularly assigned to them."[49]

Illinois Central officers realized that successful personnel management required justice, impartiality, and consistency in the treatment of employees. James Clarke stressed the importance of these qualities in an 1883 letter to his superintendent of machinery in which he laboriously outlined the principles which he thought should govern the treatment of engineers. Clarke wrote:

> My own idea is
>
> 1st All men should have justice done them.
>
> 2d No officer controlling men should have any favorites or permit his personal feelings to enter into his official duties. He should be a fair and impartial judge between the co[mpany] and the men and between the claims or grievances of those under his authority.
>
> 3d Merit should be fully recognized, and where . . . Merits of Men are Equal in all respects, seniority in service should have preference.

> 4th When work upon the Road does not give employment for all . . . it should be fairly divided so as to do the best we can for all. . . .
>
> . . . .
>
> 10th Please see if Master Mechanics . . . all understand and allow . . . time and pay alike. It should be uniform if it is not. . . .
>
> 11th If you find any conflicting orders or customs prevailing . . . instructions [are] to be given in order to produce uniformity. . . .
>
> 12th . . . Engines [are] to run as much and as often as the wants of the Road may require, [but] of course you will consider due regard for mens physical ability and proper rest, and [you are] not to over work your men.
>
> 13th Have it distinctly understood every Master Mechanic shall be responsible if he keeps an Engineer in the service who drinks liquor on duty or is a drunkard and Rowdy off duty.
>
> 14th Let it be distinctly understood we dont want discontented men to work for this company, but request them if any to quit our service.[50]

Edward Jeffery subscribed to the same general principles as Clarke, but in addition Jeffery believed that officers should endeavor to maintain close personal relationships with the men under their charge. In 1888 he remarked to Stuyvesant Fish:

> In my 28 years experience with men, working beside them in the shop and subsequently managing them in the various depts. of which I have had control, I am led to the belief that, ordinarily, with the exercise of good sense, kindness, firmness and justice on the part of the Company's officers, and by the Company's

> officers holding themselves in close relationship with the men, so as to inspire their confidence and esteem, that serious troubles are not liable to occur.[51]

The difference in attitude between Jeffery and Clarke was small but significant, and nowhere was it more apparent than in their handling of discipline problems.

In the 1880's Clarke continued to favor the same strict discipline policy that he had introduced to the Illinois Central in its earliest years. Because he was convinced that firmness in discipline prevented accidents, he urged his subordinates to enforce all regulations zealously.[52] Sometimes the occurrence of a serious accident would lead him to express his attitude in rash terms. When a collision of trains on February 24, 1885 resulted in one death, several injuries, and $30,000 in damages, Clarke said it was the

> worst wreck and most disreputable that has occurred on the line north of Cairo in ten years--all the result of failing to obey standing rules and regulations. . . .
>
> I wish we had power to kill men who violate rules and are guilty of gross negligence in Rail Road service.[53]

Clarke could not kill men who caused accidents, but he could and did dismiss them. He never allowed his personal feelings to affect his decisions in such matters. To a woman who had begged him to reinstate her husband, who had been fired following an accident, Clarke wrote:

> Your appeal is a very earnest one, and I should be glad if I could, consistently with my duty, offer your husband employment; but the truth is, I should not be justified in doing this. That unfortunate mistake of his cost this co. over $30,000, and I could not offer him employment in this service again.

But Clarke did add that he was very sorry for the woman and her children, and he enclosed a gift of $10 which he said she was "very welcome to."[54]

In contrast to Clarke, Edward Jeffery believed that when dismissals were being considered it was "wise always to inquire into the personal qualities of men as well as their official ability."[55] Once Jeffery intervened on behalf of an engineer who had been fired, pointing out to the superintendent of machinery that the man in question had "a good record" and a "very nice family" and was "pleasantly situated" in his community.[56] Jeffery thought that these facts ought to be taken into account. He said:

> Where men are well disposed, capable, honest, temperate and reliable, have good families with whom they live happily, and have comfortable homes, it is desirable to so discipline them as not to lose them from the ranks. . . . Men who have not the qualifications herein outlined, are not entitled to consideration at our hands when breaches of discipline occur, of a serious character.[57]

Another example of Jeffery's willingness to take personal factors into account occurred in the summer of 1888 when an epidemic of yellow fever in Mississippi caused some engineers to refuse to run trains through the towns where the pestilence was acute. As soon as he learned of the situation, James Clarke telegraphed a local officer that he should allow engineers to lay off if they were afraid to make their runs, but he also told the official to inform the frightened employees that no class of men were so apt to escape infection as were engineers and trainmen, "owing to the continual change of air they enjoy and which is the best disinfectant." Clarke added, "Tell your men not to become nervous and demoralized, but stand up to their duties and posts as brave and honest men, and they will come through all right."[58] Apparently some of the engineers did not share

Clarke's faith in fresh air, for a month later, as the sickness was at last subsiding, Edward Jeffery wrote that at the height of the epidemic many engineers had abandoned their engines in the middle of their runs.[59] Because to leave one's locomotive before completing a trip was a most serious infraction of company rules, it is easy to understand why Stuyvesant Fish felt certain that Jeffery would "with his usual thoroughness sift the matter to the bottom and make examples of the delinquents."[60] But Jeffery considered the situation a singular one, and he decided to "give the whole subject a very careful scrutiny" and "act with justice" in disposing of each individual case.[61] We do not know the precise outcome of Jeffery's deliberations. Probably he did not fulfill Fish's expectations, for he wrote:

> I regret exceedingly the action of the engineers on the Mississippi Division but feel like making some allowances for those who had large families, and who were not only laboring under excitement themselves, but were also upset by the fears and pleadings of wives and children. These family matters are things that railroad officers cannot control, and men are at times influenced by their families to do that which is afterwards seen to have been unwise. . . .
>
> The time has been a trying one.[62]

Had James Clarke handled this affair, it is unlikely that he would have acted with such forbearance. When Clarke showed restraint in discipline, it was not out of compassion but for reasons of practicality.

One illustration of Clarke's practical approach was his reaction to the idea of having employees legally indicted for criminal negligence in cases where their carelessness had caused accidents. This innovation was suggested to Clarke in 1885 by Stuyvesant Fish, who said:

> by once making examples of the guilty you would more easily maintain discipline in the future. . . . We are all obliged to work with such tools as we can obtain. All men are fallible. . . . We must . . . pay heavily for their neglect, [so] why not make them pay also?[63]

Fish pointed out also that if a negligent employee were hanged or imprisoned for life, he would not be likely to bother the Illinois Central with a damage suit.[64] Clarke responded negatively to the idea of prosecuting negligent men, not because it offended his sensibilities, but simply because he considered it infeasible. He told Fish:

> It is doubtful if you could procure an indictment or conviction in a court that

> would punish men for such carelessness. When such things occur public sentiment is for the moment against the careless men. It soon reacts in sympathy for the men who have been heretofore regarded as reliable men. Then avarice and cupidity begins to figure how much can be made out of the Rail Road in the shape of damages.[65]

Clarke's judgment was supported by the company's chief attorney, who noted that in supplying evidence for the prosecution of employees the company would be publicizing information which could be used against the railroad in damage suits from injured passengers and shippers.[66]

Only a single scrap of evidence survives of another disciplinary innovation of the 1880's: the formal blacklisting of discharged employees. The evidence consists in an 1885 letter which Superintendent of Machinery Henry Schlacks wrote to James Clarke concerning a request by C. H. Edwards, a former engineer, to be removed from "the black list of the Ill. Cent. R.R." Schlacks told Clarke that he could not find Edwards' name on the list kept in his office and suggested that Edwards might have been included in "the old list formerly kept by the Chicago St.Louis and New Orleans Railroad," the southern line absorbed by the Illinois Central in

1883. Schlacks said that anyone guilty of Edwards' offense--erasing his name from the board on which runs were scheduled--"would be dismissed from the service and his name would surely be entered in the black book." But Schlacks added, "This black-book has nothing to do nor does it interfere with a man's career outside of the Ill. Cent. R.R., [and] consequently it ought to make no difference to Mr. Edwards."[67] Schlacks' letter clearly shows: (1) that by 1885 the Illinois Central maintained a formal blacklist, at least in its machinery department; (2) that a similar list had been kept on the southern line prior to the merger of 1883; and (3) that on the Illinois Central the blacklist was considered an internal matter and the names of blacklisted men were not divulged to other employers.

Living with Labor Unions

In the 'eighties the relationship between the Illinois Central and organized labor underwent significant development. Both in reaction to the events of the decade and as a reflection of the differing personalities of James Clarke and Edward

Jeffery, management attitudes changed. From an initial posture of distrust and hostility, compounded by ignorance, the policy of the railroad managers toward unions moved in the direction of a more sophisticated and tolerant outlook, particularly in their relations with the Brotherhood of Locomotive Engineers.

While managing the lines south of Cairo in the early 'eighties, James Clarke was not inclined to be patient in his dealings with the Brotherhood, although in 1883 he did consent to meet with a committee representing that organization.[68] After the meeting he urged his subordinates to investigate the various grievances presented by the engineers, including the claim that they were overworked at times. Clarke was perfectly willing to do this much, for he believed that it was not in the company's interest to overtax its workers.[69] But once he had taken the steps that he considered appropriate, Clarke expected to hear no more from the Brotherhood. He resented it very much when he learned that the engineers were not satisfied with his response. To Edward Jeffery, Clarke wrote:

> There is not a single Man or officer in this Service south of Cairo who has just cause for complaint[;] our Engineers are on duty less hours and get more pay for what they do than engineers similarly occupied on any Rail Road south of the Ohio and east of the Miss[issippi] River. They have allways [sic] been treated Kindly and Liberally in all things. There is six or eight sore heads among our men south of Cairo. They must either stop fomenting discord or I will dismiss them from our service. . . . We have had none of this dissatisfaction during the past five years until recently[;] there is no cause for it. I am getting tired of it. It must and shall stop.[70]

Clarke said that any employee was free to quit the service of the Illinois Central whenever he chose but that he was not free to remain in the service and at the same time "agitate and produce discord and dissatisfaction."[71] He added that the committeemen with whom he had conferred were "good men and competent engineers" and that he respected their union. "But," he said, "neither they nor it shall designate . . . how or in what manner we will operate this Road."[72]

Clarke's distrust and resentment of the Brotherhood stemmed in part from the fact that he was unsure just what the organization wanted and how far it was willing to go in pursuit of its objectives. He was alarmed by rumors that the engineers of the southern line had the "cooperation of all Engineers on [the] ICRR north of Cairo to carry their views," but he did not know whether they were true or not.[73] Also, he had no idea what proportion of his engineers were B.L.E. members,[74] and he even showed uncertainty as to the precise name of that organization.[75] But Clarke knew the Brotherhood well enough to know that he did not like it, and that feeling stayed with him throughout his term as president of the Illinois Central, from August 1883 to May 1887.

As president, Clarke had to cope with the Chicago strikes of 1886, and that experience did not increase his love for labor unions. Clarke did not deal directly with any organizations other than the engineers' Brotherhood, but he knew that the 1886 strikes by freight handlers and other employees against the Illinois Central and other Chicago railroads were connected with even if not formally sanctioned by labor unions, especially certain affiliates of the Knights of Labor. And Clarke blamed the trouble on union agitation. He said, "These damned infernal organizations known as labor unions, Brotherhoods, and Knights of Labor are I am afraid destined to give all R[ail] R[oa]ds trouble in the future."[76]

At this time the Knights were leading a great strike by 60,000 shopmen, switchmen, track hands, and other employees against Jay Gould's southwestern railroad system.[77] James Fentress, chief legal officer of the Illinois Central, urged Clarke to give all possible encouragement to the Gould system in its battle with the Knights of Labor, for Fentress believed that the defeat of the southwest strike would break the backbone of the Knights and spare the Illinois Central a strike of its own later on.[78] There is no evidence that Clarke took Fentress' advice, although he did express concern over the traffic losses which the Illinois Central suffered as a result of the stoppage on the Gould lines.[79]

An alternative to the position advanced by Fentress was suggested by Sidney Webster, a member of the Illinois Central board of directors. Webster urged Clarke to adopt a conciliatory attitude toward labor organizations and not to worry at all about the labor troubles of other railroads. Webster argued that the Knights of Labor and other unions would in time learn their duties as well as their rights and that when workers were well organized and led by competent men, then relations between them and their employers could be more easily adjusted. Webster remarked that while it was true that there was sometimes an absence of good sense on the part of employees, there was also "a good deal of stupidity in the conduct of some employers." He suggested that Clarke simply decide how the Illinois Central might obtain for itself "the most contented, effective, and therefore the cheapest labor." And he had his own answer to that rather loaded question:

> In the rivalry which now exists between railway corporations it does not seem to me that the Illinois Central is bound to consider the welfare of its competitors. If we can really improve our own condition, and elevate our own reputation, by conciliating those who are in our employ, or by conciliating labor organizations, I certainly would do it. Our object is to carry freight and passengers at a cheaper rate than our rivals. If, therefore, a policy of conciliation, and even a higher rate of wages than other railway companies pay, will bring to us a more efficient, and therefore in the end a cheaper

> service, it does seem to me that good policy would prompt that line of action.[80]

Of course Webster's thinking was far ahead of its time. And nothing is so weak as an idea whose time has not come. To James Clarke, the business of a railroad was to make money for its owners, and money was not made by paying high wages or coddling labor unions. In 1886 Clarke vigorously beat back the efforts of Illinois Central employees to win wage increases, and he also took steps to see that the workers on his railroad did not become well organized and led by competent men. In July he told James Fentress that he intended to instruct Edward Jeffery "to weed out all disaffected persons" from the service of the Illinois Central.[81] If Clarke carried out this intention, it was probably over the objections of Jeffery, who was always more complaisant than Clarke in his dealings with organized labor.[82]

During a bitter strike by the Brotherhood of Locomotive Engineers against the Chicago Burlington and Quincy Railroad in 1888, Jeffery expressed sympathy for the union side of the controversy. Even while he was having trouble persuading the

Illinois Central's own engineers not to join in a sympathetic boycott of Burlington rolling stock, he wrote to James Clarke that he could not understand the motives of the Burlington managers in precipitating the strike through their "injudicious conduct."[83] Jeffery tried to bring about a settlement of the dispute and in the course of serving as mediator acquired even more respect for the Brotherhood. He told Stuyvesant Fish that his conciliatory efforts involved "a struggle with prejudice and temper," a disproportionate share of which came from the C.B.& Q. management:

> The labor leaders have conceded to me several points, but the C.B.+Q. management are not as conciliatory as I would like. . . . they can't quite get up to the plane of magnanimity yet. . . . I incline to think that the labor leaders are disposed to concede more than the C.B.+Q. The latter so far will not go 1/2 or even 1/3 way to a settlement.[84]

Perhaps the best proof of Jeffery's growing sympathy for the engineers lies in the fact that during the strike he wrote letters of reference for some former Burlington engineers who had decided to seek employment on other railroads.[85]

During the Burlington strike and afterwards, Jeffery carried on a friendly correspondence with A. B. Minton, an Illinois Central foreman at Cairo who was active in the engineers' brotherhood.[86] Minton told Jeffery about any feelings of dissatisfaction among engineers or other employees, and Jeffery used this information to prevent labor difficulties. For example, in one letter Jeffery promised Minton that he would look into the case of a dismissed engineer ("Your endorsement of him as a man and as an engineer has great weight with me, because I know you are an honest reliable man yourself") and at the same time accepted Minton's explanation of his failure to perform a favor requested by Jeffery ("I am sorry you did not know in time about the petition from the switchmen . . . as I thought you were in a position to be of assistance").[87] In this way Jeffery kept himself informed of the attitudes and desires of workers and their organizations in a manner which stands in sharp contrast to the ignorance displayed by James Clarke early in the decade. In further contrast to Clarke, Jeffery was anxious to deal with all employees, both individually and collectively, in an atmosphere of cordiality.

When representatives of the Order of Railway Conductors presented Jeffery with a list of grievances in October 1888, he immediately granted many of their requests and promised to have General Superintendent C. A. Beck take up the remaining points with them "in a friendly spirit and with a desire to do what is right for men and Company." Jeffery concluded his gracious reply to the conductors' petition by saying:

> I wish to reiterate what I said to you verbally, and have always and at all times said to our men, that I want the family feeling to prevail in this service, and both officers and men to realize that all are working in a common interest, and for the same employer, and that justice and right must be the basis of all relations which are established between officers and men and company.[88]

Apparently Jeffery was willing not only to consider the grievances of the conductors but also to engage in real collective bargaining with their union spokesmen. It is not likely that the Illinois Central's relations with labor organizations other than those of the engineers and the conductors had reached such a level of maturity, but there is some indication that Jeffery was anxious to maintain good relations with other unions, in that in 1888 and 1889 he granted free passes over the Illinois Central lines to national officers and convention delegates of the Brotherhood of Railroad Brakemen, the Brotherhood of Locomotive Firemen, the Switchmen's Mutual Aid Association, and the Order of Railway Telegraphers, as well as the Order of Railway Conductors and the Brotherhood of Locomotive Engineers.[89]

Tempering the Fortunes of War

Train accidents and other mishaps continued to take a heavy toll among Illinois Central employees in the 1880's. In the middle of the decade, the officer responsible for settling personal injury claims against the company mentioned that in recent times an average of two employees per year had been totally disabled, while eight others had suffered the amputation of legs as a result of injuries sustained on the job.[90] Some statistics assembled at the request of Edward Jeffery in 1884 bear grim testimony to the terrible risks under which many railroad workers labored.[91] Based upon records for the preceding ten years and excluding "the cases of lesser importance," these figures show that each year on the Illinois Central the proportion of employees suffering a disabling injury was:

1 in 167 office and station workers

1 in 36 machinery department employees

1 in 30 road department employees

1 in 10 men in train service

1 in 7 men in switching service.

The mortality rate was no less shocking. Each year the proportion of men killed on the job was:

1 in 2,120 office and station workers

1 in 1,090 machinery department employees

1 in 360 road department employees

1 in 120 men in train service

1 in 90 men in switching service.

In the face of these melancholy statistics, it is easy to see why the threat of disablement or even death was taken for granted among men working in such high risk occupations as switchman or brakeman. Once, when the father of a brakeman complained to

President William Ackerman of an injury which his son had received in falling from the top of a moving car, Ackerman replied that a brakeman had to expect such things. "I am sorry indeed that the accident happened," Ackerman said, "but it is one of the fortunes of war that a young man must encounter in accepting a position of the kind he did."[92]

Under prevailing legal doctrines, an employer was not liable to an employee for an injury sustained on the job except where the injury could be attributed solely to negligence on the part of the employer. To railroad officers this seemed entirely reasonable. When the 1881 Illinois legislature considered enacting a law which would have broadened employer liability so as to include injuries resulting from the negligence of either the victim or one of his fellow workers, William Ackerman was astonished that such a thing should even be considered. Why, he exclaimed,

> It amounts to saying that if one of the men in our Weldon shops, for instance, should drop a piece of hot iron upon the foot of the man he happened to be working with, our company would be liable to the injured party. Such things are happening of course every day. A case in point happened yesterday at our Clinton Shops, when a mechanic

> had his eye put out, while hammering iron, from a red hot flake of the material.[93]

But Ackerman was not worried, for he felt sure that the railroad interests had "enough friends in the Senate" to defeat such "foolish and hostile bills."[94] He recalled that "a similar bill was introduced two years ago and defeated through our influence."[95] History repeated itself in 1881, for when the legislature ended its five month session Ackerman was "happy to say that no legislation hostile to the Railways was passed."[96]

Occasionally a crippled worker did succeed in collecting damages from the company by proving that his injury was the result of employer negligence.[97] In this way a brakeman named Boyd won a $1,000 judgement against the Illinois Central by proving that he had been hurt by a defective brake which the company had failed to keep in proper repair. James Clarke was annoyed by this particular case, for it seemed to him that if Boyd had not known the brake was defective then it was hardly possible for the company to have been aware of it.[98] "I suppose we are stuck," Clarke admitted. "The only thing to be regretted is that Boyd was not killed instead of being hurt."[99]

While trying its best to escape legal responsibility for employee injuries, the railroad nevertheless was willing to provide some voluntary help to accident victims and their families. For example, Edward Jeffery once mentioned that when switchmen at the Chicago yard were severely injured they nearly always were taken to nearby St. Luke's Hospital, where they were treated at company expense. In 1883 the Illinois Central donated $5,000 to the hospital to endow a bed to be used by injured employees of the road.[100]

When the death of an employee left his family without means of support, the company sometimes made donations to his survivors.[101] In 1883 Mrs. Mary E. Cross appealed to James Clarke for aid following the death of her son, who had been killed a few days after beginning work as a brakeman. "I am so completely broken down and distressed I hardly know what to do or say," she wrote. "I am a widow with two little boys, and my lost son has been my stay and support."[102] Clarke responded with an expression of sympathy, a donation of money, and a disclaimer of liability:

> I enclose you herewith copy of report . . . from which you will see that the accident was caused by the error and unthoughtful act of Mr. Cross in jumping off the tender, which resulted in his falling across the track, when the tender passed over his left leg and groin, killing him instantly. . . .
>
> It was very unfortunate that the young man placed himself in the position he did; evidently he did not realize the danger he was incurring.
>
> . . . you will see that no blame or fault could attach to the Company for the unfortunate accident resulting in your son's death. But, as you write to me and say that you were greatly dependent on him for support &c., I will recommend to the company to give you a sum of two hundred and fifty dollars. . . . You will readily understand that this donation would not be made in consideration of the death of your son--because no amount of money could compensate for so sad an accident--but it is to help you that I make this offer.[103]

Record has survived of two other instances in which Clarke made donations of this kind. In 1883 he granted $300 to the widow and orphan of switchman James Haverty, who had slipped while coupling some cars, and in 1887 he donated $250 to Mrs. Ella Moody, the widow of a brakeman who had been knocked from the top of a car as it passed under a bridge.[104] Clarke's action seems to have satisfied Mrs. Haverty, but Mrs. Moody protested that $250 "would not purchase a Respectable Tomb Stone" for her "poor darling husband."[105] Among the letters of Edward Jeffery there is evidence of one other donation to the indigent survivors of an employee: On March 4, 1888, just three weeks after P. B. Rambo had taken a job with the Illinois Central, the mangled body of this twenty-two year old brakeman was found along the tracks near Jackson, Tennessee. As apparently Rambo had lost his footing and fallen from his train, a coroner's jury found the railroad in no way responsible for his death. Nevertheless, because his relatives were very poor, the Illinois Central paid the costs of his burial--$28.75--and later donated $250 to his father.[106]

Although the disablement or death of a breadwinner was a crushing blow to any workingclass family, the voluntary donations of the Illinois Central company were confined to a relatively few cases of acute need. The vast majority of injured employees received no such assistance from the railroad. Nor, in most cases, did they secure aid from any other source. A hundred or so Illinois Central employees were enrolled in the all but moribund I.C.R.R. Mutual Benefit Association and perhaps a larger number purchased insurance from private companies, but for the rest there was no help.[107] The situation was similar for the men who worked for other American railroads at that time, except for a few companies which began in the late 'seventies and early 'eighties to furnish accident and death benefits to all of their employees through company-sponsored insurance systems. On the Illinois Central, William Ackerman was at first the only officer who gave any thought to such a possibility. As early as 1877 Ackerman had taken the trouble to inquire about the workings of an insurance plan introduced by the Reading Railroad, and by 1882 he was mulling over the practicability of introducing some sort of insurance scheme on his own railroad.[108] Then, in 1883, Ackerman resigned the presidency of the Illinois Central without having taken any positive action on the matter. But within the next few years another company officer, Stuyvesant Fish, did make a serious attempt to bring about the inauguration of an insurance system for Illinois Central workers.

Vice President Fish tried very hard to sell

President Clarke on the idea of establishing a company supported relief plan. When Fish learned that the Pennsylvania Railroad intended to introduce such a system early in 1886, he suggested that it would be very good for the morale of Illinois Central employees if, before they learned of the intentions of the Pennsylvania, Clarke were to tell them that their own employer was going to sponsor a relief system.[109] Although Clarke failed to respond to this suggestion, Fish did not abandon his efforts. Repeatedly he urged Clarke to reconsider the idea.[110] Even during the strikes of 1886, Fish continued his campaign. He wrote to Edward Jeffery:

> While I am perfectly in accord with you that this is not the proper time . . . a time will come when it will be right and therefore necessary to increase the pay of employees. When this arrives we ought to have a plan well matured and thoroughly digested, and make the increase in the form of a payment by the Company to the Relief Fund for the benefit of the men; each man's interest in the Fund and in the benefits to be derived therefrom to be conditioned on his remaining in the service, or, on his leaving it, with a proper discharge from the constituted authorities.[111]

Here Fish implied that the establishment of a relief fund might be a means of preventing strikes, since employees would risk the loss of their insurance benefits if they walked off the job. Fish also believed that a company sponsored insurance plan would be a means of combatting labor unions. Shortly after the 1886 troubles had ended, he told Clarke:

> Recent experience ought to teach us that laborers are combining against capital and will continue to do so with greater unanimity and intelligence, and that it behoves us as large employers of labor to forestall this tendency, keep our men out of Trades Unions by giving them at less expense better security against accident, sickness, death and superannuation; and we ought to be manly enough to come out frankly with our proposition and say we have learnt this much.[112]

Perhaps Clarke had learnt that much. At any rate he now said that he would favor the establishment of a relief system, and he instructed Edward Jeffery to devise an insurance program into which employees could be enrolled on a voluntary basis.[113]

For several weeks Jeffery undertook an exhaustive review of the relief systems already in operation on the Baltimore and Ohio Railroad, the Pennsylvania system, and on several railways in France and Great Britain. He also employed an actuary to estimate how much the sponsorship of such a program would cost the Illinois Central. Finally, after pondering all of the information which he had acquired, Jeffery concluded that the Illinois Central should not attempt to sponsor insurance protection for its employees. In a report to Clarke, he said that in his opinion a relief system could not be operated on a voluntary basis unless the company was prepared to bear at least half of its costs, because not enough men would participate to make the plan anywhere near self-supporting. On the other hand, if membership were made compulsory, the men would resent being forced to contribute to the insurance fund. Furthermore, no matter which course were adopted, company-sponsored insurance would be expensive to the Illinois Central because it had extensive mileage in the southern states, where sickness was common and where the company's more than 1,000 black employees would be a heavy burden because, Jeffery said, their "lack of thrift, ignorance and liability of sickness" was greater than was the case among white laborers.[114]

As a result of Jeffery's negative findings,

the Illinois Central abandoned all thought of sponsoring a relief system. After 1886 although company officers remained well aware of the dangers inherent in railroad work, they made only half-hearted efforts to shield their workers from those hazards. In 1888 Edward Jeffery made a gesture towards reviving the old I.C.R.R. Mutual Benefit Association, the self-supporting life insurance society which had nearly died aborning in the 1870's, but his announcement that the company might subsidize the association if 500 or more men joined it elicited no response.[115] Toward the close of the decade, Jeffery began to allow the agents of private insurance companies to enter the Illinois Central's shops in order to solicit business among employees. He also permitted the insurance companies to make arrangements with the Illinois Central paymaster whereby that official would collect premiums on their behalf.[116]

At the close of the decade the railroad worker was scarcely better off than he had been at its beginning, so far as accident protection was concerned. The significance of the attempt of

Stuyvesant Fish to bring about an insurance program organized and subsidized by the railroad company lies not in its result, which was barren, but in its proof that some railroad officers had come to see that labor was combining against capital, that only increased attention to the welfare of workingmen could forestall the tendency toward conflict, and that employers would be wise to admit those facts. Much the same point emerges from an examination of other employee welfare measures that were considered by Illinois Central officers of the 1880's.

Promoting Employee Morals and Morale

William Ackerman was the first Illinois Central president to concern himself seriously with the welfare of employees off as well as on the job. In the 'seventies he had witnessed, with much misgiving, the emergence of labor organization and the great upheaval of 1877, and like Stuyvesant Fish he had come to realize that the welfare of employees was a necessary concern of management. In boldness, Ackerman's thoughts generally outran his actions, but in the early 'eighties he did take some practical steps to promote the welfare of employees by supporting the work of the Young Men's Christian Association among railroaders. After the strikes and riots of 1877, the Chicago Y.M.C.A. had set up a special department to serve the thousands of railroad workers concentrated at that city, the railroad capital of the nation. The Y.M.C.A. established centers to which railroaders were lured by the promise of clean beds, hot baths, and comfortable reading rooms. Thus enticed, the men were rapidly ensnared in a sticky web of edifying lectures, salubrious entertainments, Bible study groups, hymn fests, and similar agonies, all calculated to improve the mind or nourish the spirit, just as baths and beds ministered to bodily needs.[117]

In 1882 William Ackerman was one of ten railway executives who agreed to serve on a newly formed advisory committee set up to furnish aid and counsel to the Railroad Department of the Chicago Y.M.C.A., and the following year he authorized a donation of $200 as the Illinois Central's contritribution towards outfitting a new Y.M.C.A. facility in Chicago.[118] In 1882 Ackerman also helped to bring the blessings of the Y.M.C.A. to railroad men elsewhere in Illinois. He told Edward Jeffery, "I have authorized the Young Men's Christian Association to station an Evangelist at Cairo and have agreed to pay for six months $50 per month. I hope that he will be able to accomplish some good in that ungodly place."[119] A year earlier Ackerman had censured Jeffery for working some men on the Sabbath at Cairo and Jeffery had defended his action on the grounds that in that community workers viewed a Sunday holiday merely as on opportunity for a bacchanalia, often resulting in "the loss of their services not only for that day, but for a part or all of the following day also."[120] Thus Ackerman knew that Jeffery would be interested in his campaign to clean up Cairo. Unfortunately, the campaign was short-lived, for the evangelist who was sent south died within a few months.[121] Ackerman, undaunted, determined to try again.

In the spring of 1883 a second Y.M.C.A. worker was dispatched to Cairo, with a promise from

Ackerman that the Illinois Central would donate $600 to support his activities for one year.[122] Edward Jeffery assured Ackerman that he would report on the man's work and give him whatever assistance he could, for he believed that there was no place more in need of such work than was Cairo.[123] At about this same time, Ackerman also agreed to pay $50 a month to support a Y.M.C.A. organizer at Amboy for six months. The latter experiment was not a success, for in November the local division superintendent wrote Ackerman that at Amboy few employees had attended Y.M.C.A. meetings or visited the organization's reading room.[124] At Cairo too the results must have been disappointing, for in November Ackerman decided that he would not extend his subsidy to the Y.M.C.A. at either place beyond the commitments he had already made.[125] When first he became interested in the Y.M.C.A. Railroad Department, Ackerman had been quite optimistic about the good influence that the Y.M.C.A. might have upon Illinois Central employees. He said that it seemed to him that the morale of railway workers throughout the United States had risen markedly since the early 'seventies; that now there was less drunkenness, more respect for the Lord's Day, and a generally higher standard of morality among the railroaders; and that much of the improvement could be attributed to the efforts made by the officers of the nation's leading railroads to afford their men the advantages of reading rooms and other conveniences.[126] But very quickly, and doubtless without comprehending what had happened, Ackerman came up against the hard fact that the problems of bad morale, intemperance, and moral laxity among workingmen reflected social ills too deep to be cured by so simple a remedy as he had proffered.

James Clarke, who succeeded Ackerman as president in 1883, never suffered disappointment in trying to improve the morals and morale of the labor force, for the simple reason that he never attempted any such thing. When he was asked to subsidize Y.M.C.A. work, Clarke refused, on the grounds that the railroad received no equivalent benefit when it spent money in that way.[127] In Clarke's view, an employer's only clear obligation to an employee was to pay whatever wages had been promised. Occasionally some extra reward might be given to an employee for faithful service, but beyond that the employer had no legitimate reason for meddling in the private life of the worker. A few examples will serve to illustrate Clarke's attitude. In the spring of 1887, when a railroad in which Clarke had a modest personal investment encountered financial difficulties, Clarke urged the president of the beleaguered road to consider wage payments as having first claim on any available funds. Clarke said that persons like himself "who have bought the securities of this line with the view of speculation can better afford to stand the losses, if any are to be made, than the white and colored laborers who have put their labor upon the property."[128] In 1885 Clarke cheerfully presided over the distribution among numerous Illinois Central switchmen, firemen, brakemen, conductors, and low level officers of $5,000 voted by the board of directors as a special bonus to meritorious employees.[129] But when it was suggested to Clarke that the company allow its Chicago employees the privilege of riding free on Illinois Central commuter trains, Clarke opposed the idea. He said:

> I can see no good reason why we ought to furnish free transportation to employes living out on the road any more than we should pay the streetcar fare for those living in the city. . . . If we furnish free transportation then we ought to pay less compensation for their services. . . . I believe in liberality to employes founded on strict and impartial justice, recognizing merit by promotion . . . and in compensating men in ratio to the services performed.[130]

Obviously Clarke's attitude was different from that of Ackerman. It is altogether typical of the two men that at the time the latter officer was busying himself with Y.M.C.A. work Clarke, in telling Ackerman about some construction work underway on the southern lines, remarked that "a great deal can be done by pinching, long hours, short grub time, some cussin and a fair am[oun]t of Persuasion and praying."[131] And clearly most of the labor policies of the Illinois Central Railroad had more in common with the hard-headed, profit-and-loss approach of James Clarke than they did with the benevolent experimentation of William Ackerman.

In general Illinois Central officers had no use for employer paternalism, a fact which is evident in their handling of certain property at McComb City, Mississippi, which came under their jurisdiction at the time the southern lines were merged into the Illinois Central system. McComb City, located in the piney woods 100 miles north of the Gulf, had been established in 1872 when the southern line decided to move its shop facilities from New Orleans to a place where it was hoped a higher altitude, better drainage, and improved sanitation would bring relief from yellow fever and other diseases.[132] By 1882 the town contained more than fifty houses, some stores and offices, a livery stable, a church, and a schoolhouse, and the whole town belonged to the railroad company.[133] It was, said Edward Jeffery, "a railway village in every sense of the word."[134] To the people living at this isolated location, the railroad was employer, landlord, and virtually the only institution linking their tiny hamlet with the outside world. The railroad company allowed McComb City residents reduced freight rates on food, clothing, furniture, and such other necessities as had to be hauled in from New Orleans. It also furnished the local schoolhouse free of rent and contributed to the salary of the teacher.[135]

When McComb City came under the control of Illinois Central officers, the new managers showed no enthusiasm for playing the role of town proprietors. As soon as they could, they began an effort to sell the houses at McComb City to the employees who heretofore had rented the properties. James Clarke initiated this policy in 1887 when he allowed a locomotive engineer named C. J. Miller to purchase his home. "Mr. Miller is a very good man and has been faithful to the Company," wrote Clarke, "and we name the low price of $1500 for the property although it is considered worth more."[136] Stuyvesant Fish suggested that the company should not sell any McComb City property to real estate speculators but should instead, so long as might be necessary, "continue to take the trouble and risk of renting homes to the men employed in the Company's shops," while encouraging them to buy their homes at reasonable rates and on easy terms, "thus enabling them while receiving sufficient wages to support and educate their families, ultimately to own their homes in the neighborhood of their work."[137] Clarke agreed, saying that "such a course would identify the employees with the Company and its interests to a greater degree than if they were merely renters."[138] Fish named the low figure of 4 per cent as the interest rate to be charged the employees for deferred payments on their houses. "We dont want to make money in this way, and we do want them to understand this fact," he said, but "we do want them to pay some interest in order to preserve their self-respect."[139]

***

By the close of the 1880's the rudiments of many aspects of the modern industrial relations environment had appeared on the Illinois Central. Systematic personnel management had become apparent in such innovations as careful control over the consumption of fuel by engineers, the formal testing of candidates for promotion, and the examination of trainmen for visual defects. Collective action by workingmen had been evidenced by strikes which were not spontaneous outbursts but rather systematic attempts to achieve stated objectives. Worker organizations had grown in size and influence, and the Knights of Labor and the Order of Railway Conductors had joined the Brotherhood of Locomotive Engineers as powers to be reckoned with by railroad managers. As the years went by Illinois Central officers had been compelled to take cognizance of unions, and their attitude had shifted from blind hostility toward informed acceptance of the fact of labor organization.

Collective action by workers had had a mixed effect upon management policies. It had led Illinois Central officers to join with the managers of other railroads in a combined resistance to labor demands, but it also had led some officers to give serious thought to plans for easing worker discontent through such innovations as the sponsorship of Y.M.C.A. work and the subsidization of an insurance program. By the close of the decade, the increased strength as well as the conservative behavior of some of the leading labor organizations had so impressed Edward Jeffery that he was willing to engage in real collective bargaining with union spokesmen.

In these eventful years both managers and men had come a long way toward carrying out the industrial imperatives of organization and rationalization. In many ways the working environment on the Illinois Central had been transformed and the modern era was already underway.

[1]Corliss, Main Line of Mid-America, pp. 173, 218-31. The financial complexities involved in the expansion of the Illinois Central are summarized in Henry V. Poor, Manual of the Railroads of the United States (30th ed.; New York: H.V. and H.W. Poor, 1897), pp. 454-62.

[2]Edward T. Jeffery, General Manager, to Stuyvesant Fish, Vice-Pres., Chicago, February 25, 1887, IC-1F2.2.

[3]Fish to James C. Clarke, Pres., New York, January 13, 1885, IC-1C5.5.

[4]Clarke to Fish, Chicago, January 17, 1885, IC-1C5.2.

[5]Fish to Clarke, New York, January 2, 1886, IC-1C5.5.

[6]"Report of James C. Clarke, General Manager, to Stockholders of Chicago, St.Louis, and New Orleans Railroad Co., New Orleans, January 1, 1883," printed in Ackerman, Historical Sketch, pp. 122-23.

[7]Ibid.

[8]Clarke to T. Morris Chester, Chicago, April 29, 1886, IC-1C5.2. Chester, president of a railroad being built by Negroes in North Carolina, had written Clarke to urge the employment of Negroes as a means of combatting labor unions. Chester to Clarke, Harrisburg, Pa., April 23, 1886, IC-1C5.5. In 1886 Jeffery mentioned that the Illinois Central had between 1000 and 1200 black employees. Jeffery to Clarke, Chicago, June 8, 1886, IC-1F2.2.

[9]Clarke to Chester, Chicago, April 29, 1886, IC-1C5.2.

[10]Ibid.

[11]Clarke to Fish, Chicago, December 22, 1886, IC-1C5.2.

[12]The statistics presented in Fig. 5 are

given in a memorandum from A. G. Bruen to Fish, Chicago, May 17, 1897, IC-1F2.2.

[13]I.C.R.R., Schedule of Wages of Locomotive Engineers and Firemen, 1885, file 33 1880 3.1, Burlington Archives, Newberry Library.

[14]Henry B. Stone, Supt. of Locomotive and Car Depts. of Chicago Burlington and Quincy R.R., to Thomas J. Potter, Asst. General Manager of C.B.& Q., Aurora, Ill., June 2, 1880, file 33 1880 3.2, Burlington Archives, Newberry Library. According to Stone's figures, engineers and firemen in the Illinois Central's passenger service earned considerably more than their counterparts on the C.B.& Q., who had annual incomes of $1175 and $617, respectively. But for men in freight service, the C.B.& Q. was the more generous employer: Burlington freight engineers and firemen earned $1431 and $750, respectively. File 33 1880 3.1 in the Burlington Archives contains tables listing the wages paid to enginemen in 1885 by the Illinois Central, the Burlington, and several other Chicago railroads. However, the figures are useless for comparative purposes because each railroad had its own unique way of calculating statistics on mileage and pay.

[15]William K. Ackerman, Pres., to Lewis V. F. Randolph, Treas., Chicago, September 13, 1880, IC-1A2.1.

[16]John Jacobs, Supervisor, to M. Gilleas, Roadmaster, Fort Dodge, September 21, 1880, IC-1A2.4. Gilleas to D. W. Parker, Division Supt., Dubuque, September 23, 1880, IC-1A2.4. Parker to Jeffery, Dubuque, September 24, 1880, IC-1A2.4.

[17]Albert W. Sullivan, Supt. of Lines in Illinois, to J. C. Jacobs, Division Supt., Chicago, December 21, 1887, IC-1D6.1.

[18]Historical Statistics of the U.S., p. 127.

[19]Ackerman to Randolph, Chicago, April 23, 1881, IC-1A2.1.

[20]Ackerman to Randolph, Chicago, April 28, 1881, IC-1A2.1.

[21]Ackerman to Clarke, Chicago, April 23, 1881, IC-1A2.1. See also Ackerman to William H. Osborn, Director, Chicago, April 23, 1881, IC-1A2.1.

[22]Ackerman to Fish, Chicago, May 23, 1881, IC-1A2.1.

[23]Ackerman to Randolph, Chicago, April 28, 1881, IC-1A2.1. Switchmen of the Burlington railroad asked for a wage of $3.00 for a ten-hour day, "owing to the great increase in rent and other expenses of living at the present time." Copy of petition from committee [of switchmen] to E. Ryder, Supt. of C.B.& Q., n.p., n.d., included in letter from Ryder to Potter, Chicago, April 29, 1881, file 33 1880 3.2, Burlington Archives, Newberry Library.

[24]This meeting is described in the letter from Ryder to Potter just cited.

[25]Ackerman to Randolph, Chicago, May 3, 1881, IC-1A2.1.

[26]_Ibid_. Jeffery to Ackerman, Chicago, May 9, 1881; May 14, 1881, IC-1A2.4. Quotation from letter of May 9.

[27]Ackerman to Randolph, Chicago, May 16, 1881, IC-1A2.1.

[28]A strike by freight handlers at New Orleans in 1883 was defeated by importing 200 laborers from along the line north of the city. R. S. Charles, Local Treas., to Clarke, New Orleans, November 28, 1883, IC-1A2.4. S. B. McConnico, Agent, to Clarke, New Orleans, November 30, 1883, IC-1A2.4. J. G. Mann, Chief Engineer, to Clarke, Jackson, Tenn., December 1, 1883, IC-1F2.2. James Fentress, General Solicitor, to Clarke, n.p., December 14, 1883, IC-1F2.2. Early in 1886 a short strike by twenty-four brakemen in Louisiana was settled quickly by Clarke, who persuaded the men to return to work with-

out making any concession to them. Clarke to Fish, New Orleans, February 23, 1886, IC-1F2.2. Jeffery to Fish, Chicago, March 5, 1886, IC-1F2.2.

[29]Clarke to Fish, Chicago, May 1, 1886, IC-1F2.2. Jeffery to Fish, Chicago, May 4, 1886, IC-1F2.2.

[30]Jeffery to Fish, Chicago, May 4, 1886, IC-1F2.2. Clarke to Fish, Chicago, May 10, 1886, IC-1F2.2.

[31]Clarke to Fish, Chicago, May 10, 1886, IC-1F2.2.

[32]Jeffery to Fish, Chicago, May 4, 1886, IC-1F2.2.

[33]Clarke to Fish, Chicago, May 1, 1886, IC-1F2.2.

[34]Jeffery to Fish, Chicago, May 4, 1886, IC-1F2.2.

[35]Clarke to Fish, Chicago, May 10, 1886, IC-1F2.2.

[36]Clarke to Fish, Chicago, July 8, 1886, IC-1F2.2.

[37]Pullman hoped to raise a total of $500,000 from Chicago railroads and banks and from the Pullman and McCormick companies. Fish favored the plan but "drew Pullman's attention to the inexpediency of saying anything about RRs' and capitalists subscribing for this purpose at this time and he explained how he hoped to keep the matter in confidence." Fish to Clarke, New York, March 24, 1886, IC-1C5.5.

[38]Clarke to Fish, Chicago, March 26, 1886, IC-1C5.2. Fish to Clarke, New York, March 26, 1886, IC-1C5.5.

[39]Clarke to George Pullman, Chicago, March 26, 1886, IC-1C5.2, says that at a special meeting the

I.C. board of directors authorized the subscription. Clarke to Fish, Chicago, July 8, 1886, IC-1F2.2, says that the I.C. has been called upon for its $15,000 contribution.

[40]Clarke to Fish, Chicago, May 10, 1886, IC-1F2.2. Clarke had proposed an anti-strike law as early as April 1886 in a letter to U.S. Senator Shelby M. Cullom, Chicago, April 28, 1886, IC-1C5.2.

[41]Clarke's incoming letters for May and June of 1886, IC-1C5.5, contain numerous replies from southern railroad officials.

[42]"While it seems the majority of the Senate feel it their duty to regulate railroads in conducting inter-state commerce, they have not yet reached the point where they feel it their duty to protect them, while they are thus engaged," wrote a Congressman who had supported the strike ban. Joseph E. Brown, U.S. Senator, to Clarke, Washington, May 15, 1886, IC-1C5.5.

[43]In March 1881 Ackerman said, "As a rule we retain all the oldest men in our employ if they are found worthy and competent, but we have adopted a new rule to take in only young men in the future." If there really was a new rule, it merely confirmed a practice dating back to the earliest years of the company. As a matter of fact, in February Ackerman had told a job applicant that it was "an established rule of this company to employ very young men and have them work their way up in the service." Ackerman to Mrs. E. G. Ryerson, Chicago, March 5, 1881, IC-1A2.1. Ackerman to H. P. Bender, Chicago, February 5, 1881, IC-1A2.1.

[44]C. J. Headley to Ackerman, Mattoon, Ill., February 23, 1881, IC-1A2.4. With this letter is the "partial list of questions," which is dated February 18, 1881.

[45]Report of John E. Owens, Superintending Surgeon, to Jeffery, Chicago, August 9, 1880, printed in "Color Blindness on the Illinois Central

Railroad," Railroad Gazette, XXIV (September 3, 1880), 465.

[46]Ibid., statistical table.

[47]Jeffery to Fish, Chicago, June 6, 1888, IC-1F2.2.

[48]Jeffery to Fish, Chicago, September 28, 1887, IC-1F2.2. The shortage of motive power was acute in Iowa, where many engines were being used to haul materials for the branch lines then under construction.

[49]Jeffery to Fish, Chicago, September 4, 1888, IC-1J4.1. This time the shortage was worst on the Chicago division, where thirty-two freight engine crews were making as many as thirty-six trips a day, yet using only twenty-four locomotives.

[50]Clarke to Sheafe, Supt., and Henry Schlacks, Supt. of Machinery, Chicago, April 16, 1883, IC-1C5.2. Points 5-9, not quoted, deal with technical matters involved in determining the pay of engineers.

[51]Jeffery to Fish, Chicago, March 5, 1886, IC-1F2.2.

[52]Noting a large number of employee injuries in 1884, Clarke asked his general superintendent to "see if heads of Depts. and officers are not remiss in enforcing regulations among employees." Clarke to Jeffery, Chicago, November 5, 1884, IC-1C5.2.

[53]Clarke to Fish, Chicago, February 25, 1885, IC-1C5.2.

[54]Clarke to Mrs. I. Smith, Chicago, December 24, 1885, IC-1C5.2.

[55]Jeffery to Schlacks, Chicago, August 31, 1888, IC-1J4.1.

[56]Jeffery to Schlacks, Chicago, August 29, 1888, IC-1J4.1.

[57]Jeffery to Schlacks, Chicago, August 31, 1888, IC-1J4.1.

[58]Clarke to R. N. Colyquhoun, [Master Mechanic?], Chicago, August 28, 1888, IC-1C5.2.

[59]Jeffery to Fentress, Bolivar, Tenn., October 1, 1888, IC-1J4.1.

[60]Fish to Fentress, New York, October 13, 1888, IC-1F2.1.

[61]Jeffery to Fentress, Bolivar, Tenn., October 1, 1888, IC-1J4.1.

[62]Jeffery to A. B. Minton, [foreman], Chicago, October 2, 1888, IC-1J4.1.

[63]Fish to Clarke, New York, March 23, 1885, IC-1C5.5.

[64]Fish here referred to the case of engineer John Smalley, who, having escaped indictment despite a great public outcry following an 1883 accident, was now suing the Illinois Central for damages. Fish to Clarke, New York, February 28, 1885, IC-1C5.5. The 1883 accident, which killed two persons and injured thirty others, was caused by Smalley's having ignored a signal and pulled his train out of a station without orders. His carelessness resulted in a spectacular collision, in which the two locomotives stood up on end, wheels to wheels. Mann to Clarke, Jackson, Tenn., November 18, 1883, IC-1A2.4. Jeffery to Clarke, Bradford, Tenn., November 19, 1883, IC-1A2.4.

[65]Clarke to Fish, Chicago, March 20, 1885, IC-1F2.2.

[66]Fentress to Fish, Washington, D.C., March 9, 1885, IC-1F2.2.

[67]Schlacks to Clarke, Chicago, October 17, 1885, IC-1C5.5.

[68]Clarke to Schlacks, Chicago, April 10,

1883, IC-1C5.2.

[69]Clarke to Sheafe and Schlacks, Chicago, April 16, 1883, IC-1C5.2.

[70]Clarke to Jeffery, Chicago, May 16, 1883, IC-1C5.2.

[71]*Ibid*.

[72]*Ibid*. The day before, Clarke had written that he intended to dismiss some men employed at Jackson, Tenn., "as I believe they produce as much dissension as they are competent to do." Clarke to Jonathan W. Buford, Mayor of Jackson, Chicago, May 15, 1883, IC-1C5.2.

[73]Clarke to Jeffery, Chicago, May 16, 1883, IC-1C5.2.

[74]Clarke to Sheafe and Schlacks, Chicago, April 16, 1883, IC-1C5.2.

[75]As when he referred to his respect for the engineers' "Brotherhood Order." Clarke to Jeffery, Chicago, May 16, 1883, IC-1C5.2.

[76]Clarke to Fish, New Orleans, February 23, 1886, IC-1F2.2.

[77]Philip Taft, *Organized Labor in American History* (New York: Harper and Row, 1964), pp. 100-103.

[78]Fentress to Clarke, Bolivar, Tenn., March 25, 1886, IC-1C5.5.

[79]"It hurts bad. dmnd bad." Clarke to Fish, Chicago, May 11, 1886, IC-1C5.5.

[80]Sidney Webster, Director, to Clarke, New York, May 1, 1886, IC-1C5.5.

[81]Clarke to Fentress, Chicago, July 14, 1886, IC-1C5.2.

[82]In his public appearances Jeffery liked to stress his own humble origin and to claim a deep interest in the welfare of workingmen. See, for example, Remarks of E. T. Jeffery, General Manager of the Illinois Central Railroad Co. before the Senate Committee on Railroads of the Iowa Legislature, at Des Moines, February 9, 1888 (Chicago: Rand McNally & Co., n.d.), and Remarks of E. T. Jeffery, General Manager of the Illinois Central Railroad before the City Council of New Orleans, La., November 28th, 1888 (New Orleans: L. Graham and Sons, n.d.), IC-1F2.2.

[83]Jeffery to Clarke, Chicago, March 16, 1888, IC-1J4.1. Jeffery's activities are discussed in Donald L. McMurry, The Great Burlington Strike of 1888: A Case History in Labor Relations (Cambridge: Harvard University Press, 1956), pp. 150-52, 220-22.

[84]Jeffery to Fish, Chicago, April 7, 1888, IC-1F2.2.

[85]Jeffery, unaddressed letters of reference on behalf of A. P. Smith and M. Commons, former C.B.& Q. engineers, Chicago, August 28, 1888, IC-1J4.1.

[86]Jeffery to Minton, Chicago, August 29, 1888; September 20, 1888; October 2, 1888, IC-1J4.1. See also C. A. Beck, General Supt., to Minton, Chicago, August 24, 1888, IC-1D6.1. In 1883 James Clarke had mentioned Minton as one of the nine Brotherhood agitators who were causing trouble on the southern lines. Clarke to Jeffery, Chicago, May 16, 1883, IC-1C5.2.

[87]Jeffery to Minton, Chicago, August 29, 1888, IC-1J4.1.

[88]Jeffery to C. J. Malone, P. C. Parrington, D. Maroney, and J. Lineman, [committeemen of Order of Railway Conductors], Chicago, October 1, 1888, IC-1J4.1.

[89]Jeffery to William P. Daniels, Grand Sec. of Order of Railway Conductors, Chicago, March 3,

1888, IC-1J4.1. Jeffery to E. F. O'Shea, Grand Sec.-Treas. of Brotherhood of Railroad Brakemen, Chicago, September 4, 1888, IC-1J4.1. Jeffery to R. B. Losie, locomotive engineer, Chicago, September 14, 1888, IC-1J4.1. Jeffery to F. P. Sargent and Eugene V. Debs, national officers of Brotherhood of Locomotive Firemen, Chicago, October 6, 1888, IC-1J4.1. Jeffery to A. D. Thurston, Grand Chief Telegrapher of Order of Railway Telegraphers, Chicago, April 19, 1889, IC-1J4.1. Jeffery to William A. Simsrott, Grand Sec.-Treas. of Switchmen's Mutual Aid Association of North America, Chicago, June 27, 1889, IC-1J4.1.

[90]W. R. Head, Personal Injury Agent, to William J. Mauriac, Secretary, Chicago, January 31, 1885, IC-11N1.3.

[91]The following statistics are given in Jeffery to Mauriac, Chicago, December 22, 1884, IC-11N1.3. That the figures on disablements do not include "the cases of lesser importance" is mentioned in Head to Mauriac, Chicago, January 5, 1885, IC-11N1.3.

[92]Ackerman to Henry B. Carrington, Chicago, September 14, 1880, IC-1A2.1. See also: Carrington to Ackerman, Bridgeport, Conn., September 3, 1880, IC-1A2.4. Ackerman to John E. Owens, Superintending Surgeon, Chicago, September 6, 1880, IC-1A2.1. Owens to Ackerman, Chicago, September 14, 1880, IC-1A2.4.

[93]Ackerman to Randolph, Springfield, February 26, 1881, IC-1A2.1.

[94]Ackerman to Clarke, March 30, 1881, IC-1A2.1.

[95]Ackerman to Randolph, Springfield, February 26, 1881, IC-1A2.1.

[96]Ackerman to Albert Fink, [Pres. of Louisville and Nashville R.R.], Chicago, June 6, 1881, IC-1A2.1.

[97]Damage suits by injured employees were infrequent. Of the 127 suits handled by the company's legal department in 1889, only two are identified as personal injury suits by employees in "Annual Report of the General Solicitor of the Illinois Central R.R. Co. as of December 1st, 1889," typed copy, IC-1F2.2.

[98]Clarke to R. A. Hill, Chicago, January 27, 1885, IC-1C5.2.

[99]Clarke to Fentress, Chicago, February 9, 1885, IC-1C5.2. See also Hill to Fentress, Oxford, Miss., January 16, 1885, IC-1C5.5. Fentress to Hill, n.p., January 19, 1885, IC-1C5.5. Clarke to Fentress, Chicago, March 21, 1888, IC-1C5.2.

[100]Jeffery to G. M. Beach, General Manager of Chicago and Atlantic Railway, Chicago, July 23, 1889, IC-1J4.1. Ackerman to N. K. Fairbanks, Treas. of St. Luke's Hospital, Chicago, April 28, 1883, IC-1A2.1.

[101]Although the cases cited here all occurred on the southern lines, similar donations doubtless were made to the families of some men killed in Illinois and Iowa. Personal injury cases on the northern lines were handled by Personal Injury Agent W. R. Head, whose letters are not extant.

[102]Mrs. Mary E. Cross to Clarke, Water Valley, Miss., October 30, 1883, IC-1A2.4.

[103]Clarke to Cross, Chicago, November 10, 1883, IC-1C5.2. See also Clarke to John Myers, Trainmaster, Chicago, November 7, 1883, IC-1A2.4. Myers to Clarke, McComb City, Miss., November 8, 1883, IC-1A2.4. Clarke to Cross, Chicago, January 27, 1884; February 25, 1884, IC-1C5.2.

[104]H. W. Clarke, Asst. Division Supt., to James Clarke, New Orleans, October 25, 1883, IC-1A2.4. C. W. Sheafe to James Clarke, Yazoo City, Miss., November 1883, IC-1A2.4. James Clarke to V. B. Watts, Chicago, January 12, 1887, IC-1C5.2. James Clarke to Mrs. Ella Moody, Chicago, April 18,

1887, IC-1C5.2.

[105]Moody to James Clarke, Beauregard, Miss., March 24, 1887, IC-1C5.5.

[106]Jeffery to Fish, Chicago, January 25, 1889, IC-1J4.1. Jeffery to Fentress, Chicago, February 15, 1889, IC-1J4.1.

[107]Some I.C. employees probably belonged to the "Railway Employees Mutual Benefit Association," which provided life insurance for Chicago railroaders from 1870 until 1884, when it disbanded. Two Illinois Central officers, John Dunn and W. R. Head, served as officials of this organization. Mauriac to Fish, Chicago, September 6, 1883, IC-1F2.2, encloses a copy of the bylaws of the R.E.M.B.A. See also printed circular announcing dissolution of the association, November 25, 1884, IC-11N1.3.

[108]Ackerman to William T. Barnard, Sec. of Baltimore and Ohio Railroad Employes' Relief Association, Chicago, March 6, 1882, IC-1A2.4.

[109]Fish to James Clarke, New York, December 30, 1885, IC-1F2.2.

[110]Fish to James Clarke, New York, January 26, 1886, IC-1C5.5.

[111]Fish to Jeffery, New York, May 8, 1886, IC-1F2.2.

[112]Fish to James Clarke, New York, May 11, 1886, IC-1F2.2.

[113]James Clarke to Jeffery, Chicago, May 13, 1886, IC-1F2.2.

[114]Jeffery to James Clarke, Chicago, June 8, 1886, IC-1F2.2. Accompanying Jeffery's report are materials relating to relief plans in use on various railroads and a copy of J. H. Kellogg, Illinois Central Railway Relief Association Plan: Report of Actuary (n.p., n.d.).

[115]Jeffery to employees of I.C.R.R., Chicago, September 14, 1888, IC-1J4.1.

[116]Jeffery to Beck, Chicago, August 31, 1888, IC-1J4.1. Jeffery's correspondence for 1888 and 1889 contains several letters pertaining to this subject.

[117]The work of the Y.M.C.A. is described in a printed circular letter from Railroad Department of Y.M.C.A. to managers of Chicago railroads, Chicago, February 5, 1883, IC-1A2.4, which lists Ackerman as a member of the newly formed advisory committee.

[118]H. E. Sargent, Pres. of Fargo and Southern Railway Co., to Ackerman, Chicago, September 31, 1883, IC-1A2.1. W. I. Miller, Sec. of Railway Executive Committee of Y.M.C.A., to Ackerman, Chicago, November 1, 1883, IC-1A2.1. Ackerman to Sargent, Chicago, December 4, 1883, IC-1A2.1.

[119]Ackerman to Jeffery, Chicago, June 30, 1882, IC-1A2.1.

[120]Jeffery to Ackerman, Chicago, June 3, 1881, IC-1A2.4.

[121]Weekly Bulletin of the Young Men's Christian Association (Chicago), November 15, 1882, IC-1A2.4.

[122]George W. Strode, Baptist minister at Cairo, to Ackerman, Cairo, March 13, 1883, IC-1A2.4. Ackerman to Strode, Chicago, March 26, 1883, IC-1A2.1.

[123]Jeffery to Ackerman, Cairo, March 24, 1883, IC-1A2.4.

[124]John C. Jacobs, Divison Supt., to Ackerman, Amboy, November 17, 1883, IC-1A2.1.

[125]Ackerman to I. E. Brown, State Secretary of Y.M.C.A., Chicago, November 7, 1883, IC-1A2.1.

[126]Ackerman to Rufus W. Clark, clergyman at Albany, N.Y., Chicago, November 25, 1882, IC-1A2.1.

[127]James Clarke to A. T. Hemingway, Y.M.C.A. Secretary, Chicago, March 13, 1885, IC-1C5.2.

[128]James Clarke to Thomas T. A. Lyon, Pres. of Memphis and Northwestern Railroad, Chicago, March 21, 1887, IC-1C5.2.

[129]Fish to James Clarke, New York, March 9, 1885, IC-1C5.5. James Clarke to Fish, Chicago, March 11, 1885, IC-1F2.2. Minutes of the Board of Directors, January 21, 1885, *IC-+3.1.

[130]James Clarke to Potter, Chicago, July 11, 1885, IC-1C5.2.

[131]James Clarke to Ackerman, Chicago, October 12, 1883, IC-1F2.2, commenting on construction of Canton Aberdeen and Nashville branch.

[132]McConnico to Fish, New Orleans, June 27, 1887, IC-1F2.2. Jeffery to Thomas M. Cooley, Chairman of Interstate Commerce Commission, Chicago, July 17, 1882, IC-1J4.1.

[133]"List of Properties of the Mississippi Valley Co.," April 1, 1887, IC-1F2.2.

[134]Jeffery to Cooley, Chicago, July 17, 1882, IC-1J4.1.

[135]Ibid.

[136]James Clarke to McConnico, Chicago, March 21, [1887], IC-1C5.2.

[137]Fish to McConnico, New York, May 23, 1887, IC-1C5.5.

[138]James Clarke to Fish, Chicago, May 28, 1887, IC-1F2.2.

[139]Fish to McConnico, New York, May 31, 1887, IC-1F2.1. The going rate had been 8 per cent. McConnico to Fish, New Orleans, May 27, 1887, IC-1F2.2.

CHAPTER V

PANIC, PULLMAN, AND THE BRYAN CRUSADE

The Illinois Central continued to expand in the early 1890's. The railroad managers, having greatly augmented the trackage of their northern lines during the preceding decade, now set out to strengthen their competitive position in the South by making strategic additions to the southern system. In the fall of 1892, they purchased the Louisville, New Orleans, and Texas Railroad, at a cost of $25,000,000. This acquisition removed an important competitor and made the Illinois Central the leading railroad at the port of New Orleans and in the state of Mississippi. It also provided the equivalent of a double track from New Orleans to Memphis and carried the system into Arkansas.[1] A year later, the Illinois Central extended its territory into Kentucky by buying a controlling interest in the Chesapeake, Ohio, and Southwestern Railroad, which linked Memphis to Louisville and also had several branches in Kentucky.[2] Still further expansion might have been undertaken but for the panic and depression of 1893, which compelled the railroad managers to turn from expansion to retrenchment.

The Panic of 1893 had an immediate impact upon the labor policies of the railroad managers. Moreover, it ushered in a three-year depression in which economic distress and social unrest resulted in two other events that affected railroad labor policies. One of the two was the Pullman strike of 1894, in which organized labor mounted an unprecedented assault upon organized capital. The other event was the famous Free Silver election of 1896, in which William Jennings Bryan campaigned for the presidency upon a platform that terrified those whom he accused of pressing down upon the brow of labor a crown of thorns. The manner in which the railroad managers responded to each of these three occurrences--the Panic of 1893, the Pullman strike, and the presidential campaign--had important consequences for the railroad labor force.

The Panic of 1893: Work Force and Wages, before and after

Prior to the expansion of the southern lines in 1892 and 1893, the Illinois Central labor force had already grown to almost 17,000 men (see Table 6). There were now 4,339 employees in the transportation department and 6,113 in the road department, while the machinery department included 4,119 shopmen and 1,479 engineers and firemen. All of these, together with 949 office workers, telegraphers, and other employees, brought the total work force in June, 1892, to 16,997, triple the number that had been employed ten years before. For most of these workers, rates of pay either held steady or else increased moderately between 1890 and 1893. The wages of road department employees varied, as always, according to local conditions, but generally section hands in Illinois and Iowa received $1.25 for a ten-hour day. That figure was above what company officers still referred to as the "standard wage" of $1.10 a day, but ever since the early 1880's, the so-called standard had

TABLE 6

COMPARATIVE STATEMENT OF FORCE EMPLOYED ON THE ILLINOIS CENTRAL RAILROAD IN JUNE 1891 AND 1892

Branch of Service	June 1891		June 1892	
	No.	Pay	No.	Pay
General Offices	414	$ 43,665	491	$ 49,611
Transportation Department				
Chicago	1848	101,832	1743	98,686
Amboy	344	18,696	353	19,592
Springfield	166	8,112	162	7,968
Pontiac	58	3,039	53	2,700
Freeport	285	15,438	322	17,846
Dubuque	285	15,503	322	18,120
Cherokee	183	9,991	203	11,463
Mississippi	448	25,973	404	25,270
Louisiana	512	30,039	636	37,552
Memphis	142	6,228	141	6,343

TABLE 6--Continued

Branch of Service	June 1891		June 1892	
	No.	Pay	No.	Pay
Road Department				
Division 1	937	$ 46,554	725	$ 33,918
Division 2	948	32,122	435	15,118
Division 3	282	9,501	331	11,649
Division 4	258	8,410	239	8,139
Division 5	111	3,675	101	3,642
Division 6	420	15,557	438	15,927
Division 8	416	15,609	737	29,439
Division 9	449	16,794	439	15,251
Division 11	925	32,130	1011	32,409
Division 12	544	17,688	1378	47,636
Division 13	248	4,930	279	5,205
Machinery Department				
Shopmen				
North	2043	92,264	2233	96,499
West	523	21,275	651	24,594
South	1041	42,890	1235	48,357

TABLE 6--Continued

Branch of Service	June 1891		June 1892	
	No.	Pay	No.	Pay
Enginemen				
North	819	$ 52,858	693	$ 54,094
West	277	20,217	329	24,215
South	416	30,111	457	34,341
Telegraph Department	326	14,450	348	15,918
Miscellaneous	120	6,663	110	4,920
Total	15788	$762,113	16997	$816,726

Source: Comparative Statement of Force Employed, form dated August 2, 1892, IC-1F2.2.

often been exceeded. On the southern lines, a lower pay scale prevailed, 90 cents a day being the usual wage for common laborers (see Table 7).[3]

Information on the wages of trainmen is scanty. In the summer of 1890, the Illinois Central's general manager told his counterpart on another railroad that I.C. conductors and brakemen on the northern lines were paid $75 and $50 a month, respectively, based upon their making runs totalling 2600 miles. When their monthly mileage exceeded that figure, they received additional compensation. On the lines south of Cairo, trainmen normally were expected to cover 3000 miles in a month's time. Conductors whose runs totalled that amount were paid $85, while brakemen received $50 if they were white men, $45 if they were black.[4] These pay scales were revised as a result of conferences held in 1890, 1891, and 1892 between Illinois Central officers and representatives of the Order of Railway Conductors and the Brotherhood of Railroad Trainmen. The agreements which resulted from these negotiations have not been preserved, but apparently

TABLE 7

DAILY WAGES OF ROAD DEPARTMENT

EMPLOYEES 1892-96

Year	Ordinary Laborers	Superior Laborers	Painters	Masons	Black-smiths
		Northern Lines			
1892	$1.25	$1.40	$2.75	$3.00	$2.50
1893	$1.25	$1.40	$2.75	$3.00	$2.50
1894	$1.10	$1.25	$2.75	$3.00	$2.50
1895	$1.10	$1.25	$2.75	$3.00	$2.50
1896	$1.10	$1.25	$2.75	$3.00	$2.50
		Southern Lines			
1892	$0.90	$1.10	$2.75	$3.00	$2.50
1893	$0.90	$1.10	$2.75	$3.00	$2.50
1894	$0.90	$1.00	$2.75	$3.00	$2.50
1895	$0.80	$0.90	$2.75	$3.00	$2.50
1896	$0.90	$1.00	$2.75	$3.00	$2.50

Source: A. G. Bruen to Stuyvesant Fish, Chicago, May 17, 1897, IC-1F2.2.

some pay increases were made. In the spring of 1891 a company clerk attributed a rise in the expenses of the transportation department to the new schedule of wages for trainmen that had been adopted the previous fall, and after the negotiations held in November 1891 the general manager mentioned that the pay of some conductors had been increased $5 per month.[5]

The wages of enginemen increased slightly during the early 'nineties. In 1892 the pay scale for all of the regular freight and passenger runs was revised for the first time since 1876. Under the new schedule, firemen received increased compensation for most of their runs. There were fewer changes in the rates paid to engineers, but they did receive more money for some runs, particularly in the passenger service.[6] Of course the actual earnings of an engineman depended on the particular runs to which he was assigned. One fireman for whom records happen to have been preserved averaged about $55 a month in earnings during the years 1890-95.[7] An engineer making the same runs probably would have earned in the neighborhood of $95 a month.[8] Whether these figures are at all typical of the earnings of enginemen during those years is, of course, a moot point.

Other classes of employees sought wage increases in the early 'nineties but failed to get them. In 1890 switchmen at Memphis, Tennessee, and at numerous points in Illinois and Iowa petitioned for raises that would have made their earnings near or equal to those of yardmen at Chicago, where an unusually high rate was paid.[9] At Chicago the foreman, so-called, of each switching crew received 27 cents an hour for day work and 29 cents at night. His two assistants each were paid 25 cents an hour in the daytime and 27 cents at night.[10] These rates were much higher than those prevailing at Memphis, where foremen received 25 cents an hour for both day and night work and their helpers earned 21-1/2 cents for day work and 22 cents at night.[11] However, the company refused to grant any of the requests for wage increases because, in the words of the general manager, there was "no more reason why Chicago rates should be paid at Memphis than wages at New York, Boston, or any other far distant point."[12] Even though they were being paid more than switchmen at other locations, the Chicago yardmen themselves sought a wage increase in the spring of 1893. Their request for a raise of about 5 cents an hour was denied by the general manager, who asserted that because of more regular employment and overtime work their average earnings had increased 50 per cent in the last ten years even though they had received no wage increase since 1881.[13]

All of the railroads at Chicago joined with the Illinois Central in refusing to raise wages. General Manager James T. Harahan of the Illinois Central and the managers of the other roads arranged for the importation of 1,000 men, who would have replaced the Chicago switchmen had they gone out on strike.[14] Several months later, Harahan wrote that by presenting a united front against labor demands, the Chicago roads had been able to resist all pressures for wage increases. He said that the backing of the Chicago General Managers' Association had enabled the Illinois Central to refuse requests for increased compensation by shop workers and baggage handlers as well as switchmen, and he urged President Stuyvesant Fish to support a plan to establish organizations similar to the General Managers' Association at other railroad centers,

> the object being to get organized all over the country to meet the demands of organized labor. If this had been done, years ago, the Railroads of this country would not be in the condition they are today . . . and Labor organizations would not be as strong as they are at present.[15]

Another demand for higher wages in 1892 was made by the Illinois Central's freight handlers at New Orleans. These men asked that the company pay them $2.00 a day and agree to employ only men belonging to their labor organization, Freight Handlers Protective Union No. 5782 of the American Federation of Labor. The freight handlers joined with most New Orleans workingmen in a general strike against local employers, but the Illinois Central was able to continue its operations by bringing in men from points north of the city.[16] Partly through the influence of Stuyvesant Fish, a suit was filed against the Workingmen's Amalgamated Council of New Orleans, seeking an injunction prohibiting that body from interfering with interstate commerce.[17] Although the general strike collapsed long before the case was resolved in the courts, an important legal precedent was established when the U.S. District Court ruled that the injunction could be issued because the strike was a conspiracy in restraint of trade and was therefore unlawful under the terms of the Sherman Antitrust Act of 1890.[18] In this way a law aimed at business monopolies became a powerful weapon against organized labor.

A major reason for the railroad managers' firm resistance to wage demands in the early 'nineties was the fact that in those years a business recession reduced the earnings of many railroads. On the Illinois Central, traffic fell off so much that operating expenses, which had amounted to 60 per cent of gross earnings in July 1889, rose to 70 per cent in 1890, 73 per cent in 1891, and 80 per cent in 1892. Company officers were so alarmed by these mounting costs that in the fall of 1892 they took steps to reduce the work force in the road and machinery departments "to the lowest practicable point."[19] Further reductions were made in

March 1893, as company officers went over "each name, on each roll, to see what could be cut, to reduce expenses" in the transportation department of the southern lines.[20] Thus the Illinois Central was already operating on a lean basis when the collapse of the New York stock market on June 27 heralded the coming of the Panic of 1893.

During the depression of 1893-97 there were, it hardly need be said, no wage increases for railroad employees. Instead, wage reductions were considered. In January 1894, James Harahan told Stuyvesant Fish that the General Managers' Association was discussing the possibility of a 10 per cent cut for all engineers, firemen, brakemen, and yardmen. But, said Harahan, there was a problem in that several roads were "in the same fix" as the Illinois Central, in that their current earnings were not quite low enough to justify a cut.[21] Earlier, Harahan had suggested a means of overcoming this difficulty:

> While our earnings show up so well, do you not think it would be a good idea not to publish them? The indications are that after the World's Fair is over, business will be light, and if our men have the published statements of earnings showing the increases

> we are making, should there be a necessity for the reduction of wages, I am afraid we would have difficulty in carrying such a proposition through, with those facts in their hands to use against us. As you know, the Labor Organizations take advantage of everything they can to protect their own interests.[22]

However, Fish had not adopted this suggestion. By the time Harahan met with committeemen of the Order of Railway Conductors and the Brotherhood of Railroad Trainmen in February 1894, there no longer was any cause for concealing the company's earnings from the union representatives. Harahan told the labor spokesmen:

> Gentlemen, I am very glad to see you. . . . We are passing through quite a hard time and the indications are that times will be worse. . . . So far as our own business is concerned, we did very well up to the first of December; since then we have not done well at all. In December, we were $129,867.53 behind the receipts of the same month of the previous year. As I have said to the other committees that have been here, I am always glad to let you know just exactly what we are doing, so you can understand the situation as well as I do.

Harahan asked the committeemen to urge the members of their lodges to do everything possible to avoid accidents and otherwise save the railroad money, and he reminded them that the company shops were running only eight hours a day and that the track force had been pared to the bone.[23] After the meeting, Harahan wrote to Fish that he had sent the union men home "without giving them anything" and had intimated to them the possibility of a wage cut "so as to prepare them for it, in case it should come."[24]

The cut for which Harahan had laid the groundwork was never made, primarily because the railroad managers remembered the strikes and riots that pay cuts had provoked in 1877, and they knew that now there could be more organized, massive resistance to wage reductions, because of the great power that had been attained by labor unions in the twenty years since the Panic of 1873.[25] "We are, of course, all of the same mind that wages should be reduced," wrote Harahan to Fish in February 1895, "but how to do it and whether or not we can do it without co-operation, is a question I think we should seriously consider."[26] Fear of strikes caused the Illinois Central officers to turn to means other than wage cuts for reducing expenses. In this way there emerged a new kind of depression policy, which Stuyvesant Fish later described in these words:

> No reductions in pay were made by the Illinois Central Railroad during the long period of depression (1893 to 1897) from which we are emerging, excepting that, in some parts of the Country, the fall in the wages of farm laborers necessarily affected, for a short season, those of our track hands. But many of our men suffered severely through our diminished need of their services. Making less of our cars and engines, we had less of them to repair, and both the number employed and the hours of work in the shops were reduced. It seemed to me then, and it seems to me now, that it would have been better for the men, if it had been possible for us, by reducing the scale of wages a little, to have employed more men or to give them work on full time.[27]

Fish said that if wages had been reduced, the railroad could have employed more shop hands to build cars and engines. But since they were not, it was cheaper to buy them--and the Illinois Central did in fact buy 180 locomotives, 63 passenger cars, and 8,272 freight cars between 1893 and 1897. In the same period, the company built for itself only 241 cars and no locomotives.[28]

The Pullman Boycott

Not all employers had learned the lesson of 1877 so well as had the officers of the Illinois

Central. One who had not was George M. Pullman, head of the Pullman Palace Car Company, a major manufacturer of sleeping cars and other rolling stock. When the Panic of 1893 caused a sharp drop in his company's car-building business, Pullman reduced the wages of his shopmen by an average of 25 per cent. This sharp cut was particularly hard on the Pullman workers because most of them lived in the company-owned town of Pullman, where house rents had always been 20 to 25 per cent higher than in other Chicago suburbs and were not now reduced, despite the wage cut. Soon many employees found themselves falling deeply into debt to their employer-landlord. The total arrears in rent at Pullman eventually reached $100,000. Finally, in desperation, the Pullman workers went out on strike in an effort to bring about the restoration of their former wages.[29] The walkout by the Pullman employees, which occurred on June 11, 1894, was the beginning of a major event in American labor history. It became such because between March and May of 1894 some 4,000 Pullman workers had been enrolled into a new and phenomenally successful labor organization, the American Railway Union. The A.R.U. had been founded on June 30, 1893, under the leadership of Eugene V. Debs, a former national officer of the Brotherhood of Locomotive Firemen who had come to believe that all railroad workers must be combined into one big union if organized labor was to cope effectively with the entrenched power of the railroad operators. Many railroaders agreed with Debs, and well over 100,000 of them joined the A.R.U. during the first year of its existence. A successful strike against the Northern Pacific Railroad boosted the prestige of the organization, so that when delegates to the first convention of the union met at Chicago in June 1894, they were in an ebullient and aggressive mood. Consequently, when the delegates were informed of the circumstances of the Pullman strike, they voted to notify the Pullman managers that unless the wage cuts of 1893 were rescinded, the A.R.U. would call upon its members to institute a boycott of all Pullman cars. The Pullman company refused to entertain this demand. The stage was now set for a test of strength between the nation's first great industrial union and the combined powers of the railroad industry.[30]

The Illinois Central Railroad was selected as the first target of the Pullman boycott movement, for the American Railway Union had numerous adherents within the company's labor force. A Chicago newspaper quoted a locomotive engineer as saying, "The Illinois Central is the best organized road in the country. We all belong to the American Railway Union--that is, the switchmen, switchtenders, and tower men--and there are a good many engineers and firemen in it, too."[31] When A.R.U. leaders announced that the boycott of Pullman cars would begin on July 26, Illinois Central officers declared that any employee who disregarded an order to handle such cars would be discharged.[32] General Manager Harahan told President Fish that he had "no sympathy with Mr. Pullman" but that the railroad was obligated to "accommodate the travelling public."[33] Chief Attorney James Fentress wrote bitterly that Pullman was "as usual, selfish" and "little concerned about the distress of those who are attempting, in good faith, to carry his cars." But Fentress agreed with Harahan that the Illinois Central had to insist that its employees perform their duties or else face dismissal.[34]

The Pullman boycott began on June 26, when some switchmen at the Illinois Central's Chicago yard refused to attach Pullman sleepers to a passenger train. For this offense they were immediately fired, and the firings precipitated a walkout by nearly all of the Chicago switchmen.[35] The next day more than 100 shopmen joined in the strike, and the day after that 1,000 more tradesmen, or about two-thirds of all the men employed at the Chicago shops, ceased work.[36] During the first week in July, some trainmen in the Illinois Central suburban service quit work, and there were a few incidents of vandalism against suburban and other trains.[37] Meanwhile, the strike was spreading to other locations. By the end of the week, switchmen had ceased work at Kankakee, Freeport, Mounds, and Clinton. Clerks and telegraphers had struck at Mounds, shopmen were out at Clinton, and a few men had ceased work as far away as Memphis, Tennessee.[38] At Cairo and at Sioux City only a few Illinois Central employees went out on strike, but mob action interrupted traffic until state militia were called in to restore order.[39]

The managers of the Illinois Central considered the action of the striking employees to be totally without justification. On June 27, Harahan issued a circular in which he pointed out that the Illinois Central could do nothing to influence the relations between the Pullman company and its workers, for if the Illinois Central declined to haul Pullman cars on its trains it would violate its contract with the Pullman company and become liable for damages. Therefore such action would injure the Illinois Central but would have no material effect upon Pullman. Harahan appealed for men to fill the places of the strikers, promising to give preference to former employees who had been laid off because of the depression.[40] Some Illinois Central workers decided that Harahan's position made sense. At Cherokee, Iowa, twenty-two engineers and firemen publicly rejected an appeal from Eugene Debs to join in the boycott. They said:

> We have always been well treated by the Company. When grievances existed, we have

> had them adjusted to our entire satisfaction. We do not work for the Pullman Company and think this strike unjust and uncalled for on the Illinois Central System. We propose to remain with our engines and the Company and will do our utmost to protect the Company's property when called on to do so.[41]

Similar action was taken by the local lodges of the Order of Railway Conductors at Freeport and at Jackson, Tennessee, and by engineers and firemen at Centralia and Cairo.[42] When a few employees at McComb City, Mississippi, set up a local unit of the American Railway Union, the rest of the men joined it and then promptly voted to abolish the organization.[43] In the midst of the strike, Harahan wrote Fish that it was "very gratifying" to know that there were "so many loyal men in the service." He said that the aid of these men was a great help to the management "in putting down the uprising of some of the Company's employees."[44] Although more than 3,500 Illinois Central employees ceased work at one time another during the month of July, the company's business was at no time completely abandoned. Officers and clerks did the work of switchmen at several locations, and at Chicago about sixty office workers were sworn in as U.S. deputy marshals in order to protect company property from mob violence.[45] Also, the Illinois Central joined with the other roads belonging to the General Managers' Association in successful efforts to recruit replacements for strikers and to seek legal action against the organizers of the Pullman boycott.[46]

Intervention by the federal government was a decisive factor in turning the tide of battle against the strikers. On July 2, a federal judge issued an injunction commanding the leaders of the American Railway Union and all other persons combining and conspiring with them to cease obstructing the business of the railroads. The next day President Grover Cleveland ordered federal troops into Chicago, over the protests of Governor John Peter Altgeld.[47] An Illinois Central officer hailed these events as "the beginning of the end" of the strike and predicted that the troubles would be over within a few weeks.[48] Stuyvesant Fish agreed that the end was near. The most important thing now, he said, was to see to it that the ring leaders in the strike were apprehended and severely punished. Fish was determined that the strike should be utterly crushed, whatever the cost. He said that fortunately for the Illinois Central,

> our financial position is such that we need have no apprehension as to the future, but rather than yield in any way I would prefer to see a reduction, or even an entire suspension, of dividends on Illinois Central stock; this for the reason that to yield would be to turn over the management of this property to any mob which may at any time be incited to make demands, however unreasonable.[49]

On July 17, Eugene Debs and other A.R.U. officers were arrested on contempt charges because of their defiance of the injunction that had been issued against them. The arrest of the union leaders soon led to the collapse of the boycott and strike movements, which were already faltering.

By July 20, more than 500 Illinois Central shopmen had returned to work at Chicago, and by the end of the month the shop force was back to normal.[50] On July 31, Harahan wrote that thirty firemen in the suburban service were back at work. Seventy firemen remained out, as did seventeen engineers, sixteen conductors, and about forty brakemen.[51] Two days later, Harahan noted that matters were "getting along very well," so well in fact that he took time off from his own company's affairs in order to witness the reopening of the Pullman shops. Many of the Illinois Central's 150 Chicago switchmen now were asking to be re-employed, but Harahan said that he was "going very slowly in taking any of them back, and then only on our own terms, treating them as individuals, without any of the rights or agreements that existed before the strike."[52] Of the nearly 2,000 Illinois Central employees who had been active strikers, about 1,300 were dismissed from the service of the company.[53] Although Harahan denied that the dismissed men subsequently were blacklisted, it is clear that many of them were. J. W. Higgins, superintendent of terminals, drew up a list of 524 names of men who had been fired and who were not to be reemployed by the company. A messenger boy in Higgins' office later testified that not only was the list circulated among Illinois Central officers but also copies marked "private" were sent to every railroad at Chicago. Harahan's denial that blacklisting had occurred probably was based on the fact that the general managers of the

Chicago roads had not conspired to deny jobs to former strikers; instead, they had merely agreed to inform one another of the identity of the strikers and not to hire men who could not secure a clearance from their former employers. To draw such a distinction was entirely fatuous, for the practical result was the same in either case: the strikers were barred from further employment on any of the railroads.[54]

The 1894 strike cost the Illinois Central Railroad $50,000 in claims for freight detained and destroyed, $50,000 in property damages, and $500,000 in lost revenues; cost 1,300 Illinois Central employees their jobs; and cost the American Railway Union its existence. The strike had been an unprecedented test of will between organized labor and organized capital. As an example of workingclass solidarity, the decision by the A.R.U. to boycott Pullman cars had been an inspiration. But as an effort to attain practical ends it was a disaster.[55]

The Bryan Crusade

Throughout its history the Illinois Central

Railroad had refrained from interference in the political activities of its employees. In the 1860's President John Douglas had said that it was "always the rule of this company to allow its employees the greatest freedom and liberty in the exercise of the rights of suffrage," and a decade later William Ackerman had forbidden any officer "to interfere in any manner with any of his employees' political opinions. In the management of a large railway like ours," Ackerman said, "we must let politics and religion alone."[56] But in 1896 the free silver platform of the Democratic Party so alarmed some Illinois Central officers that they found it difficult to restrain themselves. Even Stuyvesant Fish was affected. Fish did not like the platform of the Republican Party because it called for a high protective tariff, which was not in the interest of the railroad industry; Fish therefore viewed the possible election of William McKinley with misgivings. But, he said,

> I prefer bad government to chaos. I may be wrong but Bryan's election holds out to me, first, panic; secondly, repudiation; thirdly, the man on horseback; and fourthly, a despotic form of government.[57]

Many lesser officers shared Fish's fears, and some of them took steps to convince the employees under their charge that a vote for Bryan was a vote for virtual anarchy.

At Cherokee, Iowa, an Illinois Central shop foreman helped to organize a local Republican campaign club into which many railroad employees were enrolled. A few days after the founding of the club, the foreman proudly reported to Master Mechanic T. W. Place that all but two of the machinery department employees at Cherokee had joined the club. And the next day he said that the two "doubtful" men had decided to join after all. "Therefore," he told Place, "you may erase the marks opposite their names."[58] Apparently Place had asked local shop foreman throughout Iowa to poll their men as to their position on the free silver question, for in August he sent the head of the Illinois Central machinery department an elaborate statement of the results of such a survey among the engineers, firemen, and shopmen at Dubuque, Waterloo, Fort Dodge, Cherokee, and Sioux City (see Table 8). The poll showed that an over-

TABLE 8

POLL OF IOWA MACHINERY DEPARTMENT EMPLOYEES

ON THE MONEY QUESTION, AUGUST 1896

Class of Employee	For Gold Standard	For Free Silver	Doubtful	No Vote (under-age or alien)	Total
Dubuque					
Shopmen	57	0	2	3	62
Engineers	4	0	1	0	5
Firemen	5	0	0	0	5
Waterloo					
Shopmen	161	2	19	41	223
Engineers	43	0	0	0	43
Firemen	43	0	0	0	43
Fort Dodge					
Shopmen	36	3	0	0	39
Engineers	19	0	2	0	21
Firemen	14	1	1	0	16
Cherokee					
Shopmen	39	1	2	3	45
Engineers	16	0	0	0	16
Firemen	13	0	1	0	14

TABLE 8--Continued

Class of Employee	For Gold Standard	For Free Silver	Doubtful	No Vote (underage or alien)	Total
Sioux City					
Shopmen	15	0	0	0	15
Engineers	1	0	0	0	1
Firemen	1	0	0	0	1
Grand Total, All Locations					
All	467	7	28	47	549

Source: T. W. Place, Master Mechanic, to W. Renshaw, Superintendent of Machinery, Waterloo, August 23, 1896, IC-1P6.1.

whelming majority of the men at each location backed McKinley and the gold standard. At Sioux City not a single man was listed as pro-Bryan or undecided. It is a matter of conjecture as to whether these figures reflected the real feelings of the men involved or if they merely illustrated the old adage that the better part of valor is discretion. Certainly the employees could not have been unaware of the political preference of their employer. On October 23, the Illinois Central donated $1,000 to the Iowa Republican State Committee.[59] A week later, Master Mechanic Place ordered his foremen to post on shop bulletin boards copies of a statement in which the national president of the Brotherhood of Locomotive Firemen had supported the gold standard. The statement had been sent to Place by Superintendent of Machinery William Renshaw in a confidential letter. Renshaw told Place:

> Of course you will understand that the Officers of this road have not taken any active steps in the political issue of the day [and] neither do we intend to but if you can arrange in your own way to have these circulars posted on bulletin board[s] at terminals it would be the means of showing the firemen, especially[,] of the action and policy of their chief.[60]

The Iowa lines were not the only part of the Illinois Central system on which efforts were made to drum up enthusiasm for the anti-Bryan cause. At Champaign, Illinois, the head of the local pro-McKinley club wrote President Fish that he had recruited many employees into his organization, although he vigorously denied a local newspaper's allegation that some men had been coerced into joining. He said:

> We have organized a "Sound Money Club" of the I.C.R.R. employees, now have 132 members and more to follow. . . . In my address last night I . . . told the men if any official had intimidated them into joining this club, to give me their names and I would make it known to you personally, That I was personally acquainted with you and knew that you would not tolerate any such action, It was not the intention of any official of this Co to intimidate the employees into voting for either Candidate, Free vote is American's glory and pride, which no vandle hand shall destroy, nor devide. This brought down the house.[61]

The writer went on to say that he was lining up speakers for future club meetings and that he himself would be one of them:

> We have a fight and must give this gigantic "Silver Trust" [such] a slap that it will not stick its head above water for a hundred years to come. I am requested to roast Debs, as I was Secy of the A.R.U. and refused to call the men out but kept them in the ser-

> vice. I am capable of replying to Mr. Debs. . . . My attack on Altgeld and Debs will not be of abuse or ridicule. The question must be brought to the boys in a clear truthful manner, so they can look at these gentlemen both ways.[62]

Similar efforts to influence the political allegiance of Illinois Central workers were made in the state of Mississippi and also at St. Louis, where a company agent wrote Fish that he had mustered 400 employees for a sound money parade held shortly before the election.[63]

Not all company officers believed that it was wise for the railroad to meddle in the politics of its men. General Solicitor James Fentress was an outspoken opponent of all such activity. In August 1895, Fentress advised Fish not to distribute sound money leaflets under company auspices, although he thought it would be all right to make a list of Illinois Central employees available to a committee of the New York Chamber of Commerce which was disseminating this propaganda.[64] A year later, when the governor of Mississippi complained to Fentress that some railroad officers in his state were interfering in the politics of their men, Fentress asked Fish to support him in putting a stop to such activity. Fentress pointed out that the Illinois Central had extensive mileage in states that were certain to be carried by Bryan and that it would be foolish to arouse dissension within the company and antagonism among customers by becoming involved in politics.[65] Fentress tried to restrain the activity of pro-McKinley officers on the Iowa lines by ordering them to make it clear that they were acting only as individuals and not on behalf of the company. Of these officers, Fentress wrote:

> They all denied to me that they had mixed the Company in, but I insisted that when they talked with any of the men under them that they should explicitly state that the Company had nothing to do with politics, and what they stated was their own individual opinion, and that every man had a right to his own views, and that he would not be prejudiced in any way, no matter which political party he was with, nor how active he was in its interest, provided he discharged his duties to this Co.[66]

In the middle of October, Fentress wrote Fish a detailed explanation and defense of his actions. He said that although his restraint of some officers had resulted in wounded feelings, he was convinced that much good had resulted. He said that in his opinion "there would not have been a single ballot by any self respecting employee in favor of the republican ticket had it not been that partisan officers wisely changed their attitude to one of personal influence rather than railroad officers' coercion." Fentress added that he himself did not like the platform of either party but that a victory by neither one would bring disaster or dishonor.[67]

Although Fish did not share Fentress' disinterest in the outcome of the election, he did support the latter's efforts to halt the coercion of employees. The results of the election subsequently showed that Fentress' position had been as sound as a McKinley dollar. In the ten states served by the Illinois Central Railroad, the Republican Party attracted many more votes than it had in 1892. Fish considered the election statistics very gratifying, and in passing them on to another officer he showed that Fentress had taught him caution in political matters: he marked his letter "confidential" and advised its recipient not to publicize the material it contained, "as it might look as if the Corporation had been taking an interest in politics."[68]

[1]Corliss, Main Line of Mid-America, p. 243.

[2]Ibid., p. 261.

[3]A. G. Bruen to Stuyvesant Fish, President, Chicago, May 17, 1897, IC-1F2.2, gives the wage statistics shown in Table 7. Bruen's figures on the pay of laborers in Illinois and Iowa are corroborated by the papers of Roadmaster F. R. Doty, IC-1D6.1, which include dozens of letters discussing the pay of section laborers.

[4]C. A. Beck, General Manager, to J. G. Metcalfe, General Manager of Louisville and Nashville Railroad, Chicago, July 15, 1890, IC-1B4.1.

[5]Bruen to John C. Welling, Auditor, Chicago, May 16, 1891, IC-1W3.3. James T. Harahan, Second Vice-Pres. [and General Manager], to Fish, Chicago, November 10, 1891, IC-1F2.2.

[6]I.C.R.R., Schedule of Wages of Locomotive Engineers and Firemen, 1892 (n.p., n.d.), IC-3.93, gives the new schedules.

[7][F. B. Harriman], Supt., to T. W. Place, Master Mechanic, Dubuque, December 31, 1895, IC-1P6.1, giving monthly earnings of fireman W. T. Wood from June 1890 to June 1895.

[8]Place to A. C. Goodrich, General Manager of K[eokuk] and W[estern] Railroad, Waterloo, October 21, 1896, IC-1P6.1, mentions that Illinois Central firemen average 57 per cent of engineers' pay on passenger runs, 58 per cent on freight runs.

[9]Beck to Harahan (then General Manager of Louisville New Orleans and Texas Railroad), Chicago, June 14, 1890, IC-1B4.1, and Beck to A. W. Sullivan, General Superintendent, Chicago, June 17, 1890, IC-1B4.1, deal with demands at Memphis. Beck to J. N. Henry, Yardmaster, Chicago, September 9, 1890, IC-1B4.1, and Beck to Sullivan, Chicago, September 10, 1890, IC-1B4.1, mention petitions from Decatur, Clinton, Bloomington, Minonk, La Salle, Amboy, Freeport, Rockford, Springfield, and Gilman. Beck to M. E. Mayer and H. M. Shull, Chicago, Sep-

tember 30, 1890, IC-1B4.1, mentions demands at Champaign, Centralia, and Du Quoin. See also copy of petition from switchmen at Dubuque, Waterloo, and Sioux City, [ca. October 24, 1890], IC-1B4.1.

[10]Harahan to Fish, Chicago, February 14, 1893, IC-1F2.3.

[11]Beck to Sullivan, Chicago, June 17, 1890, IC-1B4.1.

[12]Beck to Harahan, Chicago, June 14, 1890, IC-1B4.1. In 1892 the Memphis switchmen again petitioned for an increase, but Beck obtained the support of other Memphis railroads in refusing this request. Harahan to Fish, Chicago, February 26, 1892, IC-1F2.2.

[13]Harahan to George Hough, E. M. Hutchinson, H. S. Isaacs, J. H. Phillips, and W. C. Walsh, committeemen of I.C. switchmen in Chicago terminal district, Chicago, March 9, 1893, IC-1F2.2.

[14]Harahan to Fish, Chicago, February 25, 1893; February 27, 1893; March 8, 1893, IC-1F2.2.

[15]Harahan to Fish, Chicago, August 21, 1893, IC-1F2.2.

[16]James Fentress, General Solicitor, to Fish, New Orleans, November 7, 1892, IC-1F2.2. Harahan to Fish, New Orleans, November 12, 1892, IC-1F2.2.

[17]Fentress to Fish, Chicago, December 23, 1892, IC-1F2.2. W. H. Miller, U.S. Attorney General, to Levi P. Morton, Vice Pres. of U.S., Washington, December 27, 1892, IC-1F2.2. Farrar and Leake, Local Attorneys, to Fish, New Orleans, December 27, 1892, IC-1F2.2.

[18]*New Orleans Times-Democrat*, March 26, 1893, clipping in IC-1F2.2.

[19]Welling to Fish, September 12, 1892, IC-1F2.2.

[20]Harahan to Fish, Chicago, March 11, 1893, IC-1F2.2.

[21]Harahan to Fish, Chicago, January 28, 1894, IC-1F2.2.

[22]Harahan to Fish, Chicago, September 8, 1893, IC-1F2.2.

[23]"Meeting with Committee of Train-men, in Second Vice President's Office, Chicago, February 1st, 1894," IC-1F2.2.

[24]Harahan to Fish, Chicago, February 12, 1894, IC-1F2.2.

[25]Fentress to Fish, Chicago, February 5, 1894, IC-1F2.2.

[26]Harahan to Fish, New Orleans, February 22, 1895, IC-1F2.2.

[27]Stuyvesant Fish, _Statement to the U.S. Industrial Commission_ (n.p., 1899), pp. 11-12.

[28]_Ibid._, p. 13.

[29]U.S. Strike Commission, _Report on the Strike of June-July, 1894_, Senate Executive Document No. 7 (Washington: Government Printing Office, 1895), pp. xxxiii, 79, 550, 564, 611. Almont Lindsey, _The Pullman Strike: The Story of a Unique Experiment and of a Great Labor Upheaval_ (Chicago: University of Chicago Press, 1942), pp. 92-122.

[30]U.S. Strike Commission, _Report_, pp. 6, 58, 80, 87-94, 134-35, 590.

[31]_Chicago Tribune_, June 27, 1894, clipping in IC-1F2.2.

[32]Fentress to Fish, Chicago, June 23, 1894, IC-1F2.2.

[33]Harahan to Fish, Chicago, June 23, 1894, IC-1F2.2.

[34]Fentress to Fish, Chicago, June 28, 1894, IC-1F2.2.

[35]Fentress to Fish, Chicago, June 27, 1894, IC-1F2.2. Harvey Wish, "The Pullman Strike: A Study in Industrial Warfare," Illinois State Historical Society _Journal_, XXXII (September, 1939), 293.

[36]Fentress to Fish, Chicago, June 27, 1894, IC-1F2.2. Harahan to Fish, Chicago, June 28, 1894, IC-1F2.2. _Chicago Herald_, June 28, 1894, clipping in IC-1F2.2.

[37]_Chicago Herald_, July 2, 1894, clipping in IC-1F2.2. John Dunn, Assistant to Pres., to Fish, Chicago, July 2, 1894; July 3, 1894, IC-1F2.2. Sullivan to J. H. Bilbert, Sheriff of Cook County, T. E. Milchrist, U.S. District Attorney, J. P. Hopkins, Mayor of Chicago, and J. W. Arnold, U.S. Marshal, Chicago, July 6, 1894, IC-1F2.2.

[38]Harahan to Fish, Chicago, June 28, 1894, IC-1F2.2. _Chicago Inter-Ocean_, July 2, 1894, clipping in IC-1F2.2. Dunn to Fish, Chicago, July 3, 1894, IC-1F2.2. Dunn to A. G. Hackstaff, Secretary, Chicago, July 5, 1894, IC-11N1.3.

[39]_Bloomington Weekly Pantagraph_, June 29, 1894. _Chicago Inter-Ocean_, July 2, 1894, clipping in IC-1F2.2. J. F. Duncombe, Attorney, to Fentress, Fort Dodge, July 11, 1894, IC-1F2.2.

[40]Harahan to I.C. employees, Chicago, June 27, 1894, IC-1F2.2.

[41]Harahan to Fish, Chicago, July 1, 1894, IC-1F2.2, quoting statement sent Eugene V. Debs by Cherokee enginemen.

[42]Harahan to I.C. employees, Chicago, July 2, 1894, IC-1F2.2.

[43]Harahan to Fish, Chicago, July 31, 1894, IC-1F2.2.

[44]Harahan to Fish, Chicago, July 12, 1894, IC-1F2.2.

[45]Sullivan estimated that 1,990 employees were strikers and that another 1,609 quit work "through intimidation or persuasion of the strikers." U.S. Strike Commission, Report, p. 326. Eleven documents relating to the volunteer guards are located in IC-2.91. That the strike did not totally cripple the railroad is apparent from the fact that total train movements in July 1894 were down only 25 per cent from those of July 1893. Dunn to Fish, Chicago, August 7, 1894, IC-1F2.2.

[46]Fentress to Fish, Chicago, June 28, 1894, IC-1F2.2. M. J. Carpenter, Treasurer of committee of General Managers' Association, to Harahan, Chicago, June 29, 1894, IC-1W3.3. U.S. Strike Commission, Report, pp. 250, 271.

[47]U.S. Strike Commission, Report, pp. 48-49. Harry Barnard, Eagle Forgotten: The Life of John Peter Altgeld (Indianapolis: Bobbs-Merrill Co., 1938), pp. 306-310.

[48]Dunn to Fish, Chicago, July 3, 1894, IC-1F2.2.

[49]Fish to Welling, New York, June 29, 1894, IC-1W3.3.

[50]Daily letters from Dunn to Fish, Chicago, July 19-August 1, 1894, IC-1F2.2, give the number of men back at work each day.

[51]Harahan to Fish, Chicago, July 31, 1894, IC-1F2.2.

[52]Harahan to Fish, Chicago, August 2, 1894, IC-1F2.2.

[53]U.S. Strike Commission, Report, p. 328.

[54]Harahan to Fish, Chicago, June 29, 1896, IC-1F2.2, denies blacklisting. William J. Strong, "Blacklisting: The New Slavery," The Arena, XXI (March,

1899), 273-292, includes a facsimile of a part of Higgins' list and quotes the testimony of the office boy, Norman Ford. Some blacklisted men sued the Illinois Central for damages, but the Illinois State Supreme Court ruled that the railroads had the lawful right to inform one another of the identity of the strikers. See Fentress to Fish, Chicago, February 24, 1896; April 19, 1897; November 17, 1898; October 27, 1899, and accompanying briefs and other documents in IC-1F2.2.

[55]On the cost of the strike to the Illinois Central, see U.S. Strike Commission, Report, p. 330.

[56]John M. Douglas, Pres., to J. W. Merritt, Chicago, October 31, 1866, IC-1D7.1. William K. Ackerman, Pres., to Edward T. Jeffery, General Supt., Chicago, October 5, 1878, IC-1A2.1.

[57]Fish to Duncombe, New Orleans, October 28, 1896, IC-1F2.2.

[58]T. F. Shannon, Foreman, to Place, Cherokee, August 16, 1896, IC-1P6.1. See also Shannon to T. W. Knicely, Master Mechanic, Cherokee, August 16, 1896, IC-1P6.1. An "Illinois Central Sound Money Club" was organized at Waterloo, and both the Cherokee and Waterloo clubs distributed campaign badges which had been obtained through Illinois Central officers. H. S. Reynolds to E. H. Harriman, Waterloo, September 9, 1896, IC-1P6.1. C. K. Dixon, Supt., to Welling, Cherokee, August 16, 1896, IC-1P6.1.

[59]Dunn to Fish, Chicago, October 23, 1896; October 31, 1896, IC-1F2.2.

[60]William Renshaw, Supt. of Machinery, to Place, Chicago, October 29, 1896, IC-1P6.1.

[61]J. A. Reeves, Pres. of Sound Money Club, to Fish, Champaign, September 15, 1896, IC-1W3.3.

[62]Ibid.

[63]Fentress to Fish, n.p., September 3, 1896, IC-1F2.2. C. S. Parker, General Agent, to Fish, St. Louis, November 2, 1896, IC-1F2.2.

[64] Fentress to Fish, Chicago, August 10, 1895, IC-1F2.2. Francis L. Chrisman of Special Committee on Sound Financial Legislation of New York State Chamber of Commerce, to Fish, New York, August 7, 1895, IC-1F2.2.

[65] Fentress to Fish, n.p., September 3, 1896, IC-1F2.2. Two weeks later when the Mississippi Railroad Commission ordered a cut in railroad tariffs, Fentress viewed that action as retaliation for political meddling by the railroads. Fentress to Fish, n.p., September 18, 1896, IC-1F2.2.

[66] Fentress to W. J. Knight, Attorney at Dubuque, n.p., October 7, 1896, copy in IC-1F2.2.

[67] Fentress to Fish, Chicago, October 13, 1896, IC-1F2.2. Five weeks later in discussing hostile public sentiment towards railroads in Iowa, Fentress said, "It is undoubtedly true that some of our officers and employees went entirely too far in the late election." Fentress to Fish, Chicago, November 20, 1896, IC-1F2.2.

[68] Fish to Welling, New York, November 9, 1896, IC-1W3.3.

CHAPTER VI

A MODERN INDUSTRIAL ENVIRONMENT

While dramatic events capture newspaper headlines and become enshrined in history books, some important developments take place so gradually as to be unheralded by contemporaries and unnoticed by historians. To the railroad worker of the 1890's such events as the Pullman boycott and the Bryan crusade were important, yet they did not affect him to the same degree as did the continued quiet evolution of his working environment.

Personnel Management and Discipline

By 1890 the Illinois Central had already attained a high degree of rationalization in its personnel policies. Therefore, most development in this area between 1890 and 1900 merely continued and extended earlier innovations. For example, the policy of requiring train employees to pass a visual examination, an innovation of 1886, was given wider application in the 'nineties. In 1892 all master mechanics and trainmasters were supplied with materials with which to test the color perception of job seekers and they were ordered to refer all doubtful cases to a company physician for a definitive examination.[1] In 1896 a company surgeon travelled over the southern lines, checking the vision of train employees in the same way that the men of the Illinois and Iowa lines had been tested ten years before. General Manager Harahan considered this action necessary because of the increased speed of trains and the growing use of block signals. He later reported to President Fish that the examinations "resulted in removing from the service quite a number of employees whose visual powers and color perception was not normal."[2] At about this same time, according to Harahan, the company "adopted a system of physical examination to determine whether applicants for employment are physically sound in every particular. Those failing are rejected."[3] By 1898 all applicants for employment as station agents, telegraphers, engineers, firemen, hostlers, conductors, collectors, baggagemen, brakemen, porters, switchmen, and towermen were required to pass a thorough examination of their vision, color perception, hearing, and general physical condition.[4] Another innovation of the 1880's that saw further development was the practice of giving formal examinations to firemen seeking promotion to the position of locomotive engineer. In 1891 the practice was instituted of requiring firemen to try for advancement even if they were not inclined to do so. Moreover, any fireman who failed the examination twice was dismissed from the company's service.[5] Presumably such testing was a fairer way to determine promotions than was the old method in which master mechanics had simply relied upon their own judgment. But abuse was still possible. In 1896 the superintendent of machinery wrote a master mechanic about two troublesome firemen who were about to take the examination:

> I do not propose to make engineers of either Brown or Fluent, and to prevent discussion or comment it is better to make the examination sufficiently severe to prevent their passing.[6]

One of the few real innovations of the 1890's was the inauguration of a new system of wage payment. Since its earliest days the Illinois Central had always paid its employees in cash. Each month the paymaster travelled over the lines in a special car, often carrying thirty or forty thousand dollars in coin and currency. An engineer on the Iowa lines recalled that when the day arrived for the pay car to reach Waterloo, the local merchants kept special hours "in order that the boys [might] spend their money," and there was "a greater celebration than the fourth of July."[7] Similar scenes occurred at many another railroad town on the Illinois Central system. But in the 'nineties this bit of Americana came to an end, as payment by check was introduced first on the northern and then on the southern lines. Employees in Illinois and Iowa ceased to receive cash beginning with the payrolls for May 1896.[8] For a time company officers hesitated to abandon cash payments in the South, where there were relatively few banks and where it was feared that local merchants would insist on discounting the checks, especially when they were presented by black employees. The superintendent of the southern lines said:

> In considering this question it must be born in mind that the conditions south of the [Ohio] river are not so favorable for doing business in the way proposed as they are north of the river for the reason that a very large percentage of our employes are illiterate, a great many of them being negroes, and among certain classes of business men in the south it is considered no sin to rob a negro of every cent possible.[9]

However, in 1897 quarantines resulting from a yellow fever epidemic necessitated payment by check as a temporary expedient, and when the emergency had passed company officers decided that they might as well make the system permanent. There were some difficulties. When checks were first issued at New Orleans, the local treasurer reported that the men "flocked to the bank in droves," making it "unable to transact any other business" for several days and leaving the place "smelling anything other than like otter [_sic_] of roses."[10] Yet soon the new system was taken for granted. Not all steps toward rationalization were accepted so easily.

In the 'nineties there was considerable indication that many railroad employees were bothered by their increasingly formalized, impersonal working environment. When a railroad executive rhapsodized in the public prints about the happy lot of railroad workers, one not-so-happy worker was incensed by his assertion that all railroad men would be well off if they would only cease drinking and gambling. The worker defended the railroaders' inalienable right to the pursuit of happiness ("The above men are flesh and blood . . . and if they want to enjoy themselves I guess they will") and he claimed that their jobs were "not what they are cracked up to be." He said:

> The engineers and firemen have to get their scrappy engines over the road without making a smoke. . . . The engineer must keep his engine machinery just so and the fireman must keep this engine clean. . . . The passenger conductor can't take a 5-cent fare without being spotted. The freight conductor and brakeman have to run over icy cars on which a misstep means death, or worse than that, mangled so your relatives can't identify you.[11]

In 1893 the Illinois Central introduced the use of turnstiles at its suburban stations in order to halt the embezzlement of cash fares by conductors. This action touched off much public comment and prompted some of the conductors to bemoan the close controls to which they were subjected. In a Chicago newspaper, the disgruntled men said:

> To the Editor: The Conductors of the Illinois Central railroad would like to thank you in a body for the kindness you have shown them. . . .
>
> We do not dare say a word or the "hogs" would chop our heads off for the least provocation. The men would give them the little nickels and dimes if they would pay living wages. . . . They bother the lives nearly out of us with red tape and abuse. We are treated more like cattle than men. Tell them to take off their spotters, take off their cash-fare slips, take off the man they call an "inspector," take down the turnstiles, do away with their immense ball of red tape, and you can gamble on it the men will do the square thing by the road.[12]

Many employees longed for the bygone days when personal relationships between officers and men had been more common than they now were. Some men still felt strong attachment to certain officers and were upset when the upper echelons of management disturbed customary relationships. Thus in 1892 a New Orleans newspaper reported widespread demoralization among employees on the southern lines as a result of a management shake-up in which several officers had been displaced.[13] More serious discontent arose in the summer of 1890 when the firing of Trainmaster C. A. Berry of the Chicago division touched off a strike by conductors, brakemen, and switchmen which halted traffic on the division for four days and cost the company some $80,000 in lost earnings. An officer who investigated the circumstances of the strike described it as "the most unreasonable, senseless, and ill-advised of any" that he had ever heard of. He said that the men knew perfectly well that any time they presented a grievance it would be looked into but that meanwhile the trains should continue running. The officer was at a loss to explain why the strike had occurred; he noted that it had not been sanctioned by any labor organization. He could only point to two factors that had contributed to the trouble. He said that his investigation showed:

> 1st. That some of the complaints . . . were not founded on facts, but from rumor or hearsay evidence.
> 2nd. That some of the men were uneasy and irritable under reasonable restraint, evincing a peculiar sensitiveness at being corrected or reprimanded for fault or for neglect of duty by acts of commission or omission.[14]

Evidently some employees were much discomfitted by the rationalized, bureaucratic personnel policies of the modern era.

By the mid-1890's, disciplinary procedures on the Illinois Central had become thoroughly rationalized. Printed forms were used both for providing references for workers leaving the employ of the company under "honorable" circumstances and for recording the names of men who were dismissed.[15] The latter form was in essence a sophisticated form of blacklisting. Whenever a man was fired, copies of a form giving his name and a brief notation on the reasons for his discharge were sent to the first and second vice-presidents, the chief engineer, the superintendent of machinery, the superintendent of lines, the superintendent of telegraph, and to each division superintendent, "these officers in turn to notify those under them who employ men."[16] The causes for dismissals were much the same as in earlier decades: negligence resulting in accidents, habitual drunkenness, insubordination, repeated garnishment of wages, embezzlement or theft, poor workmanship, and--in a few cases--labor agitation.[17] Less serious offenses usually were punished by means of formal reprimands or temporary suspensions. On the Iowa lines, for example, locomotive engineers were suspended for from five to fifteen days for such things as carrying unauthorized persons in the locomotive cab, scratching the side of a train, and running at excessive speeds.[18] After serious accidents or upon the request of committeemen from the railroad brotherhoods, local company officers organized themselves into formal "boards of inquiry," which took the testimony of witnesses in an effort to ascertain appropriate disciplinary measures.[19] In a typical case, a board of inquiry composed of Master Mechanic T. W. Place and Trainmaster G. R. Turner concluded that a derailment in which engineer J. C. Payne suffered a broken leg had been caused by the negligence of switchman C. C. Gardner, who had failed to properly secure a switch lever, and of Payne himself, who had been on the wrong side of his cab and therefore had not seen that the switch was improperly set. The board recommended that Gardner and Payne be suspended for fifteen and thirty days, respectively.[20] In another case, a board of inquiry conducted a thorough inquiry into the disappearance of some watermelons from a freight car at Iowa Falls. The investigation was conducted with all the solemnity of a military court martial and resulted in suspensions for all of the train crew except for the engineer, who had refused to take a slice of melon brought to him by the fireman. The engineer testified, incidentally, that he was sure that his fireman had never committed such an offense before, because "a man couldnt have a melon on the engine without my seeing the seeds when it came daylight."[21]

A most significant disciplinary innovation of the 1890's was the introduction of the "Brown System," named after its originator, George R. Brown of the Fall Brook Railway.[22] Under this system, when an employee was given a suspension he no longer was actually dropped from the service for the designated period of time. Instead, it was merely recorded that he had been so disciplined and he was allowed to continue working. If he then succeeded in avoiding any further offenses, he eventually could have his suspension erased. A simple reprimand could be extinguished by three months' good conduct, a five day suspension by six months' good conduct, ten days by nine months, thirty days by twelve months, and sixty days by eighteen months without an infraction. On the other hand, an employee who kept piling one suspension on top of another could expect to be called before a board of inquiry and perhaps be dismissed from the service, even though he had committed no single offense that would in itself warrant dismissal.[23] Major offenses, such as theft, drunkenness, insubordination, and gross misconduct, remained punishable by immediate discharge, and the new system did not involve any change in the operations of the boards of inquiry, which continued to function as before.[24] The Brown system saved the company the bother of replacing suspended men and gave all employees greater employment stability.[25]

Relations with Unions

Perhaps the most striking aspect of the mature industrial environment that had come into existence on the Illinois Central was the relationship which now existed between the company management and the railroad brotherhoods representing engineers, conductors, firemen, and brakemen. In the 'nineties, Illinois Central officers met with the representatives of these organizations whenever the latter requested a conference. Bargaining with unions was now an accepted practice and the railroad officers had learned to approach such matters with tact and skill. When General Superintendent Albert Sullivan had to postpone a meeting with representatives of the brakemen's brotherhood, he saw to it that the union spokesmen received a full and courteous explanation; and when General Manager Harahan had a conference with the Order of Railway Conductors, he was careful to forearm himself with a quantity of statistics showing how much the earnings of the trainmen had increased in the preceding year.[26]

Lower level officers met frequently with committeemen representing the local lodges of the brotherhoods in order to consider grievances arising from disciplinary measures, changes in working conditions, and the interpretation of rules. When a question could not be settled at the local level, it was carried to higher authorities.[27] For example, in 1898 committeemen representing the conductors at

Cherokee objected to their local trainmaster's refusal to allow them extra compensation when they made a run which extended over parts of two operating districts. The conductors felt that such a run should be considered two separate trips, in which case they were entitled to considerably more pay than if it was viewed as one continuous trip. This grievance was taken up first with the division superintendent and then with the general superintendent. It was settled finally in a conference between General Manager Harahan of the Illinois Central and E. E. Clark, national president of the Order of Railway Conductors, at which the original ruling of the local trainmaster was upheld.[28] In most cases it was not necessary to go to such lengths in order to resolve a grievance. For instance, when the run of conductors operating out of Madison, Wisconsin, was extended to Rockford, Illinois, instead of terminating at Freeport as formerly, the general superintendent readily agreed to grant the affected men a special allowance of $10 a month in order to pay for their lodging and breakfast at Rockford.[29]

Although the railroad managers now recognized the major brotherhoods as the legitimate spokesmen for trainmen and enginemen, they did not adopt a similar attitude toward all labor organizations. Stuyvesant Fish perhaps had the American Railway Union in mind when, in testifying before a federal commission, he denounced militant labor organizations that sought to impose their demands upon employers. He made this condemnation while outlining his general views on collective bargaining and on the practicability of government mediation in labor disputes:

> It does not seem to me that disputes over wages form so vital a question as to exclude arbitration, so absolutely and universally as does the maintenance of proper discipline. The duty of safely carrying passengers and freight has been by the State committed to corporations. They cannot share that responsibility with others, much less arbitrate. . . . Wages, on the other hand, have been generally controlled by supply and demand, to the great gain in recent years of the employed. That natural law will always control, except as its operation may be influenced by labor trusts seeking to prevent free men from selling their only capital, labor, in the best market. By labor trusts I do not mean organized labor as exemplified by the Brotherhood of Locomotive Engineers, the Order of Railroad Conductors and like useful and honorable organizations of intelligent railroad men, but the lawless and disorganized bodies of outsiders who know nothing of, and care nothing

> for, either the railroads or the high class of men whom they employ.[30]

In the early 1890's the Order of Railway Telegraphers began enrolling considerable numbers of Illinois Central telegraph operators and train dispatchers. Company officers did not view this development favorably, especially when the Order began pressing the company to cut back somewhat on its long-standing policy of hiring large numbers of young men as telegraphers, paying them only $35 a month while giving them on-the-job training, and then promoting them to the position of dispatcher. At a meeting of company officers in the fall of 1892, the superintendents of the Dubuque and Cherokee divisions said that they had never heard of the O.R.T., but the superintendent of lines in Illinois reported that he was having much difficulty with it. After the officers had discussed the matter,

> Mr. Harahan said he wanted them to keep on teaching telegraphy to students, and to watch the organization and not let it get any more foothold than possible.[31]

Later Harahan decided to deprive the O.R.T. of such foothold as it had already secured. In the spring of 1893, he told Stuyvesant Fish:

> After quite a long fight, we have at last received written assurances from all the Train Despatchers on our road, who have been members of the Order of Railway Telegraphers, that they have withdrawn from it. This leaves our line free, so far as the Despatchers are concerned, of this pernicious Order. We had quite a number who very foolishly joined the order, but they were given to understand that they had to either leave the service or the Order and they concluded that it was to their interest to leave the Order, rather than the service of the company.
>
> This places us now in a very good position to meet any demands which may be made by our Operators and it will have a tendency to prevent demands being made. . . .
>
> This matter was put in the hands of our two Assistant General Superintendents to handle, personally, and they did it very well.[32]

Thus while company officers were friendly to the major brotherhoods or at least recognized their existence as a _fait accompli_, they did not welcome inroads by other labor organizations.

Accidents and Compensation

Through the 'nineties, the Illinois Central labor force continued to suffer the consequences of working in a hazardous environment. More than 350 employees were killed on the job in the years 1888 to 1894, and thousands more sustained disabling injuries.[33] In 1891 the company's personal injury agent reported "a fearful increase" in accidents over the preceding year, a development which he attributed in part to the use of heavier locomotives and the greater speed at which trains were run.[34] In 1894 James Harahan claimed that the steady increase in accidents on the Illinois Central probably was not out of line with the increase in the company's traffic.[35] But even if that was true, the situation was alarming. In the year in which Harahan made his assertion, 51 workers were killed on the job, 22 received injuries requiring the amputation of arms or legs, 40 suffered broken limbs, and 118 sustained other injuries that required surgical attention. In addition, more than 1,000 employees received injuries that were classified as slight.[36] It might be mentioned that some of the latter injuries were minor only in a very relative sense. For example, Harahan once referred to a derailment in which a fireman

> was slightly injured, receiving a cut in the back of the head and on left cheek, 3 or more ribs broken and internal shock reported. He is, however, said to be improving.[37]

Accidents continued to take a heavy toll of life and limb throughout the decade despite the steps which company officers took in an effort to remove their causes.[38]

Through the 1880's, the managers had relied almost entirely upon the strict enforcement of rules and regulations as the means of preventing accidents and injuries. At no time had company officers shown any serious interest in experimenting with technical devices intended to provide greater safety to railroad workers. This indifference is understandable to some degree, in that the officers were busy men and certainly could not have tried out every invention that was brought to their attention. Nevertheless, it must be said that had progress depended upon the Illinois Central, it is by no means clear that such valuable innovations as air brakes, automatic couplers, and block signals would ever have been given a trial. Even when devices had been proved workable and worthwhile through use on other railways, the Illinois Central was slow to adopt them.

Not until 1890 did the Illinois Central

consider the installation of "telltales," strips of leather or rope hung over the track as a warning to trainmen to look out for low bridges or other obstructions. By this time, according to General Manager C. A. Beck, the device had long been in use on the Pennsylvania, the Burlington, the Chicago and Northwestern, the Chicago Minneapolis and St. Paul, "and no doubt a great many other first class railroads."[39] Yet it was only after decades of deaths and injuries that the Illinois Central at last decided to utilize this simple device. There was only one invention in which the Illinois Central was something of a pioneer: the automatic, electrically operated block signal, a device which was far superior to the old-fashioned signal operated by a towerman and thus subject to human error. But when the company decided to install automatic signals at Chicago in 1893 it was not so much to improve safety as to expedite the handling of the huge volume of traffic generated by the World's Fair of that year.[40]

The company adopted two other safety

devices only because of legal compulsion. In 1890 and 1893, respectively, the Iowa legislature and then the U.S. Congress enacted statutes ordering that railroad cars be equipped with air brakes and automatic couplers.[41] Although the Illinois Central joined with other railroads in successful efforts to postpone the implementation of these laws, it had no choice but to conform to them.[42] In 1890 the company installed air brakes on 100 locomotives and 1500 freight cars.[43] By June 1896, it had equipped 7,616 cars with automatic brakes and it also had outfitted 7,535 cars with automatic couplers, but that still left nearly two-thirds of the company's rolling stock without one or both of these appliances.[44] Two years later, 64 per cent of the cars had safety couplers, but only 46 per cent had as yet been fitted with air brakes.[45] In 1899 the Illinois Central equipped the last of its cars with automatic couplers, but it continued to use cars not equipped with safety brakes until into the twentieth century.[46] During the years in which some cars had air brakes and some did not, the cars equipped with the device had to be grouped together at the forward end of trains in order that their air hoses could be connected. Railroad officials found that if at least one-fifth of the cars on a train were fitted with air brakes, it was possible for the engineer to control his train by using them, so long as the regular brakemen stood ready to assist him, if the need arose, by screwing on the manual brakes of the rear cars. The simultaneous use of both the old and the new systems of braking required careful coordination, for if the engineer released the automatic brakes before the brakemen released the manual brakes, the rear part of the train would break off from the front portion.[47]

The interest of the railroad managers in safety devices was increased as a result of the weakening of the legal barriers which had in the past excused railroad companies from liability to many injured employees. For example, the courts had always held that the possibility of losing a finger while operating a link-and-pin coupler was an "assumed risk" inherent in the occupation of a brakeman or switchman, but there was some question as to whether such rulings made sense now that automatic couplers were readily available. It happened that laws required the Illinois Central to introduce automatic couplers before judicial doctrine changed, but there was at least one safety device which the company began using as a direct result of judicial decisions. The device was the safety frog, a mechanism which prevented workers from getting their feet caught at places where one rail crossed over another. In 1894 chief attorney James Fentress urged the installation of the new frogs because judges were beginning to hold that railroads were negligent if they did not use them. Fentress told Harahan that there occurred on the Illinois Central "a good many accidents where the switchmen and others claim that their feet have been caught in the frogs" and so he considered it important to call attention

> to the fact that we are almost certain to lose cases where the party's foot has been caught in an unblocked frog, before juries; and that the courts are hesitating more and more in holding that it is not necessarily negligence on the part of the company in leaving the frogs unblocked.[48]

In the 1890's several state legislatures considered the enactment of bills that would have increased employer liability by weakening or voiding altogether the doctrines of assumed risk, fellow servant, and contributory negligence. As might be expected, such bills were opposed by railroad officers. James Fentress wrote numerous letters in which he condemned bills of this kind when they were proposed in the state legislatures of Illinois, Louisiana, Kentucky, Mississippi, and Tennessee. Although the fellow servant doctrine actually had not been formulated until nearly the middle of the nineteenth century, Fentress maintained that if Tennessee passed a law abolishing that doctrine it would "overturn a principle of law which has obtained for centuries the approval of all right-minded men."[49] And when Illinois considered enacting a similar statute he said, "It is always unwise for legislators to rush into the delicate china-shop of settled law that has been built up by centuries of wise men, and arbitrarily upset things."[50] Fentress also used pragmatic arguments. In opposing the Illinois bill he said that the fellow servant doctrine was sound law because it made it to the interest of workmen to see that their fellow employees did their jobs in a proper manner.[51] When the Louisiana legislature considered voiding the fellow servant rule, Fentress said simply that the rule was "founded upon reason and right" and that to make the state "the guardian for employees as against the corporation" was "wrong in principle and reason."[52] When the state of Mississippi considered a bill to modify the contributory negligence doctrine, Fentress condemned the bill as unreasonable and he also maintained that it was discriminatory because it applied only to railroads rather than to all employers. He lamented the fact that in many states the courts were "stretching away and away from this doctrine, and, like the blind Sampson, pulling down the posts which uphold the great structure of law established by the ages."[53]

Although Fentress was strongly opposed to employer liability legislation, he was even more opposed to the use of bribery or corruption to prevent the enactment of such laws. He instructed the company's local attorneys in Mississippi to make it clear to all parties concerned that the Illinois Central would not cooperate in any way with any persons who might desire to "form a lobby or in any manner directly or indirectly to corrupt members of the legislature." He said that if the legislature passed a law, even one "which we think is ruinous, then we propose to submit to it." He continued:

> From 1876 up to the present time there has been much legislation in Mississippi granted to Companies connected with the Illinois Central Railroad; and, as I had charge of most of it, I can state, as a fact, that not one cent was ever offered or paid or asked, and that everything was done openly and honestly and fearlessly. And so, I trust, it will be, as long as the State and the Railroad Company exist.[54]

Fentress gave similar instructions to attorneys in Kentucky. He said, "It would be our duty, where we thought the Company was being hurt, to represent the facts. . . . But when that is done we are done." He insisted that the local attorneys must do nothing

> to give the slightest coloring to the idea that we were adopting the well-known policy of the Louisville and Nashville Road, in maintaining a lobby, or attempting improperly to influence legislation.[55]

Fentress claimed that other company officers supported him in his opposition to lobbying in the southern states. He said:

> I have been the General Solicitor of the Illinois Central Railroad over its Southern Lines since 1877; and I know of what I speak, that matters of legislation were left to the Legal Department, and that the President of the Company and the Board of Directors agreed promptly and consistently with the views of the General Solicitor, that no matter what wrong we might suffer, it was essentially wrong for the Company or its officers to engage in a lobby, or to assist in maintaining a lobby, or to do anything that would have a tendency to corrupt legislation.56

While Fentress forbade lobbying in the states under his jurisdiction, he does not seem to have been upset by the fact, apparently well known to him, that the Illinois Central did engage in such activity elsewhere. He once remarked to Stuyvesant Fish that within Illinois

> Mr. Dunn and others have heretofore dealt with legislators, &c.
>
> Of course you understand that the Legislature of Illinois are [sic] very far in advance of any of the other Legislatures along our system of roads on the line of being generally on the make and ready to trade honor for money, law for filthy lucre. It may be the others will progress to the same degree of proficiency in these evil lines; but when they do, you can deal with each particular case as it arises.57

The Mr. Dunn to whom Fentress referred was John Dunn, assistant to the president of the Illinois Central. That Dunn had no compunctions about lobbying is evident in his remarks to another company officer at a time when the Illinois state legislature was considering an employer liability bill:

> As you know, for some years past we have had an arrangement in the Senate whereby a good deal of this legislation could be blocked. Nothing of this sort exists now and we are subject to the passage of such legislation in both houses. . . .
>
> I would strongly urge you to see Mr. Goddard [of the Burlington Railroad] and have a talk with him without delay about these matters. If no understanding can be arrived at we must certainly have some one down there to represent our co. independently.[58]

Although the vigorous action of John Dunn and the gentler suasion of James Fentress helped to stop some employer liability legislation, enough laws were passed to affect significantly the Illinois Central's expenditures for personal injury suits.[59] In 1899 the company's chief claim agent reported that in the fiscal year ended June 30 the corporation had paid out $52,564 in order to settle personal injury cases involving 1,833 employees. That was nearly double the amount expended the year before, in which a total of $26,902 had been paid to 411 injured men. The claim agent cited as a reason for the increase the

> crystallization of prejudice against railroads, fostered, in many places by the bar and judiciary, and encouraged by adverse legislation, which, in certain classes of injuries, deprives the railway of defence, regardless of the recklessness of the injured, and also by the fact that the hitherto protecting plea of fellow servant has, through _judicial legislation_, ceased to be available.[60]

The change in the legal environment was especially marked in Mississippi, where a company official described the employer liability laws as "by all odds the worst in any state in which we operate." The official told Stuyvesant Fish of a case in which an engineer named Lilly had been killed at McComb City when his train ran into some cars that had rolled from a siding because another employee had failed to set their brakes properly. The officer said that the local attorney at Hazlehurst recommended that inasmuch as the fellow-servant doctrine no longer applied in Mississippi it would be best to settle a suit by Lilly's heirs for

$11,000. The officer added:

> From all I can learn Miller [the local attorney] is one of our best fighters in that State, yet he does not hesitate to recommend the payment of this enormous sum as a compromise.[61]

As the weakening of the old legal defenses made the railroad legally liable to an increased proportion of injured employees, Illinois Central officers became increasingly reluctant to make voluntary donations in those cases where the company was not legally responsible. When Stuyvesant Fish complained about the large increase in personal injury expenditures in 1891 as opposed to the preceding year, James Harahan replied that he had made every effort to hold the costs down. He said:

> I issued instructions on the 20th of November, 1890, which I believe have had the effect of reducing the amounts paid, especially where there was no liability on the part of the company, or where the question of liability was doubtful. . . . I found that it had been the practice of the Personal Injury Agent, on conference with heads of sub-departments, to make vouchers in numbers of cases where the money paid was regarded merely as a donation based upon charity, or upon appreciation of previous meritorious service on the part of the injured employee. Since the date mentioned all such claims have been passed upon by me personally, and only in exceptional cases, approved.[62]

Under special circumstances, donations continued to be allowed. In December 1893, brakeman J. Jordan, who had been injured while trying to put two tramps off a train, was allowed his full wages of $150 for the 107 days that he was incapacitated. Harahan said that it was not customary to allow men more than half-time while laid up as a result of injuries, but that he would make an exception "in view of the peculiar circumstances in this instance."[63] At about this same time, the citizens of Matteson, Illinois, got up a petition asking aid for Mrs. Henry Trautt, the widow of a section hand who had been killed while extinguishing switch lamps in the Chicago yard. Company officers decided to give Mrs. Trautt $75, in view of the fact that her husband had been a "sober, honest, and industrious" employee for six years and that his family was "in very poor circumstances and the children too small to take care of themselves."[64]

While Harahan reduced the practice of making cash donations, he did not alter the company's long-standing policy of furnishing free medical care to men hurt while at work. Thus the Illinois Central continued to give at least the latter assistance to all injured employees. When switchmen at Chicago said that men should also be given half-pay while laid up following accidents, General Manager C. A. Beck denied that assertion and defended the company's existing policy as liberal and humane:

> No fixed general rule relating to the allowance of time by reason of injuries can be established; . . . the cases as they arise must be taken up separately and each considered on its merits. . . .
>
> This Company was one of the first to organize and establish a Surgical Department and it has maintained the same for the benefit of employes at considerable expense. In cases of injury, employes are treated by the Company's surgeon, without expense, and the medical and surgical services so rendered are from surgeons of the highest ability at the different points through which our line passes. . . . This much is done for all employes without reference to legal liability and without compulsion, for the reason that we desire to exercise humane consideration for those in our service who meet with misfortune in the performance of their duties.[65]

When the Illinois Central took over the Chesapeake Ohio and Southwestern Railroad in 1892, it continued to operate a hospital at Paducah, Kentucky, which the C. O. & S.W. had set up some years earlier. The hospital was partly supported by assessments on the wages of employees, a feature which caused some dissatisfaction, especially among white workers, who did not use the facility so much as did the black men.[66]

In the 'nineties some Illinois Central officers toyed once again with the idea of establishing a company-sponsored insurance plan to provide relief for accident victims. But as usual they took no practical steps in that direction. John C. Welling was the leading advocate of the measure, and he presented a report on the subject to Stuyvesant Fish in February, 1896.[67] Fish took enough interest in Welling's plan to make the practical suggestion that any relief fund that might be set up should be kept in New York rather than Chicago, in order to escape taxation and to make it difficult for dissatisfied employees to initiate lawsuits.[68] But there the matter rested. In April Welling wrote Fish that because the railroad was about to start paying the men employed on its northern lines by check rather than in cash it was necessary to make more formal arrangements with the private companies through which some employees obtained insurance.

And, Welling said,

> Before taking up the question with them I would like to know, in a general way, if there is any prospect of our having a Relief Department of our own. In case this question is indefinitely postponed, Mr. Harahan and I agree that we should reduce the number of Insurance Companies now working on the system to two or three good companies, so as to secure a better class of soliciting agents, and also to save much trouble in handling the details.[69]

Apparently the idea of setting up a relief fund had been abandoned, for in 1898 the Illinois Central granted the Railway Officials and Employes' Accident Association of Indianapolis the exclusive privilege of soliciting insurance subscriptions among company employees.[70] By this time, a good many employees were buying insurance, for in October 1897, Welling mentioned that the paymaster deducted about $2,500 a month from company payrolls on behalf of insurance companies.[71] The insurance issued by private companies may have provided adequate protection to many employees on the northern lines, but in the South there was so much difficulty in collecting premiums that Illinois Central officers advised the insurance agents to issue policies only to "the better class of Railway employees, such as Engineers, Firemen and Freight Conductors" and "not to insure any of the colored brakemen" or "men earning very small pay."[72]

Welfare Policies

Since William Ackerman's abortive experiments of the early 1880's, Illinois Central officers had taken no interest in the work of the Young Men's Christian Association among railroad employees. However, in 1896 Stuyvesant Fish granted an interview to Clarence J. Hicks, Railroad Secretary of the International Committee of Y.M.C.A.'s, and afterwards Fish told John Welling that he was beginning to think it would be wise for the company to spend some money to support Y.M.C.A. activity at a few of its relay stations and terminals.[73] Within the year, Fish authorized monthly subsidies of $15, $30, and $50 to Y.M.C.A. workers at East St. Louis, Louisville, and Centralia.[74] When Illinois Central workers at Waterloo asked the railroad to aid them in setting up a gymnasium club and reading room, James Harahan got in touch with a Y.M.C.A. official, who visited Waterloo and persuaded the men to convert their club into a railroad branch of the Y.M.C.A.[75] The Y.M.C.A. officer then suggested that the Illinois Central donate $4,000 towards the cost of erecting at Waterloo a $6,000 building to be equipped with reading room, social facility, library, lecture hall, classrooms, gymnasium, bowling alleys, washrooms, and sleeping rooms.[76] Stuyvesant Fish was unwilling to go that far, but he did authorize a gift of $300 to set the club up in rented quarters and a regular subsidy of $50 a month to pay the salary of a secretary.[77]

Illinois Central officers viewed the company's subsidy of the Y.M.C.A. as an investment in the moral improvement of employees, and they expected that investment to pay dividends. They therefore refused to aid the Y.M.C.A. at Water Valley, Mississippi, because, James Harahan said:

> It is the opinion of our local officers that there is not very much need for such an organization at Water Valley on account of the fact that it is a prohibition town and the people, as a rule, church membered. I am informed that there is no drunkenness or gambling and very little rowdyism to be seen in the town.[78]

At those places where Illinois Central officers did

assist the Y.M.C.A. they seem to have been satisfied with the results, although they realized that workingmen were attracted to the Y.M.C.A. facilities mostly because of the physical amenities available there rather than because of a desire to improve themselves morally or spiritually. At East St. Louis, the local secretary reported that the men took full advantage of the cheap meals, baths, and beds available at the Y.M.C.A. but were not much interested in its other services:

> During the early part of the year Gospel meetings were held . . . but the effect was of such a negative character, especially on the men whom we were most anxious to influence, that it was deemed wise not to continue. . . . We had reason to believe that they made an adjacent saloon their place of resort until the meetings were over, or later, in many cases.79

However, the secretary observed philosophically that "it is, after all, the hand to hand and heart to heart contact that exerts the greatest influence."80 The railroad men seem to have agreed, except that they thought a little glass to glass contact was also desirable.

A major welfare innovation of the 1890's was the inauguration of a program to assist Illinois

Central workers to become stockholders in the corporation by which they were employed. The program was the brainchild of Stuyvesant Fish. As early as 1886, Fish had suggested that "the faithful employes of a corporation" might be "entitled to a share in its profits, beyond and above the mere market price of their labor," and in 1893 he decided to encourage the faithful employees of his own corporation to get their share in the profits by becoming part-owners of the Illinois Central Railroad.[81] Fish's idea of promoting the sale of stock to employees was not viewed with enthusiasm by all Illinois Central officers. John Welling did not object to the idea in principle but he did think it unwise to introduce it at a time when the railroad had just finished convincing several labor organizations that the company could not afford to add to its expenditures.[82] John Dunn feared that the plan would fail because the workingmen would not understand the vagaries of the stock market. He said:

> The difficulty . . . which occurs to my mind is this: A man at the car works wants to buy one share of stock and the price at the time of his application is

> 102; within a week a man at the same bench with him wants to buy a share of stock and at the time when he makes application the price may be 103; and another week passes and another man in the same Department wants to buy a share of stock and the price may have gone down to 101; now, when they compare notes they will find it difficult to understand the causes of this, and as it looks to me this is liable to produce a good deal of confusion and annoyance.[83]

There was, however, a good deal of sentiment in favor of the stock sale plan. A station agent who heard rumors about it was so caught up by the idea that he immediately sat down and wrote President Fish a letter of support. The agent assured Fish that the ownership of stock would make employees more interested in the company. And, he said,

> another reason is that by having all classes of our employees obtain stock it would greatly do away with labor troubles, and would more closely unite the different branches of employees, and would be the means of obtaining a better and more earnest interest in its welfare and be less liable to raise questions or disturbance and if they were raised would be more easily adjusted with those having an interest in the company's welfare in addition to wages paid them for their services than without it.[84]

Once he figured out what the man had said, Fish probably was pleased.

On May 18, 1893, Fish issued a special circular to all Illinois Central employees announcing that the board of directors had authorized him to offer employees the opportunity to invest their savings in Illinois Central stock. Any employee who wished to participate in the plan had only to ask the paymaster to deduct $5.00 or more from his wages each month and apply that sum toward the purchase of a share. As soon as the employee entered the program, the company would buy a share of stock on the open market and then hold it for the employee until his monthly payments had equalled the price that the company had paid for it. The employee would then be issued a stock certificate and could, if he chose, subscribe for another share. While an employee was saving the price of his share, the company would pay him 4 per cent interest on the sums deducted from his wages. Moreover, he was free at any time to withdraw from the plan, in which event he would receive all of the installments that he had paid plus interest.[85]

Within six months, some 300 employees decided to participate in the stock purchase plan.[86] Fish pronounced himself gratified by this show of interest, especially in view of the fact that the Panic of 1893 had meanwhile occurred.[87] Although the number of shares subscribed for by employees rose only very slowly during the succeeding year and a half and actually declined in the latter part of 1895, Fish was not discouraged.[88] He was, however, somewhat concerned by the fact that most of the shares were subscribed for by clerks and office workers rather than by the men of the transportation and road departments.[89] Therefore, in 1896, he appointed M. F. Mogg as a special agent to boost stock sales among trainmen, enginemen, and shopmen. Mogg had served for many years as a paymaster's clerk and had thereby become acquainted with a great many employees.[90] Between April 1896 and October 1897, Mogg succeeded in nearly doubling the number of men participating in the plan, much to the delight of Stuyvesant Fish, who saw to it that the success of his pet program received wide publicity.[91] When asked to explain the benefits of the plan, Fish said that it tended to bring employer and employee closer together. And, he said,

> It also gives those employed in the service a direct, personal interest in the profits of the corporation, [and] affords them a safe investment, at a fair rate of interest, for their savings when deposited in very small sums. This replaces, to a certain extent, the lack of savings banks, which . . . do not exist in the rural districts of the South and West as they do in New York and New England.92

The system which Fish had devised was fair and generous, and probably it did tend to bring about the results which he claimed for it. The only problem was that it involved only a relative handful of the company's workers. Even if we ignore the fact that many of the men who subscribed for stock were officers or clerks, it is clear that the number of workingmen participating in the plan was too small to have a significant effect upon the labor force or to give the workers any role in company affairs. By 1899 about 705 employees were registered on the company's books as the owners of a total of 2,554 shares of Illinois Central stock. At the same the regular stockholders of the corporation numbered 6,526 and owned a total of 599,948 shares.93

***

The Illinois Central worker of the 1890's encountered formal procedures in every aspect of his working environment. When he was hired by the railroad, he was asked for formal references and subjected to a formal medical examination. Once he was employed, his wages and work rules were regulated by a formal agreement between his union and his employer. If he did his job well, he might be promoted on the basis of a formal examination. If he did his job badly, he might be punished through the formal method of discipline-by-record. If he suffered an injustice, he might seek redress through a formal grievance procedure. If he was involved in an accident, he could expect a thorough investigation by a formal board of inquiry. The worker was immersed in a rationalized, bureaucratic system, the like of which had not existed fifty years earlier. It was a new kind of working environment, one that was essentially modern in tone and character.

This environment had come into existence through a half century of evolution, during which the managers of the Illinois Central had learned to combat strikes and to bargain with labor unions; had experimented with accident relief, Y.M.C.A. work, and the sale of stock to employees; and had introduced a chain of managerial innovations stretching from the employment of Pinkerton detectives in the 1850's to the Brown system of discipline in the 1890's. Often the labor policy of the Illinois Central had been affected by external influences, as when war or depression shaped wage policy or when the election of 1896 led to some interference in employee politics. But far more significant in shaping labor policies had been the internal dynamics of the industrial environment. As the Illinois Central had grown into a giant industrial enterprise, its managers had been compelled to develop ever more complex, systematic methods for dealing with all aspects of labor policy. In doing so they had created an industrial environment that was, by the 1890's, strikingly modern.

[1]I.C.R.R., Minutes of Meeting of Superintendents and Heads of Departments Held in the Second Vice-President's Office, Chicago, Illinois, September 12, 13, 14, 1892 (Chicago: Press of Knight Leonard & Co., n.d.), [uncataloged copy in Illinois Central Archives, Newberry Library], p. 117.

[2]James T. Harahan, Second Vice-Pres., to Stuyvesant Fish, Pres., Chicago, September 12, 1896; September 17, 1896, IC-1F2.2. Quotation from September 12 letter.

[3]Harahan to Fish, Chicago, September 12, 1896, IC-1F2.2.

[4]Circular no. 166, issued by Albert W. Sullivan, General Supt., Chicago, February 28, 1898, IC-1 F2.2.

[5]T. W. Place, Master Mechanic, to I. B. Appleton, Secy. to Supt. of Machinery, Waterloo, December 16, 1896, IC-1P6.1. Place to A. T. Dahlin, chairman of grievance committee of Brotherhood of Locomotive Firemen, Waterloo, January 7, 1898, IC-1P2.1.

[6]William Renshaw, Supt. of Machinery, to Place, Chicago, November 21, 1896, IC-1P6.1.

[7]William Place, locomotive engineer, quoted in Waterloo Daily Courier, February 9, 1897, clipping in IC-1F2.2.

[8]John C. Welling, Vice-Pres., to Fish, Chicago, October 1, 1896, IC-1F2.2.

[9]O. M. Dunn, Supt., to R. S. Charles [Jr.], Asst. Paymaster, New Orleans, November 16, 1897, IC-1W3.3.

[10]Charles Jr. to R. S. Charles [Sr.], Local Treasurer, New Orleans, November 13, 1897, IC-1W3.3.

[11]Anonymous letter to the editor, Chicago Herald, March 11, 1893, clipping in IC-1F2.2.

[12]"ALL HATE THE 'CENTRAL': Even the Employes of the 'All Hog' Route Write to the Daily News and Criticize," Chicago Daily News, December 2, 1893, clipping in IC-1F2.2.

[13]New Orleans Daily Truth, March 11, 1892, clipping in IC-1F2.2.

[14]C. A. Beck, General Manager, to Fish, Chicago, July 7, 1890, IC-1B4.1.

[15]Several copies of such forms are located in IC-1D6.1 and IC-1P6.1.

[16]Form enclosed in F. R. Doty, Roadmaster, to Joseph Reed, Supervisor, Amboy, March 18, 1893, IC-1D6.1. All such forms carried these directions.

[17]Examples are scattered through IC-1D6.1, IC-1P6.1, IC-1F2.2, and IC-1W3.3. Doty to Reed, Amboy, March 21, 1893, IC-1D6.1, sends a form noting the dismissal of one switchman described as an "agitator" and two others because of a strike at Clinton.

[18]IC-1P6.1, passim.

[19]I.C.R.R., Minutes of Meeting of Superintendents and Heads of Departments, pp. 102-104.

[20]"Report of Board of Inquiry held at Waterloo on June 13, 1895 case of switch engine #10 derailed in Waterloo yard morning of June 11th and personal injury sustained by engineer J. C. Payne," IC-1P6.1.

[21]Statement of engineer L. Takin, Waterloo, September 25, 1900, IC-1P6.1.

[22]Circular dated November 1, 1897, IC-1F2.2.

[23]"Brown System of Discipline on the Illinois Central Railroad," The Railway and Engineering Review, XXXVII (December 4, 1897), 697-98. U.S. Industrial Commission (1898), Reports (19 vols.; Washington: Government Printing Office, 1900-1902), XVII, 803-804.

[24]Circulars effective November 1, 1897; December 1, 1897; March 1, 1898, IC-1F2.2.

[25]Harahan to Fish, Chicago, November 25, 1897, IC-1F2.2.

[26]Beck to Frank S. Stimson, chairman of committee of trainmen, Chicago, September 6, 1890, IC-1B4.1. Harahan to Welling, Chicago, October 24, 1891, IC-1W3.3.

[27]See section entitled "Grievances: Are committees given prompt hearings, and have superintendents had any trouble in adjusting local grievances?," I.C.R.R., Minutes of Meeting of Superintendents and Heads of Departments, pp. 111-112.

[28]C, B. Fletcher, Trainmaster, to G. W. McDonald, conductor, Cherokee, February 23, 1898, IC-1F2.2. J. A. McGonagle, C. H McCarthy, and A. Harrington, members of local grievance committee of Order of Railway Conductors, to C. K. Dixon, Division Supt., Cherokee, March 8, 1898, IC-1F2.2. Sullivan to J. G. Hartigan, Assistant General Supt., Chicago, April 13, 1898, IC-1F2.2. Harahan to McGonagle, Chicago, June 9, 1898, IC-1F2.2.

[29]Sullivan to Harahan, Chicago, May 18, 1898, IC-1F2.2.

[30]Fish, Statement to the U.S. Industrial Commission, p. 11.

[31]I.C.R.R., Minutes of Meeting of Superintendents and Heads of Departments, pp. 105-107. See also Harahan to Fish, "on line," December 23, 1892, IC-1F2.2.

[32]Harahan to Fish, Chicago, February 18, 1893, IC-1F2.2. See also H. Baker, Division Supt., to Harahan, "on line," February 19, 1893, IC-1F2.2. Harahan to Fish, Chicago, February 20, 1893, IC-1F2.2.

[33]James Fentress, General Solicitor, to Harahan, Chicago, January 17, 1895, IC-1F2.2.

[34]W. R. Head, Personal Injury Agent, to Fentress, n.p., September 11, 1891, IC-1W3.3.

[35]Harahan to Fish, Chicago, February 12, 1894, IC-1W3.3.

[36]"Cases requiring considerable surgical attention for the [fiscal] year ending June 30, 1894," memorandum enclosed in Head to Welling, Chicago, August 16, 1894, IC-1W3.3. Of the seriously injured men, 67 were considered permanently injured. Fentress to Harahan, Chicago, January 17, 1895, IC-1F2.2.

[37]Harahan to Fish, Chicago, July 13, 1899, IC-1F2.2.

[38]At the start of the decade the general manager and the general superintendent conferred on "measures to lessen the number of accidents, by removing, as far as may be possible, the causes that produce them." Beck to Sullivan, Chicago, July 13, 1890, IC-1B4.1. But in 1899 the accident toll was still high: 73 men killed and nearly 3,000 injured. L. L. Losey, Chief Claim Agent, to Fish, Chicago, September 9, 1899, IC-1F2.2, reporting accidents for year ending June 30, 1899.

[39]Beck to L. T. Moore, Chief Engineer, Chicago, July 13, 1890, IC-1B4.1.

[40]Harahan to Fish, Chicago, September 9, 1893, IC-1F2.2. <u>Chicago Tribune</u>, April 17, 1892, clipping in IC-1F2.2.

[41]Beck to Sullivan, Chicago, September 2, 1890, IC-1B4.1, mentions an Iowa law enacted April 5, 1890. A number of items relating to Act of Congress of March 2, 1893, are found in IC-1W3.3. The latter law also required the installation of hand-holds on cars. Sullivan to Fentress, Chicago, July 9, 1895, IC-1F2.2. Fentress to Fish, Chicago, July 10, 1895, IC-1F2.2.

[42]On postponement see Harahan to Fish, Chicago, September 12, 1896, IC-1F2.2. John K. Cowan, Pres. of Baltimore and Ohio R.R., to Fish, Baltimore, November 24, 1897, IC-1F2.2.

[43] Beck to Sullivan, Chicago, July 7, 1890; July 14, 1890, IC-1B4.1.

[44] Harahan to Fish, Chicago, September 12, 1896, IC-1F2.2.

[45] Statement showing cars equipped and not equipped with air brakes and automatic couplers as of June 30, 1898, IC-11M2.1.

[46] Centralia Evening Sentinal, June 30, 1913.

[47] I.C.R.R., Minutes of Meeting of Superintendents and Heads of Departments, pp. 54-72.

[48] Fentress to Harahan, Chicago, June 15, 1894, IC- 1F2.2.

[49] Unaddressed letter from Fentress, probably to local attorneys in Tennessee, n.p., January 22, 1897, IC-1F2.2, enclosing copy of proposed law. One of the first cases establishing the fellow servant rule had been the Massachusetts case of Farwell v. Boston and Worcester R.R. Co. (4 Metc. 49, 1842). See U.S. Dept. of Labor, Growth of Labor Law, p. 138.

[50] Fentress to B. J. Stevens, Chicago, March 2, 1893, IC-1F2.2.

[51] Ibid.

[52] Fentress to Thomas J. Kernan, n.p., June 18, 1896, IC-1F2.2.

[53] Fentress to Harahan, n.p., February 5, 1896, IC-1F2.2. See also Harris, Local Attorney, to Luther Manship, member of Miss. legislature, Jackson, [February 1896], IC-1F2.2.

[54] Fentress to Mayes and Harris, attorneys at Jackson, n.p., February 6, 1896, IC-1F2.2.

[55] Fentress to Pirtle and Trabue, attorneys at Louisville, n.p., January 27, 1898, IC-1F2.2. The Chesapeake Ohio and Southwestern Railroad had

been a member of the Kentucky Railroad Association, which maintained a lobby at Louisville, but when Illinois Central officers assumed full control of the C. O. & S.W. in 1896, they refused to continue supporting the work of this lobby. Fentress to Fish, Chicago, November 9, 1896, IC-1F2.2. Harahan to Fish, Chicago, February 27, 1897, IC-1F2.2.

[56]Fentress to Yarger and Percy, attorneys at Greenville, Miss., n.p., January 8, 1898, IC-1F2.2.

[57]Fentress to Fish, Chicago, August 11, 1897, IC-1F2.2.

[58]John Dunn, Assistant to Pres., to Welling, Kankakee, March 1, 1897, IC-1F2.2.

[59]In 1897 such bills were defeated in Tennessee and Illinois. See Fentress and Cooper, Local Attorneys, to James Fentress, Memphis, February 13, 1897, IC-1F2.2. J. H. Paddock, Secretary of Illinois Senate, to Fish, Springfield, April 17, 1897, IC-1F2.2.

[60]Losey to Fish, Chicago, September 9, 1899, IC-1F2.2.

[61]Sidney F. Andrews, Assistant General Solicitor, to Fish, Chicago, March 25, 1899, IC-1F2.2.

[62]Harahan to Fish, Chicago, September 8, 1891, IC-1F2.2.

[63]Harahan to Fish, Chicago, December 22, 1893, IC-1F2.2.

[64]William A. Kellond, [clerk?], to Fish, Chicago, December 16, 1893, IC-1F2.2. Other donations are mentioned in Doty to Jerry O'Connor, Supervisor, Amboy, December 16, 1892, IC-1D6.1. Place to J. T. Tait, Personal Injury Agent, Waterloo, November 27, 1895; November 29, 1895; December 6, 1895, IC-1P6.1. In 1896 Harahan refused to allow a donation to the mother of brakeman Robert B. Cook, who had been murdered. Harahan to Mrs. L. E. Morris, n.p., March 9, 1896, IC-1F2.2.

[65] Beck to A. A. Allen, General Manager of Chicago and Northern Pacific Railroad, Chicago, October 11, 1890, IC-1B4.1, paraphrasing his reply to a demand made by the switchmen "some time ago."

[66] Fish to Welling, New York, February 8, 1896, IC-1W3.3. Harahan to Fish, Chicago, November 25, 1899, IC-1F2.2. U.S. Industrial Commission, Report, XVII, 868.

[67] Welling to Fish, Chicago, January 25, 1896; February 8, 1896; February 15, 1896, IC-1F2.2.

[68] Fish to Welling, New York, February 11, 1896, IC-1W3.3.

[69] Welling to Fish, Chicago, May 7, 1896, IC-1F2.2.

[70] Employees could continue to insure with other companies if they wished, but the Illinois Central would make deduction on payrolls only for the company that had been granted exclusive privileges. Circular issued by General Superintendent Sullivan, Chicago, December 31, 1897, IC-1F2.2. In 1891 the Illinois Central had refused to make a similar arrangement with another company, the American Casualty Insurance and Security Company of Baltimore. Harahan to Welling, Chicago, April 25, 1891, IC-1W3.3.

[71] Welling to Isaac Anderson, Auditor of Disbursements, Chicago, October 21, 1897, IC-1W3.3.

[72] John McAmby, General Agent for Illinois and Iowa of Standard Life and Accident Insurance Co. of Detroit, to J. T. Watkins, Paymaster, Chicago, November 21, 1894, IC-1W3.3, reporting that he has advised his company's southern agent to follow Watkins' suggestions. Much related material is in IC-1W3.3.

[73] Fish to Welling, New York, November 10, 1896, IC-1W3.3.

[74]Welling to Fish, Chicago, November 10, 1896, IC-1F2.2. A. H. Bruner, Y.M.C.A. Secretary, to Harahan, March 6, 1897, IC-1F2.2. Harahan to Fish, New Orleans, March 17, 1897, IC-1F2.2. Harahan to Fish, Chicago, June 29, 1897; July 20, 1897, IC-1F2.2. Fish to Harahan, New York, July 22, 1897, IC-1F2.2. George W. Weedon, Y.M.C.A. committee chairman, to Fish, Louisville, March 7, 1898, IC-1F2.2, enclosing copy of _The Railway Messenger_ (Louisville), V (January, 1898), reporting donation of $180 by I.C. in 1897.

[75]M. F. Cary, H. G. Searles, and J. A. Dunham, committeemen of Waterloo employees, to I.C.R.R. officials, Waterloo, March 16, 1897, IC-1P6.1. G. R. Turner, Trainmaster, to F. B. Harriman, Waterloo, March 20, 1897, IC-1P6.1. Place to Harriman, Waterloo, March 26, 1897, IC-1P6.1. Edwin L. Hamilton, Railroad Secretary of International Committee of Y.M.C.A.'s, to Harahan, Chicago, June 3, 1897, IC-1W3.3. Hamilton to Welling, Chicago, June 4, 1897, IC-1W3.3.

[76]Hamilton to Harahan, Chicago, June 3, 1897, IC-1W3.3.

[77]Fish to Harahan, New York, July 22, 1897, IC-1W3.3. _Waterloo Daily Reporter_, June 13, 1898, clipping in IC-1F2.2. _Waterloo Daily Courier_, June 15, 1898, clipping in IC-1F2.2.

[78]Harahan to Hamilton, Chicago, January 19, 1899, IC-1F2.2.

[79]Annual report of East St. Louis branch of Railroad Y.M.C.A., enclosed with C. F. Parker, General Agent, to Fish, East St. Louis, February 24, 1899, IC-1F2.2.

[80]_Ibid_.

[81]Fish to James C. Clarke, Pres., New York, May 11, 1886, IC-1F2.2. Fish made this remark in urging company sponsorship of an accident relief system.

[82] Welling to Fish, Chicago, April 11, 1893, IC-1F2.2.

[83] Dunn to Fish, Chicago, May 4, 1893, IC-1F2.2.

[84] W. L. Lighthart, Station Agent, to Fish, Freeport, April 20, 1893, IC-1F2.2.

[85] Printed circular letter, Fish to officers and employees, Chicago, May 18, 1893, IC-1W3.3.

[86] Welling to Fish, Chicago, December 21, 1893, IC-1F2.2. Monthly reports on employee stock subscriptions are given in a run of letters from Welling to Fish, 1894-96, IC-1F2.2. Ledgers and journals recording all employee stock subscriptions are in IC-+4.14 and IC-+4.15.

[87] Fish to Welling, New York, January 19, 1894, IC-1W3.3.

[88] Reports by Welling to Fish, IC-1F2.2, passim.

[89] Fish to Welling, New York, February 13, 1896, IC-1W3.3.

[90] Fish to Welling, New York, March 3, 1896; March 19, 1896, IC-1W3.3. Welling to Fish, Chicago, March 17, 1896; March 21, 1896, October 15, 1897, IC-1F2.2.

[91] Many newspaper clippings and letters testifying to Fish's publicity campaign are in IC-1F2.2.

[92] Fish to W. E. O'Bleneu, Commissioner of Iowa Bureau of Labor Statistics, New York, February 28, 1897, IC-1W3.3.

[93] Fish, Statement to the U.S. Industrial Commission, pp. 14-15.

BIBLIOGRAPHY

I. Unpublished Primary Sources

A. Burlington Railroad Archives, Newberry Library, Chicago, Illinois

1.2 Miscellaneous papers, 1854-1889.
Contains letters of I.C. officials regarding proposed regulations for employees, *ca*. 1854.

2.21 Nortwick, John Van, special file, May 4, 1849-February 9, 1851.
Includes material relating to Van Nortwick's service as division superintendent on I.C., 1855-56. Item 16a is a schedule of men employed on the I.C. third and fourth divisions in 1855.

33 1880 3.1 Engineers' grievance committee papers, 1885-86.
Includes statement of wages of engineers and firemen on I.C. and other roads, 1882, and printed I.C. wage schedule of 1885.

33 1880 3.2 Salary lists and papers, 1878-1884.
Includes wages and average annual earnings of I.C. engineers and firemen, 1880, and correspondence regarding strike by switchmen of Chicago roads, 1881.

B. Illinois Central Railroad Archives, Newberry Library, Chicago, Illinois

1A2.1 Ackerman, William K. Out-letters, 1877-1883. 8300 letters.

1A2.2 ________. Out-letters, 1854-1862. 11 letters.

1A2.3 ________. Telegrams, 1878-1880. 1000 telegrams to Ackerman and other officials.

1A2.4 ________. In-letters, 1877-1883. 6900 letters, reports, circulars, advertisements, etc.

1A2.5 ________. Out-letters, 1880-82. 150 letters.

1B2.1 Banks, Nathaniel P. Out-letters, 1861. 40 letters.

1B4.1 Beck, C. A. Out-letters, 1890. 3500 letters to division superintendents and others. Includes valuable material on wages and strikes.

1B7.1 Brayman, Mason. Out-letters, 1851-55. 150 letters. Much reference to construction problems.

1B8.1 Bruen, William G. Out-letters, 1902-1906. 1000 letters.

1B9.1 Burrall, William P. Out-letters, 1853-56. 100 letters. Useful reports on progress of construction.

1C5.1 Clarke, James C. Out-letters, 1856-59. 1700 letters.

1C5.2 ________. Out-letters, 1874-1881. 10,000 letters.

1C5.3 ________. Out-letters, 1856-58.
12 letters.

1C5.4 ________. In-letters, 1856.
150 letters.

1C5.5 ________. In-letters, 1885-87.
3500 letters, pamphlets, and advertisements sent to the president's office.

1C7.1 Crane, W. W. Out-letters, 1899.
400 letters from Jackson, Tenn., freight agent.

1D5.1 Done, John H. Out-letters, 1855-56.
25 letters.

1D6.1 Doty, F. R. In-letters, 1887-1894.
500 letters containing much information on section laborers. Also includes a few letters to A. B. Minton, 1888-89.

1D7.1 Douglas, John M. Out-letters, 1860-1877.
4700 letters.

1D7.2 ________. Telegrams, 1875-76.
500 telegrams, including series from Joseph F. Tucker on snow problems in Iowa.

1D7.3 ________. In letters, 1875.
400 letters.

1D7.4 ________. In letters, 1866-1870.
200 letters from William H. Osborn.

1F2.1 Fish, Stuyvesant. Out-letters, 1877-1906.
80,000 letters.

1F2.11 ________. Out-letters, 1895-96.
4000 letters.

*1F2.12 ________. Out-letters, 1893-97.
500 letters.

1F2.2 ________. In-letters, 1883-1906.
65,000 letters sent to the president's office. Numerous enclosures of reports, clippings, pamphlets, and advertisements.

1F2.3 ________. In-letters, 1887 and 1889-1892.
10,000 letters sent to president's office at Chicago.

1F3.1 Forbes, John M. Out-letters, 1851-56.
35 letters and telegrams.

1G7.1 Griswold, John N. A. Out-letters, 1854-56.
60 letters.

1H2.1 Harriman, E. H. In-letters, 1888.
150 letters.

1J2.1 Jacobs, John C. In-letters, 1856-57.
125 letters to superintendent at Amboy.

1J4.1 Jeffery, Edward T. Out-letters, 1888-89.
5000 letters, mainly to division superintendents and agents. Much useful material on labor matters.

1J6.1 Johnson, Benjamin F. Out-letters, 1855.
400 letters.

1J6.2 ________. Out-letters, 1853-56.
400 letters.

1J7.1 Joy, James F. Out-letters, 1851-1875.
85 letters.

1K3.1 Kirkland, Joseph. Out-letters, 1856-58.
20 letters and telegrams.

1L2.1 Lane, Ebenezer. Out-letters, 1855-58.
50 letters.

1M2.1 McClellan, George B. Out-letters, 1857-1860.
5000 letters. Much useful information on engineering department work force.

1M3.1 Mason, Roswell B. Out-letters, 1852-56.
200 letters, many containing information on labor scarcity and other problems of the construction period.

1N4.1 Neal, David A. Out-letters, 1852-58.
160 letters and telegrams.

1N6.1 Newell, John. Out-letters, 1859-1873.
4500 letters. Newell was a division engineer at Amboy from 1856 to 1863. His correspondence for those years contains much valuable information about section hands.

1N6.2 ________. Out-letters, 1874-75.
500 letters.

1N6.3 ________. In-letters, 1870-75.
1300 letters, many enclosing pamphlets, circulars, and advertisements.

106.1 Osborn, William H. Out-letters, 1855-71.
3000 letters.

106.2 ________. Out-letters, 1854-64.
400 letters to treasurer and executive committee, including some on draft problem in the Civil War.

1P2.1 Parker, D. W. Out-letters, 1878.
500 letters. Much information on wages. Also material regarding deductions from wages for damages caused by employee negligence.

1P4.1 Perkins, J. Newton. Out-letters, 1855-56.
500 letters.

1P6.1 Place, T. W. Out-letters, 1895-1902.
900 letters from master mechanic at Waterloo. Many contain extremely valuable material on wages, working conditions, and disciplinary procedures.

1R2.1 Randolph, Lewis V. F. In-letters, 1884-85.
450 letters.

1S2.1 Schuyler, Robert. Out-letters, 1852-54.
10 letters.

1S5.1 Skene, Edward P. In-telegrams, 1897.
1000 telegrams from agents at southern stations reporting on yellow fever epidemic.

1S8.1 Sturges, Jonathan. Out-letters, 1852-57.
50 letters.

1W2.1 Walker, Thomas E. Out-letters, 1863-65.
900 letters.

1W3.1 Welling, John C. Out-letters, 1893 and 1901-1903.
25,000 letters.

1W3.2 ________. Telegrams, 1892-96.
2000 telegrams.

1W3.3 ________. In-letters, 1889-1910.
30,000 letters.

1W3.4 ________. In-telegrams, 1893-97.
1000 telegrams.

1W4.1 Wentworth, John. Out-letters, 1851-55.
15 letters.

11C1.5 Chicago office. Out-letters, 1866-1897.
39 bound volumes of daily reports to New York.

11M2.1 Machinery department. In-letters, 1867-1903.
Includes memorandum on cars equipped with automatic couplers, 1898.

11M2.2 ________. In-letters concerning personnel rules, 1893-1916.
150 letters relating to shop regulations, pensions, and proposals for formal shop rules. Includes printed list of shop rules issued in 1878.

11N1.1 New York office. Out-letters, 1882-1911.
135,000 letters from assistant secretary's office, mostly on routine matters.

11N1.2 ________. Out-letters, 1895-1907.
23,000 letters from secretary and treasurer, mostly routine.

11N1.3 ________. In-letters, 1884-1905.
20,000 letters, many from officials at Chicago and on the southern lines, to the secretary and treasurer.

11N1.4 ________. In-telegrams, 1878-1907.
10,000 telegrams to New York officials, mainly from New Orleans.

11N1.5 ________. In-letters, 1851-1885.
1000 letters. Includes telegram regarding riot among construction laborers at La Salle, 1853, and letter referring to I.C. Relief Club, 1866.

11P5.1 Post office department. In-letters, 1876-1886.

+2.1 Annual reports to stockholders, 1852-1900.
A complete file of the company's printed reports.

2.12 Reports and statements, 1851-1860.
Materials used in preparing annual reports. Includes reports on construction by Roswell Mason.

2.13 Miscellaneous reports, 1882-1905.

2.14 Miscellaneous reports, 1864-1905.
Includes report on continuous running of engines by Edward Jeffery, 1876.

2.15 Annual reports to state railroad commissions, 1876-1906.

2.2 Laws and documents, 1831-1930.
40 printed volumes.

+2.21 Documents concerning incorporation, 1851.

2.22 Documents concerning organization, 1851-1938. Includes pension department rules, 1901.

2.32 Contracts, 1851-1882. Includes agreement with Pinkerton and company, 1855.

2.8 Circulars, 1853-1908. 37 scrapbooks of circulars on personnel changes, rules, etc.

+2.81 William K. Ackerman's scrapbooks, 1780-1905.

2.9 Newspaper clippings, 1871-1936. 25 scrapbooks of clippings about I.C. and other roads.

2.91 Papers used in preparing histories, 1897-98. 50 letters to W. R. Head from old employees with reminiscences, biographical sketches, etc. Includes a packet of letters concerning the Pullman strike, 1894, with list of guards sworn in as U.S. deputy marshals.

*+3.1 Minute books, 1850-1905. Minutes of meetings of incorporators, directors, stockholders, and executive committee.

3.3 Officers' letters of resignation and acceptance, 1851-1862.

*+3.4 Papers accompanying board meetings, 1850-1906. Includes report on organization of employees as volunteer guards during 1877 riots; demands of Chicago switchmen, 1893; letters on Pullman Strike, 1894; and material on relief plans, 1896.

3.6 Miscellaneous historical items, 1853-1948. 4 boxes of old records, forms, clippings, and pictures gathered from old employees.

3.61 Pamphlets, 1856-1948.

+3.8 Timetables, 1853-1916.

+3.81 Maps, 1882-1945.

3.82 Lists of stations, agents, and officials, 1872-1906.

3.9 Time books, 1859-1904.
29 time books showing wages of enginemen, shopmen, and other employees at various places and times. Includes comparative statement of total company labor force, 1880-82.

3.91 Pay roll vouchers, 1854.

3.92 Applications for positions, 1851-1862.
Includes agreement signed by Henry Phelps as agent in charge of recruitment of construction laborers.

3.93 Personnel rules, 1887-1900.
7 printed volumes of rules. Also includes schedule of wages for engineers and firemen, 1892.

+4.14 Stock ledgers of employee subscriptions, 1893-1903.

+4.15 Stock journals of employee subscriptions, 1893-1930.

6M8.7 Mississippi Valley Co. rent ledgers, 1893-1898.

C. Other Archival Materials

Ackerman, William K. Papers. Chicago Historical Society.

Brayman, Mason. Papers. Chicago Historical Society.

Dodge, Grenville M. Papers. Iowa State Department of History and Archives, Des Moines.
Includes a few items relating to Dodge's role in suppressing a strike by I.C. construction laborers in the 1850's.

Illinois Central Railroad documents. John Crerar Library, Chicago.
267 items, mostly letters to I.C. station agent at Lena, Illinois.

Lane, Ebenezer. Papers. University of Chicago Library.

Pinkerton, Allan. Papers. Chicago Historical Society.
Photostats and transcripts of Pinkerton documents. 80 items. Includes copy of contract with I.C., 1855.

II. Published Primary Sources

A. Illinois Central Railroad Publications

Annual Report, 1852-1900. (Title varies).

Code of Rules for Conducting the Business of the Illinois Central Railroad Company. Adopted by the Board of Directors December 16, 1889. In Effect from and after January 1, 1890. New York: Evening Post Job Printing Office, 1889.

Code of Rules (with Index) for Conducting the Business of the Illinois Central Railroad Company. Adopted by the Board of Directors May 21, 1902. Chicago: Rogers & Smith Co., n.d.

Dinner to the Directors and Officers of the Illinois Central Railroad Company on the Fiftieth Anniversary of the Incorporation of the Company. n.p., [1901].

Documents Relating to the Organization of the Illinois Central Rail-road Company. New York: Geo. S. Roe, 1851.

General Freight Department. Instructions to Agents and Other Employes. Chicago: Henry O. Shepard Co., 1898.

General Instruction No. 2 Issued Jointly by the General Passenger Agent, Auditor of Passenger Receipts and General Baggage Agent to Ticket Agents, Conductors, Baggage Agents and Train Baggagemen of the Illinois Central Railroad Company. Chicago: A. R. Barnes & Co., 1897.

Minutes of Meeting of Superintendents and Heads of Departments Held in the Second Vice-President's Office, Chicago, Illinois, September 12, 13, 14, 1892. Chicago: Knight, Leonard & Co., n.d.

Mutual Benefit Association. Articles of Incorporation and By-laws of the Illinois Central R.R. Mutual Benefit Association. Chicago: J. S. Thompson & Co., 1878.

Official List of Officers, Agents, Stations, Attorneys, Surgeons, Mileage, County Seats, County Lines, Etc. Chicago: Rand McNally & Co., 1887.

Pension Department. Rules and Regulations Adopted by the Board of Directors, April 24th, 1901. Effective July 1st, 1901. n.p., n.d.

Rules and Instructions for the Government of Employes of the Road Department. Chicago: Knight, Leonard & Co., 1895.

Rules Governing Employes of the Illinois Central Railroad Company. Chicago: Rand, McNally & Co., 1891.

Schedule of Wages for Trainmen in Passenger and and Freight Service in Effect February 1, 1898. n.p., n.d.

Schedule of Wages of Locomotive Engineers and Firemen, 1885. Amboy: Journal Book and Job Office, 1885.

Schedule of Wages of Locomotive Engineers and Firemen, 1892. n.p., n.d.

B. Public Documents

Illinois. Appellate Court, First District. March Term, 1898. William F. McDonald, Plaintiff in Error v. Illinois Central Railroad Company and the Chicago & North-Western Railway Company, Defendants in Error, Brief and Argument for the Illinois Central Railroad Company. Chicago: Barnard & Miller, n.d.
I.C. brief in suit over alleged blacklisting of A.R.U. strikers by the I.C. and other Chicago railroads. Copy in IC-1F2.2, vol. 217, item 69b.

Illinois. Railroad and Warehouse Commission. Annual Report. Vols. I-XXX. Springfield: Journal Printing Office, 1872-1901.
Reports for 1872-1888 list all accidents on the I.C., giving date of accident, name of person injured, occupation of the injured party, circumstances, and extent of injuries. After 1888 the reports give only the number of persons killed and injured.

Illinois. Supreme Court, Northern Grand Division. October Term, 1896. I.C.R.R. Co., appellant, v. James R. Campbell, appellee. Appeal from Appellate Court, First District. Petition for Rehearing. Chicago: Eastman Bros., n.d.
Involves a personal injury suit by a switchman whose foot was caught in an unblocked frog. Copy in IC-1F2.2, vol. 233, item 1.

Illinois. Supreme Court, Northern Grand Division, October Term, 1899. William F. McDonald, Plaintiff in Error v. I.C.R.R., Chicago & Northwestern Railway Company, Defendants in Error. Writ of Error to Appellate Court, First District. Brief and Argument for Defendant in Error, Illinois Central Railroad Company. Chicago: Barnard & Miller, n.d.
Copy in IC-1F2.2, vol. 261, item 45.

U.S. Bureau of Labor. Bulletin. Vols. I-V. Washington: Government Printing Office, 1895-1900.
Bulletin no. 8 (January, 1897) contains Emory R. Johnson, "Railway Relief Departments." No. 17 (July, 1898) contains Emory R. Johnson, "Brotherhood Relief and Insurance of Railway Employees."

U.S. Commissioner of Labor. Annual Report. Vols. I-XV. Washington: Government Printing Office, 1886-1900.
Vol. V (1889) is devoted entirely to railroad labor. It includes a great amount of statistical information on wages and some material on accidents, insurance, and welfare programs.

U.S. Congress. House. Select Committee on Depression in Labor and Business (1878). The Causes of the General Depression in Labor and Business, Etc. Washington: Government Printing Office, 1879.

U.S. Congress. Senate. Committee on Education and Labor (1883). Report of the Committee of the Senate upon the Relations between Labor and Capital, and Testimony Taken by the Committee. 5 vols. Washington: Government Printing Office, 1885.

U.S. Industrial Commission. Reports. 20 vols. Washington: Government Printing Office, 1901.
Vol. XVII, pp. 709-1135, contains Samuel M. Lindsay, "Report on Railway Labor in the United States."

U.S. Strike Commission. Report on the Chicago Strike of June-July, 1894. Senate Executive Document No. 7. Washington: Government Printing Office, 1895.
Pp. 325-338 contain testimony of Albert W. Sullivan, general superintendent of the I.C.

U.S. War Department. The War of the Rebellion: Official Records of the Union and Confederate Armies. 70 vols. in 128. Washington: Government Printing Office, 1880-1901.
Series III, vol. II (1899) has material on exemption of certain railroad workers from the draft.

C. Newspapers

Alton Daily Morning Courier.

Alton Telegraph and Madison County Record.

Amboy Times.

Bloomington Democratic News.

Bloomington Pantagraph.

Cairo Delta.

Cairo Gazette.

Cairo Sun.

Cairo Times and Delta.

Centralia Evening Sentinal.

Carlyle Calumet of Peace.

Charleston Courier.

Chicago Democrat.

Chicago Inter-Ocean.

Chicago Tribune.

Clinton De Witt Courier.

Decatur Gazette.

Decatur Illinois State Chronicle.

Dixon Telegraph.

Edwardsville Madison Weekly Advertiser.

Elgin Gazette.

Freeport Journal.

Galena Courier.

Galena Daily Evening Jeffersonian.

Galena Gazette.

Galena Northwestern Gazette

Genesco Standard.

Grayville Herald.

Hillsboro Montgomery County Herald.

Hutsonville Journal.

Jacksonville Illinois Statesman.

Jonesboro Gazette.

Kankakee Gazette.

Lockport Telegraph.

Marshall Eastern Illinoisan.

Marshall Telegraph.

Mound City National Emporium.

Olney Times.

Ottawa Republican Times.

Palestine *Ruralist*.

Peoria Daily Morning News.

Peru *La Salle County Democrat*.

Quincy Democrat.

Quincy Whig.

Quincy Daily Whig and Republican.

Rock Island Argus.

Shawneetown *Southern Illinoisan*.

Springfield *Illinois Daily Journal*.

Springfield *Illinois State Journal*.

Sterling Republican and Gazette.

Urbana Union.

Vandalia Age of Steam.

Watseka *Iroquois County Times*.

D. Periodicals

Illinois Central Magazine.

Locomotive Engineers' Monthly Journal.

Railway Conductor.

Poor's Manual of American Railroads.

Railroad Gazette.

E. Books

Benson, Robert, and Co. The Illinois Central Railway: A Historical Sketch of the Undertaking with Statistical Notes on the State of Illinois, the City of Chicago, Cairo, &c., and a Description of the Railway, Its Route and Lands. London: Smith, Elder & Co., 1855.

[Bross, William]. The Rail-roads, History and Commerce of Chicago. 2nd ed. Chicago: Democratic Press Printing Office, 1854.

Brush, Daniel H. Growing Up with Southern Illinois 1820 to 1861. Chicago: R. R. Donnelley & Sons, 1944.

Fagan, James O. Confessions of a Railroad Signalman. Boston: Houghton Mifflin Company, 1908.
Argues that government intervention is necessary to reduce railroad accidents because the rise of labor unions has made discipline by management ineffective. Attacks the "Brown system" of discipline as ineffective.

________. Labor on the Railroads. Boston: Houghton Mifflin Co., 1909.
Opposes railroad labor unions.

Fish, Stuyvesant. Statement to the U.S. Industrial Commission. n.p., n.d.
Discusses I.C. wage policy in the depression of the 1890's.

General Managers' Association of Chicago. Proceedings of the General Managers' Association of Chicago: Chicago, June 25, 1894, to July 14, 1894. Chicago: Knight Leonard & Co., n.d.
Includes at nearly all meetings a brief resume of the situation on the I.C. by General Manager James T. Harahan.

George, Charles B. Forty Years on the Rail. Chicago: R. R. Donnelley & Sons, 1887.
Reminiscences of an Illinois conductor (not on the I.C.).

Jeffery, Edward T. Remarks of E. T. Jeffery, General Manager of the Illinois Central Railroad Co., before the Senate Committee on Railroads of the Iowa Legislature, at Des Moines, February 9, 1888. Chicago: Rand McNally & Co., n.d.

Johns, Jane M. Personal Recollections of Early Decatur, Abraham Lincoln, Richard J. Oglesby, and the Civil War. Decatur, Ill.: Decatur Chapter of D.A.R., 1912.
Chapter VI, "Building Railroads," deals with German-Irish conflicts during construction of the I.C.

Reed, J. Harvey. Forty Years a Locomotive Engineer: Thrilling Tales of the Rail. Prescott, Wash.: Chas. H. O'Neil, 1912.
Memoirs of an engineer whose railroad career began in 1868. Reed worked on several western roads, but never the I.C.

Taylor, Joseph. A Fast Life on the Modern Highway; Being a Glance into the Railroad World from a New Point of View. New York: Harper & Brothers, 1874.
A delightfully humorous description of nineteenth century railroading.

III. Selected Secondary Works

A. Unpublished

Black, Paul V. "May Day in the Middle West: The Illinois Eight-hour Movement, 1866-67." Paper submitted to Professor Allan G. Bogue, History 641, University of Wisconsin, January, 1968.

_________. "Robert Harris and the Problems of Railway Labor Management, 1867-1867." Paper prepared at University of Wisconsin, February, 1968.

Gutman, Herbert G. "Social and Economic Structure and Depression: American Labor in 1873 and 1874." Ph.D. thesis, University of Wisconsin, 1959.

Perlman, Jacob. "A History of the Brotherhood of Locomotive Engineers Up to 1903." Ph.D. thesis, University of Wisconsin, 1926.

Severson, Lewis E. "Some Phases of the History of the Illinois Central Railroad Company since 1870." Ph.D. thesis, University of Chicago, 1930.

Sigmund, Elwin W. "Federal Laws Concerning Railroad Labor Disputes: A Legislative and Legal History, 1877-1934." Ph.D. thesis, University of Illinois, 1961.

Stevenson, George J. "The Brotherhood of Locomotive Engineers and Its Leaders, 1863-1920." Ph.D. thesis, Vanderbilt University, 1954.

Sutton, Robert M. "The Illinois Central Railroad in Peace and War, 1858-1868." Ph.D. thesis, University of Illinois, 1948.

B. Published

Ackerman, William K. Early Illinois Railroads, a Paper Read before the Chicago Historical Society, Tuesday evening, February 20, 1883. n.p., n.d.

________. Historical Sketch of the Illinois Central Railroad. Chicago: Fergus Printing Co., 1890.

Adams, Charles Francis Jr. Notes on Railroad Accidents. New York: G. P. Putnam's Sons, 1879.

Boulding, Kenneth E. The Organizational Revolution: A Study in the Ethics of Economic Organization. New York: Harper and Brothers, 1953.

Brownson, Howard G. History of the Illinois Central Railroad to 1870. Urbana: University of Illinois, 1915.
A financial history.

Bruce, Robert V. 1877: Year of Violence. New York: Bobbs-Merrill Co., 1959.

Chandler, Alfred D. Jr. The Railroads: The Nation's First Big Business, Sources and Readings. New York: Harcourt, Brace & World, 1965.

Part IV, "The Beginnings of Modern Labor Relations," has readings on the Brotherhoods, bargaining, and the Pullman strike.

Chief Engineers of the Illinois Central Railroad. n.p.: [I.C.R.R.], [1950?].

Clark, Thomas D. A Pioneer Southern Railroad from New Orleans to Cairo. Chapel Hill: University of North Carolina Press, 1936.

Cochran, Thomas C. Railroad Leaders 1845-1890: The Business Mind in Action. Cambridge: Harvard University Press, 1953.

Chapter XIII, pp. 173-183, analyzes the attitudes towards labor of selected railroad executives.

________ and William Miller. The Age of Enterprise: A Social History of Industrial America. New York: The Macmillan Co., 1943.

Commons, John R., et al. History of Labor in the United States. 4 vols. New York: The Macmillan Co., 1921-35.

Corliss, Carlton J. From Trails to Rails; a Story of Transportation Progress in Illinois. Chicago: Illinois Central System, 1934.

________. Main Line of Mid-America: The Story of the Illinois Central. New York: Creative Age Press, 1950.

A popular history.

Cottrell, W. Fred. The Railroader. Stanford: Stanford University Press, 1940.

An interesting sociological study of the railroader, based primarily on the personal experiences of the author, who had a railroading as well as an academic career. Includes a useful glossary of railroad jargon.

Curtis, Carolyn, and Elisabeth C. Jackson. Guide to the Burlington Archives in the Newberry Library 1851-1901. Chicago: Newberry Library, 1949.

Custer, Milo. "Asiatic Cholera in Central Illinois, 1834-1873." Illinois State Historical Society Journal, XXIII (April, 1930), 113-162.

Erickson, Charlotte. American Industry and the European Immigrant 1860-1885. Cambridge: Harvard University Press, 1957.

Fishlow, Albert. American Railroads and the Transformation of the Ante-Bellum Economy. Harvard Economic Studies, Vol. CXXVII. Cambridge: Harvard University Press, 1965.

Fogel, Robert W. Railroads and American Economic Growth: Essays in Economic History. Baltimore: Johns Hopkins Press, 1964.

Gates, Paul W. The Illinois Central Railroad and Its Colonization Work. Harvard Economic Studies, Vol. XLII. Cambridge: Harvard University Press, 1934.

Ginger, Ray. The Bending Cross: A Biography of Eugene Victor Debs. New Brunswick: Rutgers University Press, 1949.

Gutman, Herbert G. "Trouble on the Railroads in 1873-1874: Prelude to the 1877 Crisis?" Labor History, II (spring, 1961), 215-235.

Hertel, D. W. History of the Brotherhood of Maintenance of Way Employees: Its Birth and Growth 1887-1955. Washington, D.C.: Ransdall, Inc., 1955.

History of the Illinois Central Railroad Company and Representative Employes. Chicago: Railroad Historical Company, 1900.

Kirkland, Edward C. Dream and Thought in the Business Community, 1860-1890. Ithaca: Cornell University Press, 1956.

________. Industry Comes of Age: Business, Labor, and Public Policy, 1860-1897. New York: Holt, Rinehart and Winston, 1961.

Lebergott, Stanley. Manpower in Economic Growth: The American Record since 1800. New York: McGraw-Hill Book Company, 1964.

Lindsey, Almont. The Pullman Strike: The Story of a Unique Experiment and of a Great Labor Upheaval. Chicago: University of Chicago Press, 1942.

McIsaac, Archibald M. The Order of Railroad Telegraphers: A Study in Trade Unionism and Collective Bargaining. Princeton: Princeton University Press, 1933.

McMurry, Donald L. The Great Burlington Railroad Strike of 1888: A Case History in Labor Relations. Cambridge: Harvard University Press, 1956.

________. "Federation of the Railroad Brotherhoods, 1889-1894." Industrial and Labor Relations Review, VII (October, 1953), 73-92.

________. "Labor Policies of the General Managers' Association of Chicago, 1886-1894." Journal of Economic History, XIII (spring, 1953), 160-178.

Middleton, P. Harvey. Railways and Organized Labor. Chicago: Railway Business Association, 1941.

Mohr, Carolyn C. Guide to the Illinois Central Archives in the Newberry Library 1851-1906. Chicago: Newberry Library, 1951.

"Newspapers in the Illinois State Historical Library." Illinois Libraries, XLIX (June, 1967), 439-543.

Ozanne, Robert. A Century of Labor-Management Relations at McCormick and International Harvester. Madison: University of Wisconsin Press, 1967.

________. Wages in Practice and Theory: McCormick and International Harvester 1860-1960. Madison: University of Wisconsin Press, 1968.

Paxson, Frederick L. "The Railroads of the 'Old Northwest' Before the Civil War." Transactions of the Wisconsin Academy of Sciences, Arts, and Letters, Vol. XVII (1911), part I, no. 4, pp. 243-274.

Richardson, Helen R., comp. Illinois Central Railroad Company: A Centennial Bibliography, 1851-1951. Washington: Association of American Railroads Bureau of Railway Economics Library, 1950.

Richardson, Reed C. The Locomotive Engineer: 1863-1963, A Century of Railway Labor Relations and Work Rules. Ann Arbor: Bureau of Industrial Relations, University of Michigan, 1963.

Robbins, Edwin C. Railway Conductors: A Study in Organized Labor. Studies in History Economics and Public Law, Vol. LXI. New York: Columbia University Press, 1914.

Shaw, Robert B. Down Brakes: A History of Railroad Accidents, Safety Precautions and Operating Practices in the United States of America. London: P. R. Macmillan Lmtd., 1961.

Taft, Philip. Organized Labor in American History. New York: Harper & Row, 1964.

Taylor, George R., and Irene D. Neu. The American Railroad Network 1861-1890. Cambridge: Harvard University Press, 1956.

U.S. Bureau of the Census. Historical Statistics of the United States, Colonial Times to 1957. Washington: Government Printing Office, 1960.

U.S. Department of Labor. Growth of Labor Law in the United States. Washington: Government Printing Office, 1967.

Ware, Norman J. The Labor Movement in the United States, 1860-1895: A Study in Democracy. New York: D. Appleton and Company, 1929.

Wiebe, Robert H. The Search for Order 1877-1920. New York: Hill and Wang, 1957.

Wish, Harvey. "The Pullman Strike: A Study in Industrial Warfare." Illinois State Historical Society Journal, XXXII (September, 1939), 288-312.

INDEX

Dissertations in American Economic History

An Arno Press Collection

1977 Publications

Ankli, Robert Eugene. **Gross Farm Revenue in Pre-Civil War Illinois.** (Doctoral Dissertation, University of Illinois, 1969). 1977

Asher, Ephraim. **Relative Productivity, Factor-Intensity and Technology in the Manufacturing Sectors of the U.S. and the U.K. During the Nineteenth Century.** (Doctoral Dissertation, University of Rochester, 1969). 1977

Campbell, Carl. **Economic Growth, Capital Gains, and Income Distribution:** 1897-1956. (Doctoral Dissertation, University of California at Berkeley, 1964). 1977

Cederberg, Herbert R. **An Economic Analysis of English Settlement in North America, 1583-1635.** (Doctoral Dissertation, University of California at Berkeley, 1968). 1977

Dente, Leonard A. **Veblen's Theory of Social Change.** (Doctoral Dissertation, New York University, 1974). 1977

Dickey, George Edward. **Money, Prices and Growth;** The American Experience, 1869-1896. (Doctoral Dissertation, Northwestern University, 1968). 1977

Douty, Christopher Morris. **The Economics of Localized Disasters:** The 1906 San Francisco Catastrophe. (Doctoral Dissertation, Stanford University, 1969). 1977

Harper, Ann K. **The Location of the United States Steel Industry, 1879-1919.** (Doctoral Dissertation, Johns Hopkins University, 1976). 1977

Holt, Charles Frank. **The Role of State Government in the Nineteenth-Century American Economy, 1820-1902:** A Quantitative Study. (Doctoral Dissertation, Purdue University, 1970). 1977

Katz, Harold. **The Decline of Competition in the Automobile Industry, 1920-1940.** (Doctoral Dissertation, Columbia University, 1970). 1977

Lee, Susan Previant. **The Westward Movement of the Cotton Economy, 1840-1860:** Perceived Interests and Economic Realities. (Doctoral Dissertation, Columbia University, 1975). 1977

Legler, John Baxter. **Regional Distribution of Federal Receipts and Expenditures in the Nineteenth Century:** A Quantitative Study. (Doctoral Dissertation, Purdue University, 1967). 1977

Lightner, David L. **Labor on the Illinois Central Railroad, 1852-1900:** The Evolution of an Industrial Environment. (Doctoral Dissertation, Cornell University, 1969). 1977

MacMurray, Robert R. **Technological Change in the American Cotton Spinning Industry, 1790 to 1836.** (Doctoral Dissertation, University of Pennsylvania, 1970). 1977

Netschert, Bruce Carlton. **The Mineral Foreign Trade of the United States in the Twentieth Century:** A Study in Mineral Economics. (Doctoral Dissertation, Cornell University, 1949). 1977

Otenasek, Mildred. **Alexander Hamilton's Financial Policies.** (Doctoral Dissertation, Johns Hopkins University, 1939). 1977

Parks, Robert James. **European Origins of the Economic Ideas of Alexander Hamilton.** (M. A. Thesis, Michigan State University, 1963). 1977

Parsons, Burke Adrian. **British Trade Cycles and American Bank Credit:** Some Aspects of Economic Fluctuations in the United States, 1815-1840. (Doctoral Dissertation, University of Texas, 1958). 1977

Primack, Martin L. **Farm Formed Capital in American Agriculture, 1850-1910.** (Doctoral Dissertation, University of North Carolina, 1963). 1977

Pritchett, Bruce Michael. **A Study of Capital Mobilization, The Life Insurance Industry of the Nineteenth Century.** (Doctoral Dissertation, Purdue University, 1970). Revised Edition. 1977

Prosper, Peter A., Jr. **Concentration and the Rate of Change of Wages in the United States, 1950-1962.** (Doctoral Dissertation, Cornell University 1970). 1977

Schachter, Joseph. **Capital Value and Relative Wage Effects of Immigration into the United States, 1870-1930.** (Doctoral Dissertation, City University of New York, 1969). 1977

Schaefer, Donald Fred. **A Quantitative Description and Analysis of the Growth of the Pennsylvania Anthracite Coal Industry, 1820 to 1865.** (Doctoral Dissertation, University of North Carolina, 1967). 1977

Schmitz, Mark. **Economic Analysis of Antebellum Sugar Plantations in Louisiana.** (Doctoral Dissertation, University of North Carolina, 1974). 1977

Sharpless, John Burk, II. **City Growth in the United States, England and Wales, 1820-1861:** The Effects of Location, Size and Economic Structure on Inter-urban Variations in Demographic Growth. (Doctoral Dissertation, University of Michigan, 1975). 1977

Shields, Roger Elwood. **Economic Growth with Price Deflation, 1873-1896.** (Doctoral Dissertation, University of Virginia, 1969). 1977

Stettler, Henry Louis, III. **Growth and Fluctuations in the Ante-Bellum Textile Industry.** (Doctoral Dissertation, Purdue University, 1970). 1977

Sturm, James Lester. **Investing in the United States, 1798-1893:** Upper Wealth-Holders in a Market Economy. (Doctoral Dissertation, University of Wisconsin, 1969). 1977

Tenenbaum, Marcel. **(A Demographic Analysis of Interstate Labor Growth Rate Differentials;** United States, 1890-1900 to 1940-50. (Doctoral Dissertation, Columbia University, 1969). 1977

Thomas, Robert Paul. **An Analysis of the Pattern of Growth of the Automobile Industry:** 1895-1929. (Doctoral Dissertation, Northwestern University, 1965). 1977

Vickery, William Edward. **The Economics of the Negro Migration 1900-1960.** (Doctoral Dissertation, University of Chicago, 1969). 1977

Waters, Joseph Paul. **Technological Acceleration and the Great Depression.** (Doctoral Dissertation, Cornell University, 1971). 1977

Whartenby, Franklee Gilbert. **Land and Labor Productivity in United States Cotton Production, 1800-1840.** (Doctoral Dissertation, University of North Carolina, 1963). 1977

1975 Publications

Adams, Donald R., Jr. **Wage Rates in Philadelphia, 1790-1830.** (Doctoral Dissertation, University of Pennsylvania, 1967). 1975

Aldrich, Terry Mark. **Rates of Return on Investment in Technical Education in the Ante-Bellum American Economy.** (Doctoral Dissertation, The University of Texas at Austin, 1969). 1975

Anderson, Terry Lee. **The Economic Growth of Seventeenth Century New England:** A Measurement of Regional Income. (Doctoral Dissertation, University of Washington, 1972). 1975

Bean, Richard Nelson. **The British Trans-Atlantic Slave Trade, 1650-1775.** (Doctoral Dissertation, University of Washington, 1971). 1975

Brock, Leslie V. **The Currency of the American Colonies, 1700-1764:** A Study in Colonial Finance and Imperial Relations. (Doctoral Dissertation University of Michigan, 1941). 1975

Ellsworth, Lucius F. **Craft to National Industry in the Nineteenth Century:** A Case Study of the Transformation of the New York State Tanning Industry. (Doctoral Dissertation, University of Delaware, 1971). 1975

Fleisig, Heywood W. **Long Term Capital Flows and the Great Depression:** The Role of the United States, 1927-1933. (Doctoral Dissertation, Yale University, 1969). 1975

Foust, James D. **The Yeoman Farmer and Westward Expansion of U.S. Cotton Production.** (Doctoral Dissertation, University of North Carolina at Chapel Hill, 1968). 1975

Golden, James Reed. **Investment Behavior By United States Railroads, 1870-1914.** (Doctoral Thesis, Harvard University, 1971). 1975

Hill, Peter Jensen. **The Economic Impact of Immigration into the United States.** (Doctoral Dissertation, The University of Chicago, 1970). 1975

Klingaman, David C. **Colonial Virginia's Coastwise and Grain Trade.** (Doctoral Dissertation, University of Virginia, 1967). 1975

Lang, Edith Mae. **The Effects of Net Interregional Migration on Agricultural Income Growth:** The United States, 1850-1860. (Doctoral Thesis, The University of Rochester, 1971). 1975

Lindley, Lester G. **The Constitution Faces Technology:** The Relationship of the National Government to the Telegraph, 1866-1884. (Doctoral Thesis, Rice University, 1971). 1975

Lorant, John H[erman]. **The Role of Capital-Improving Innovations in American Manufacturing During the 1920's.** (Doctoral Thesis, Columbia University, 1966). 1975

Mishkin, David Joel. **The American Colonial Wine Industry:** An Economic Interpretation, Volumes I and II. (Doctoral Thesis, University of Illinois, 1966). 1975

Winkler, Donald R. **The Production of Human Capital:** A Study of Minority Achievement. (Doctoral Dissertation, University of California at Berkeley, 1972). 1977

Oates, Mary J. **The Role of the Cotton Textile Industry in the Economic Development of the American Southeast:** 1900-1940. (Doctoral Dissertation, Yale University, 1969). 1975

Passell, Peter. **Essays in the Economics of Nineteenth Century American Land Policy.** (Doctoral Dissertation, Yale University, 1970). 1975

Pope, Clayne L. **The Impact of the Ante-Bellum Tariff on Income Distribution.** (Doctoral Dissertation, The University of Chicago, 1972). 1975

Poulson, Barry Warren. **Value Added in Manufacturing, Mining, and Agriculture in the American Economy From 1809 To 1839.** (Doctoral Dissertation, The Ohio State University, 1965). 1975

Rockoff, Hugh. **The Free Banking Era: A Re-Examination.** (Doctoral Dissertation, The University of Chicago, 1972). 1975

Schumacher, Max George. **The Northern Farmer and His Markets During the Late Colonial Period.** (Doctoral Dissertation, University of California at Berkeley, 1948). 1975

Seagrave, Charles Edwin. **The Southern Negro Agricultural Worker:** 1850-1870. (Doctoral Dissertation, Stanford University, 1971). 1975

Solmon, Lewis C. **Capital Formation by Expenditures on Formal Education, 1880 and 1890.** (Doctoral Dissertation, The University of Chicago, 1968). 1975

Swan, Dale Evans. **The Structure and Profitability of the Antebellum Rice Industry:** 1859. (Doctoral Dissertation, University of North Carolina at Chapel Hill, 1972). 1975

Sylla, Richard Eugene. **The American Capital Market, 1846-1914:** A Study of the Effects of Public Policy on Economic Development. (Doctoral Thesis, Harvard University, 1968). 1975

Uselding, Paul John. **Studies in the Technological Development of the American Economy During the First Half of the Nineteenth Century.** (Doctoral Dissertation, Northwestern University, 1970). 1975

Walsh, William D[avid]. **The Diffusion of Technological Change in the Pennsylvania Pig Iron Industry, 1850-1870.** (Doctoral Dissertation, Yale University, 1967). 1975

Weiss, Thomas Joseph. **The Service Sector in the United States, 1839 Through 1899.** (Doctoral Thesis, University of North Carolina at Chapel Hill, 1967). 1975

Zevin, Robert Brooke. **The Growth of Manufacturing in Early Nineteenth Century New England.** 1975